The Master Presentation Guide

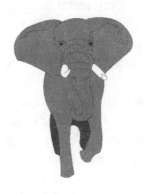

*Million Dollar Ideas
to Master the Art of Presentation!*

Proteus Press
Aspen, Colorado
USA

The Master Presentation Guide

Copyright © 2001 by Jan Ruhe

ISBN 0-9702667-1-5
LCCN: 2001092482

Published by Proteus Press
300 Puppy Smith, Suite 205-290, Aspen, CO 81611
tel. 970-927-9380
fax 970-927-0112
www.janruhe.com

About the Cover

In 2000, Jan and I traveled to South Africa. We also traveled to Zimbabwe and stayed at the magnificent, colorful, Victoria Falls Safari Lodge. Our beautiful room looked over the vast land and a waterhole where we watched the elephants at sundown. Our driver took us across the border into Botswana to meet our riverboat guide. We boarded a small flatbed boat and enjoyed lunch and a safari on the Zambezi River, weaving our way through herds of hippos and large crocodiles. In the maize fields on the Namibian side of the river, darted the most beautiful birds we had ever seen! Afterwards, we spent the rest of the day on a game drive in Botswana's massive Chobe Park.

Chobe Park boasts a burgeoning elephant population of more than 71,000 elephants! Today it's one of the best places in Africa to observe and photograph large herds of elephants. They have miles to roam freely, in unspoiled environment. Elephant viewing will never be the same as it is today in Chobe Park. While we were on the game drive with our private guide, elephants would run right in front of our vehicle many times in single file or together with their babies between them. Massed herds played in the water, spraying each other and taking care of each other. They are so interesting to watch, they are playful, frightening and awesome! When they spread their ears out they are as wide as a sail on a sailboat and their backs are humped so that we could see the curved and crested ridge of their spine beneath the grey hide and the gleam of their curved or broken off ivory. How fortunate we are to live the lifestyle and enjoy such experiences.

As we drove through the bush, a huge elephant confronted us by crashing out of the nearby trees, trumpeting loudly within six feet of our vehicle. He demonstrated his displeasure at our being in his territory intimidating us, the intruders. He reached up with his long trunk as though to pluck me from our vehicle! The pressure of the air from the elephant's movement was incredible. What an imposing creature! The elephant was so close that it certainly could have crushed our vehicle! It's ears flapped out as a warning for us to get away from his territory! It was unreal, scary, and even I felt a bit shaken.

What a *presentation*!

Jan had our camera ready and she snapped a photo of this beautiful, huge, wild beast as it charged our vehicle! Today this photo is framed in Jan's office in Aspen, as a memorable tribute to a mighty and compelling creature. *Now it's on the cover of this guide!* We think it is an appropriate symbol as we suggest that you start out making your *presentation*s boldly, like the elephant.

Happy Presenting!

Bill Ruhe
President of Jan Ruhe Productions
www.janruhe.com

Thank you Ashley for being the
inspiration for this Presentation Guide.
This is the picture of your first presentation
almost fifteen years ago. We would push a chair
for you to stand on up to the microphone as often as possible.
How lucky I am to be the one you call *"mom."*

This book is dedicated to my Bill.

Photo by Bev Burr

Jan & Bill sailing in Vancouver
2000

Acknowledgements

A very special thank you to:

Louise Adrian for being the first woman in Canada to bring me there to present my knowledge and wisdom.

Marco de la Rosa for printing my books in German and putting me in Network Press in Germany.

Sue Dupreez for being the first woman in South Africa to bring me there to present my knowledge and wisdom. Thank you for creating the most wonderful memories of Africa that a person can ever have.

John Milton Fogg for being the one who was the first person to ask me to make a public presentation in Reno, Nevada and invited me to be an Upline® Master.

Joseph Kim for printing MLM Nuts $ Bolts in Korean.

Jayne Leach for being the first woman in the UK to bring me to various parts of the UK to present my knowledge and wisdom.

John David Mann for putting me on the front cover of Network Marketing Lifestyles.

Bonnie Nelson, my Upline, who taught me her presentation over twenty years ago. Rest in peace Bon, I miss you.

Daniel Pagliari for putting on the front cover of Network Marketing News in England.

Jim Rohn and **Tom Hopkins,** my mentors. How can I ever thank you enough for helping me to see how to get out of my mediocre lifestyle and live the lifestyle of a champion?

Gavin Scott for being the first man in the UK to bring me to the UK, Ireland and Wales to present my knowledge and wisdom.

Special acknowledgements for the terrific contributions from super presenters:

Louise Adrian, Lena Akerman, Ray Aziz, Cathy Barber, Bev Burr, Jodi Carville, Jerry Clark, Lisa Combs, John Curtis, Dr. Daria Davidson, Linzi Day, Doc Eason, Teresa Epps, Pam Evans, Doug Firebaugh, John Milton Fogg, Rob Foster, Patricia Fripp, John Furhman, Debbie Gabinet, Randy Gage, Carlos Gueits, Simon Hamer, Andy Hummel, Geralyn Johnson, Hilton Johnson, Charlie "Tremendous" Jones, Lois Kelley, Edith Penniman Knowles, Jayne Leach, Melynda Lilly, Edward Ludbrook, John David Mann, Rod Nichols, Suzanne Olejnik, Asbjørn Ølnes, Peter Raynard, Kathy Riley, Dr. Joe Rubino, Tom Schreiter, Gavin Scott, Sherry Shadab, Joshua Shafran, Kathy Smith, David Stewart, Carol Waugh, Bob Webb, Dorothy Wood and **Eva Zimmerman.** Thank all of you for your significant contributions to this book.

Special praises to the leaders in my organization who have lifted me up on their shoulders. Because you are great presenters you have freed up my lifetime to do what my calling is: presenting powerful information that makes people go into motion to be the successes they are meant to and deserve to be.

To **Sarah**, **Clayton** and **Ashley**, how blessed I am to be the one you call *"Mom."* Thank you for your contributions to this book. I am so impressed with your presentation skills. I look forward to being in your audience, as there is no doubt in my mind that you all will be outstanding speakers if you so choose.

Most importantly I acknowledge my husband, **Bill**, my Gu-Ruhe, for his guidance, friendship, patience, hours of layout and proofreading of this guide. He gave me the courage to start writing books over a decade ago to share information that can change your life for the better forever. How blessed I am to have a soul mate who shares the value of contributing to others. We have loved being presenters together worldwide now for over a decade.

And to all of you who have bought over 100,000 books and tapes from JR Productions, attended our seminars; treated us all over the world, we thank you for all your love and friendship.

Happy Presenting!
Presentations are everywhere!

Jan & Bill Ruhe

Strike Up the Band!
The University of Alabama Million Dollar Band

Table of Contents

1 You Are the Ticket! 1

You Are the Ticket.

2 Prior to the Presentation 7

Attending the Presentation; Know Your Outcome; John Wesley's Thoughts; Go Over the 5-W's; Would You Buy From You?

3 Preparing the Presentation 15

The Attitude of a Champion Presenter; Keep a Positive Attitude; Have Courage; Non-verbal Cues to Use In Your Presentation to Encourage the Audience to Like You; The Benefits of an Enthusiastic Presentation; Get Enthusiastic; Using Enthusiasm; How to Present With New Enthusiasm; Red Socks; Ten Steps to a Powerful Presentation; What is an Outstanding Presentation; Use the Engage Formula; Use the Present Formula; A Successful Presentation has;

Master Flexibility In a One-On-One Presentation; Benefits of Following a Prepared Presentation Word-For-Word; Make Your Presentation Outline a Blueprint; Take Pride In; Presentation Time; Music and Your Attitude; The Power of Music; Canned Presentations Can Be Great; You Are a Performer; Master Check-List For Preparing a Presentation; Sell the Benefits; Listing Your Selling Benefit Points; How to Select the Selling Benefits For Your Presentation; How a Company Prepared List of Sales Benefits Helps; Turning Facts Into Benefits; How to Use the Benefits In Your Presentation; The Ultimate Benefit; Study Your Competition; The Presenter's Creed; Elements of Communication; Great Presentations; Make Your Presentations From; How People Listen to You; How People Listen to What You Are Saying at Different Levels; What to Do So People Come to Listen to You; Needs of Leaders Listening to Your Presentation; People With High Achievement Needs Want to Hear; Feelings People Have About Groups; Make Your Presentations Memorable; Key Points in Your Presentation; Presentation Irritants; How to Decide What Topic Would Be Great For You; Asking Questions; Encourage Participation; Ways to Present When Looking For Something New; Speaking; The Room Set Up; Using Words With Care; Use Words That Get Massive Results; Develop Important Words For Your Presentation; Pedestal Words; Words to Use in an Executive Presentation; Use You-Ability and We-Ability Words; The Basic Needs of Those to Whom You Are Presenting; Words That Convince the Other Person They Are Really the One Who Thought of It.

Introduction

Many of the thousands of people I have spoken to worldwide express an interest in being a public speaker. They have a real desire but just don't know *how to* give a dynamic presentation. So, here it is, a great guide for you on *how to* give terrific presentations! Becoming a Master speaker takes a lot of preparation and practice. For many hours of my life, in seminars, I have watched others make presentations and have become a student of presenters. I can tell you that at some seminars I have been motivated off the ceiling and at some totally turned off, leaving the presentation and never recommending them to anyone! Now, in this guide, you are going to get the fun, the best and the most exciting presentation skills found anywhere! I know, I've looked!

It's astounding but true that 20% of the salespeople bring in 80% of the sales. The top salespeople sell sixteen times as much as each average salesperson. Why? The answer lies in the way they *present* themselves to their prospects. They not only know how to make excellent presentations, but they know how to use them to get orders. An outstanding presentation separates the Master from all the average speakers.

The average salesperson may see many prospects, and spend much time explaining the benefits of what they sell and their opportunity; but, their time produces only a fraction of the sales of the leading distributors in their line of business. This is all because their presentations are mediocre or downright poor. And the sad part is, they really are not interested in improving their presentation. But the Masters know that perfecting the presentation is a huge key to success. This guide is to help you *perfect your presentation*. This guide is for you to use daily to build yourself into a great speaker. You can impact people with the information in this guide more than *you ever dreamed possible*!

It's important to give much attention to what people want to *hear* and the *knowledge they are looking for.* We need to be sensitive to our audiences. I have used the information in this guide for years, always having to look for the information in my files. In this one guide, we have selected the *best* openings, the *best* scripts and the *best* words that have been proven to get massive results. Included are the *best* notes out of my journals, the *best* presentation tips that I have gathered in my over two decades of making thousands of presentations. The information in this guide will give you bigger and better ideas to make dazzling, dynamic, exciting, and honest presentations!

Through the years I searched for this information, spent hours of reading, listened to audio tapes, attended expensive seminars and went to presentations to watch and study the

Masters. I *really wanted* to be a Master presenter. I was willing to practice, drill and rehearse my presentation and teach it to others. I found no guide like this one. Oh how I needed this guide! Now it's here for you!

Preparing a speech is not complicated. You can jot down six to ten points on a napkin prior to a speech and give a dynamic speech. And now, with this guide, you are going to get so many ideas that you will make outstanding presentations. Prepare to give presentations that will have massive impact beyond your wildest expectations.

The **most important** presentation skill is to find out *who the senior person in the room is, to honor that person, know that person's name and use it in the presentation.* Next, find out what the audience wants to know from you and deliver that information. Before starting your presentation, take a moment and put your invisible arms around the audience. Embrace the audience; come from contribution and love. One of the keys to delivering fantastic speeches is to envision a powerful world-renowned expert or famous historical figure firmly standing behind you knowing that what you have to say is most important.

Early in my career, I would drive down the streets of North Dallas, in the neighborhood where my mother grew up, Highland Park. I would see the huge homes, beautiful furniture, pretty clothes, fabulous jewelry, sports cars, and people in limousines. I wanted that lifestyle and had no hope to get it. For years I *shrunk my dreams to match our income.* When I discovered speaking in front of a group was necessary to the business I was building, I had major fear and little self-esteem. What I did have was a little guts, and a lot of nerve. I then realized I had attached my fear to the wrong thinking. I changed my thinking and attached fear to *not* being the best I could be in public speaking. I went searching for ways to improve my presentations. Today, I no longer shrink my dreams to match that old income. Because of the presentations skills that I have learned from the true presentation Masters who move people to take action, *my income increased to achieve my dreams*! It is amazing what happens when you began to study and take action on perfecting your presentation skills. Those of you who want to work on your presentation skills, buckle up and prepare for abundance and prosperity, it's headed your way!

Dream big, you can have it all! Improve your vocabulary, work on your presentation skills harder than any part of your business and watch your bank balance grow! Do you want to be wealthy? Then work on your presentation skills. Those who have worked on their presentation skills make the most money. You have to have the money to have the lifestyle. What *you will get* is far more....*you will get* amazing children who can communicate better than most adults you know ; *you will get* relationships that are much more interesting; *you will get* friends around the world, and *you will get* experiences of the rich and famous! Pay attention to the speakers who move people to take action.

Thank you Ashley, my youngest daughter, for inspiring me to write this book. Ashley called me from the University of Alabama in early 2001 and shared with me that in her major of Public Relations that she will have to take some speech courses. Upon exploring my private library to look for books for her, there was not one book or guide that would be easy for her to use. I then went to the bookstores and found not one guide for presenters that was easy to use. So, Ashley, the world thanks you because there is finally an easy guide on presentation skills for everyone to use! Happy 21st birthday in 2001!

 Tip ➜ *Next to doing things that deserve to be written, nothing gets a man more credit nor gives him more pleasure than to write things that deserve to be read.*

In the words of <u>The Millionaire Next Door</u>, *"The large majority of millionaires are not descendants of the Rockefellers or Vanderbilts. More than 80% are ordinary people who have accumulated their wealth in one generation. Today becoming a millionaire is a matter of choice, not chance!"*

By working on your presentation skills and going for greatness you too can become the millionaire next door. Come to the table of plenty—there are silver platters, heaped with abundance waiting for you! I wish you the greatest success on your pathway to being a great presenter. There is plenty of room for terrific presenters in the world. Savor the information in this book. Here is to your fun in being a Master presenter of information!

Presentations are everywhere. Be aware of them as you go through life. There are a few fun photos throughout this guide to show you pictures of some marvelous presentations.

This guide is for you.

All the best,
Go for greatness,
As I say to you now and always,
Don't be Average, be a Champion

Jan Ruhe

The Curtain Opens
Edward Ludbrook

If you attend major franchise exhibitions, you may well see an exhibit stand like the following: a stand bare except for a well dressed man, a table, a large logo on the wall and a sign saying *"Do you have $250,000?"* What a message!

The large logo is the golden arches of the McDonald's Corporation and their presentation is simple. They know that if you have the desire (and $250,000), then they have the system that will make you money. In a world where success is about presenting your business effectively, you can soon see why these guys are so successful.

So are you presenting your message effectively? In today's changing world, is your message really hitting your audience in the way you desire?

Salesmanship has entered a new era. In the 20th century, we saw new businesses establishing in all corners of the world. The world was virgin territory as few had heard of such amazing unique business opportunities. Our presentation styles were loose, raw and unseasoned. What we lacked in professionalism, we made up with enthusiasm. It may seem crazy yet it worked!

It does not work now.

The old days of *"punting"* for success are over. Welcome to the new *"professional"* age of salesmanship. To succeed now the standards must be higher, yet here's the paradox; *the opportunities are much greater now than before.* With continued economic structural change, the desire for entrepreneurial opportunities is larger now than in any other point of history. The *"New World"* of Salesmanship is bigger, more exciting and has a greater future in the 21st century than the 20th century.

Like all professions, the key to success is to become competent at what you do. 'Competence' is *'an ability to perform a skill to a set standard'*. All professions require competence. Presenting to people is a skill that you must become competent in.

To become competent, you must master the knowledge, skills and attitudes necessary to effectively achieve the result you desire time and time again. In presenting, you must convey the required message (information) effectively **every time** so that the listener acts on the information in a way that is best for them.

As I speak across the world, often through a translator, I am always aware of the different audiences' needs and reactions. I know that I must continually adapt the content and style of my speeches to ensure I get the desired result. It takes time and effort, but this is a price well worth paying for professionalism. It is the price all professionals must pay.

This book is not a rule book, it is a well constructed guide. We are all different, yet our objective is always the same. I salute Jan for her professionalism and fortitude in the production of this guide book. May it guide you in your journey. May it provide the light and confidence that many need to take those steps to delivering professional presentations. May you enjoy the 21st century boom of sales. After all, being able to present your products and opportunities in a professional way is the greatest profession on earth. You now have a guide that can be at your fingertips to help you perfect your presentations.

The future belongs to the professionals.

Well done Jan. Thank you for shining a light for others to follow.

The Presentation Pledge
Doug Firebaugh

I have just drawn a line in the sand...
There will be no more fluff, puff, or stuff...
I will no longer say only what I want to hear...
but I will empower, embolden, and embrace the prospect's heart...
I will diligently dare to display professionalism...
and carefully create a connection with my words...
The time to inform has passed...now I must improve my impact...
The way I used to present proposes problems profusely...
I must now present with purpose, passion and power...
I must now present with a radical radar feeling focus...
My words must connect, construct and consume my prospect's heart...
My words must ignite an inferno inside my prospect's mind...
I must talk possibilities, probabilities and potentialities...
I must talk with direction, diction, and destiny...
They no longer must hear my hapless, hopeless words...
But they must feel the fire and force of a focus fully embraced...
A focus that tells a story of vision, value and victory...
Not one of victim, vexing, and venting...
My words must carry a strong sense of daring destiny unleashed...
Not a weak sense of dull direction unfolding...
And the secret to a powerful presentation lies low in the dark corners of the heart...
Waking up my prospects passion and purpose...
that will propel them to a place of hot hope...
A hope on fire with change, choice, and challenge...
waking up someone's future that felt frozen forever...
My only commitment is to communicate construction...
Bending, building, bettering and believing in a beautiful future...
So the words I say and present are not only felt and heard...
but become welded to the recesses of my prospect's heart...
So their future is changed and they charge the fields of mediocrity...
With the armor of my words wrapped around their minds...
And the fire of my passion "Firing Up" the downtrodden...
And knowing that I am willing to give more than I have gotten...
For I now know that my words are life-changing tools...
and when I do my presentation...strength must rule...
So as I enter the stage arena I have only one desire...
To set my waiting audience...forever... On Fire.

"May you have all the happiness and luck

that life can hold-

And at the end of all your rainbows

may you find a pot of gold."

Irish Blessing

 Tip → *"Write your thoughts in the sand*
on the beaches of the world."
Jan Ruhe

The room is quiet.
Everyone is
looking at you.
What are you
going to say?

Chapter 1

You Are The Ticket!

"It's not who you are, but how you are."
Bob Webb

When you buy a ticket to the movies, a sporting event, a plane ticket, train ticket, theater ticket, a seminar ticket, or any ticket, what are you *really* buying? You are buying an expectation of a presentation that will change your being. Even churches, cathedrals and synagogues have figured it all out. Once you learn this and figure this out, you can make a fortune in presenting yourself. It's not about how **you** want to present; figure out what your audience expects from you and fulfill it, then they will come back over and over again to hear you!

Concert Tickets:
Your favorite group is playing in your town and you just have to buy a front row seat. Last time the tickets sold out in one hour. So you and your friends camp out at the ticket office. Think about it: What are you really buying?

What about going to:
Barbara Streisand. *What do you expect?*
Celine Dion.   *What do you expect?*
Elton John.   *What do you expect?*
Garth Brooks.   *What do you expect?*
Madonna.   *What do you expect?*
Rolling Stones.   *What do you expect?*
Widespread Panic. *What do you expect?*

You have a pre-conceived idea of what you expect. You want your expectations to be fulfilled, right? Well, what if your expectations are not fulfilled? Do you never go back to a concert? Of course not, you just say 'oh well, it wasn't what I thought it would be,' and the next time you hear about a concert you think twice of what your expectations will be. Concerts are meant to move your spirit in some way. If you are moved in spirit, you will go back again and again to a concert. And they serve refreshments. The sounds are incredible, all planned for you. And, oh yes the concerts start on time! The concert producers have figured out what the public expects; and they fulfill it! That's why the concert industry is so gigantic. They have their presentations down!

Movie Tickets:

You decide to go to a movie, there are lots of choices. You stand in line to buy a ticket. Think about it: What are you *really* buying?

What about going to:

a chick flick.	*What do you expect?*
a controversial movie.	*What do you expect?*
a happy movie.	*What do you expect?*
a movie with action.	*What do you expect?*
a sad movie.	*What do you expect?*

You have a pre-conceived idea of what you expect. You want your expectations to be fulfilled, right? Well, what if your expectations are not fulfilled? Do you never go back to a movie? Of course not, you just say 'oh well, it wasn't what I thought it would be,' and the next time you hear about a movie you think twice of what your expectations will be. Movies are meant to move your spirit in some way. If you are moved in spirit, you will go back again and again to the movies. And they serve refreshments. The sound is amazing, all planned for you. And, oh yes they start on time! The movie industry has figured out what the public expects; and they fulfill it! That's why the movie industry is so gigantic. They have their presentations down!

Sporting Events Tickets:

It's the big day of the game and you have your ticket ready to go into the stadium. Fall is in the air and you hope your team wins. Think about it: What are you *really* buying?

What about attending:

a basketball game.	*What do you expect?*
a boxing match.	*What do you expect?*
a football game.	*What do you expect?*
a golf tournament.	*What do you expect?*
a hockey game.	*What do you expect?*
a rugby match.	*What do you expect?*
a soccer match.	*What do you expect?*
the horse races.	*What do you expect?*
the Olympics.	*What do you expect?*

You have a pre-conceived idea of what you expect. You want your expectations to be fulfilled, right? Well, what if your expectations are not fulfilled? Do you never go back to a sporting event? Of course not, you just say 'oh well, it wasn't what I thought it would be,' perhaps the team you were cheering for didn't perform very well. Most real fans go back again and again. Spectator sports are meant to move your spirit in some way. If you are moved in spirit, you will go back again and again to the sporting events. And they serve refreshments. The sound is amazing, all planned for you. And, oh yes they start on time! The sporting industry has figured out what the public expects; and they fulfill it! That's why the sports industry is so gigantic. They have their presentations down!

Plane Tickets:
You are seated in the airplane, all buckled in, waiting for take off to an adventure you have been planning for a long time. Think about it: What are you *really* buying?

What about jetting to:

Aspen.	*What do you expect?*
Australia.	*What do you expect?*
Europe.	*What do you expect?*
Hawaii.	*What do you expect?*
London.	*What do you expect?*
New Zealand.	*What do you expect?*
South Africa.	*What do you expect?*

You have a pre-conceived idea of what you expect. You want your expectations to be fulfilled, right? Well, what if your expectations are not fulfilled? Do you never plan another holiday? Of course not, you just say 'oh well, it wasn't what I thought it would be,' and the next time you hear about a destination you might think twice of what your expectations will be. Vacations are meant to move your spirit in some way. If you are moved in spirit, you will dream and plan and take more holidays. And they serve refreshments. And, oh yes they do their best to be on time! The planes are orderly; the excitement builds as you take off down the runway for an adventure. It's all about expectations! The airline industry has figured out what the public expects; and they fulfill it! That's why the airline industry is so gigantic. They have their presentations down!

Train Tickets:
You are boarding a passenger train and slowly the train takes off for a new destination or even the same destination that you go to daily. Think about it: What are you *really* buying?

What about going on:

a bullet train.	*What do you expect?*
Amtrak across America.	*What do you expect?*
from Dublin to Cork.	*What do you expect?*
from London to Milton Keynes.	*What do you expect?*
from Vancouver to Whistler.	*What do you expect?*
on Africa's Rovos Rail.	*What do you expect?*
the Orient Express.	*What do you expect?*

You have a pre-conceived idea of what you expect. You want your expectations to be fulfilled, right? Well, what if your expectations are not fulfilled? Do you never go back on a train ride? Of course not, you just say 'oh well, it wasn't what I thought it would be,' and the next time you hear about a train ride you think twice of what your expectations will be. Train rides are meant to move your spirit in some way. If you are moved in spirit, you will take the train again and again. That's why the train serves you food. The sound is amazing, all planned for you. And, oh yes they start on time! The train industry has figured out what the public expects; and they fulfill it! That's why the train industry is so gigantic. They have their presentation down!

Theater Tickets:

The lights go down, the curtain rises, the orchestra begins to play and the live theater begins. Think about it: What are you really buying?

What about attending:

Aida.	*What do you expect?*
Les Miserable.	*What do you expect?*
Miss Saigon.	*What do you expect?*
Phantom of the Opera.	*What do you expect?*
Starlight Express.	*What do you expect?*
The Lion King.	*What do you expect?*

You have a pre-conceived idea of what you expect. You want your expectations to be fulfilled, right? Well, what if your expectations are not fulfilled? Do you never go back to the theater? Of course not, you just say 'oh well, it wasn't what I thought it would be,' and the next time you hear about a live theater production you think twice of what your expectations will be. The live theater is meant to move your spirit in some way. If you are moved in spirit, you will go again and again to the live production. And they serve refreshments. The sounds are amazing; all planned for you. And, oh yes, they start on time! The theater industry has figured out what the public expects! And they fulfill it, that's why the theater industry is so gigantic and popular. They have their presentation down!

4

Seminar Tickets:

The big day arrives, you think about what you are going to wear. You make sure to have a pen full of ink and a journal to take notes in. You are going to hear someone give you information that you are seeking that could make your life better forever. You are in a personal growth and development program and are anxious to hear from the top people in your industry. Think about it: What are you *really* buying?

You are going to attend a seminar by:

Jan Ruhe.	*What do you expect?*
Gavin Scott.	*What do you expect?*
Jayne Leach.	*What do you expect?*
Tom Hopkins.	*What do you expect?*
Jim Rohn.	*What do you expect?*
Continuing education.	*What do you expect?*

You have a pre-conceived idea of what you expect. You want your expectations to be fulfilled, right? Well, what if your expectations are not fulfilled? Do you never go back to another seminar? Of course not, you just say 'oh well, it wasn't what I thought it would be,' and the next time you hear about a seminar you think twice of what your expectations will be. Seminars are meant to move your spirit in some way. If you are moved in spirit, you will attend the same seminar again and again. That's why most seminars give you long breaks to have some food. The sounds are amazing, all planned for you. And, oh yes the pros start on time! They have figured out what the public expects; and they fulfill it! That's why the seminar industry is so gigantic. They have their presentations down!

Places of Worship:

You are in your house of worship. You are serene, peaceful, calm and enjoying being in the choir or listening to the choir sing and you are among like minded people. The sermon begins. Think about it: What were your expectations walking in the door?

It's holiday time.	*What do you expect?*
The Pastor or speaker looks a certain way.	*What do you expect?*
There are candles.	*What do you expect?*
There are flowers.	*What do you expect?*
There is lunch after the service.	*What do you expect?*
There is music.	*What do you expect?*
You are among like-minded believers.	*What do you expect?*
You have an order of worship.	*What do you expect?*

You have a pre-conceived idea of what you expect. You want your expectations to be fulfilled, right? Well, what if your expectations are not fulfilled? Do you never go back to another worship service? Of course not, you just say 'oh well, it wasn't what I thought it would be,' and the next time you hear about a certain church or pastor or priest you think twice of what your expectations will be. Worship services are meant to move your spirit in some way. If you are moved in spirit, you will attend the same church again and again. That's why most churches give you time to break bread together. The sounds are amazing, all planned for you. And, oh yes the worship services start on time! The religions of the world have figured out what the public expects; and they fulfill it! That's why the religion industry is so gigantic. They have their presentations down!

So, remember, **you** truly are what people buy. Your message, how you look, how you present is all about you. Find out what your public expects from you and deliver it!

You are the ticket!!!

Want people to come back over and over again. Find out what they expect. Pretty easy, wouldn't you agree?

> *"Like the small creeks that grow into mighty rivers that shape the terrain of the earth, the people who can move other's spirits will eventually shape the course of history."*
>
> **Jan Ruhe**

Chapter 2

Prior To
The Presentation

"Ponder the unthinkable."
Alma Gierke

Attending a Presentation:
Arrive Early to an Event-Don't Be Late:
- Fifteen minutes looking for parking…waste of time…
- Ten minutes in registration line….waste of time…
- Two minutes to make a name tag…waste of time…
- *Get there thirty minutes in advance and then network.*

Arrive early, register, get your name tag, meet the host, and greet the speaker. Then, keep your eyes on people's name tags. Network. Meet new people…you will become wealthy by knowing more people. Do not judge people's dress, hair style, jewelry as the average people do…focus on the name tag. Do not pre-judge people.

Going early to an event is precious *networking* time. Don't cheat yourself. One great new contact at an event can lead to mega future business. When you arrive early you can meet and talk with the registration person. They are normally a good person to know because they are acquainted with who makes the decisions to give speeches, they know the decision makers. This will give you a few minutes to get acquainted before all the average people arrive late with all their excuses. When you arrive early, and volunteer to help out, you will get to know the behind the scenes people and can observe and learn a lot about presentations. Presentations don't normally happen haphazardly, there is much preparation that is not readily seen. Every event that you attend is filled with hundreds of thousands of dollars of business opportunities, for those who don't arrive late.

Meet The Presenters:

Go early or stay late and meet the Presenter. You go to an event to gain knowledge. The presenter has knowledge. Go up to the Presenter and ask some prepared questions. Ask them information-gathering questions. You will leave the event with more information than anyone else who attended the event....learn from the presenter.

Before the Presentation - Be Prepared:

•Arrive early enough to check and/or adjust any on-site preparation.
•Complete all handouts.
•Do a couple of quick stretching exercises.
•Practice with the equipment.
•Greet your Host and ask questions about the important people in the audience.

What to Do When You Enter an Event:

Within 60 seconds after entering an event, shake hands with a stranger. Meeting strangers in events is where the new money and new business is. Average people seek out people they know. They say a few nice things to each other and talk about people they know....wasting time; catch up with those people over the phone, meet new people. Next, introduce the stranger you just met to someone new. Repeat this until the meeting starts!

What is Networking?:

Networking is the exchange of ideas, information and resources. Attend an event to gather information and make new relationships, not to try to sell someone. Networking bonds relationships. Networking is not selling, it's meeting people. You don't have time at an event to share important information, just gather information about other people and what they do. When you are a Master at Networking, you do not have to have a title. You look at everyone as if they are your peer. Treat everyone as an equal, a business partner, or someone very important.

Questions to Ask at the Presentation:

•Did you have difficulty finding a parking spot?
•Have you attended these meetings before?
•How did you hear about this event?
•How long has your company been in business?
•How long have you been with your company?
•How many people are in your organization?
•What does your company do?
•What do you know about the speaker?
•What is your position in your company?
•What is your target market?

Where to Sit at a Presentation:
- If you sit by a friend, you are missing opportunities galore. Strangers will not approach you because they feel they will be intruding on your friendship.
- In five years, 50% of all your business will come from people you have yet to meet.
- It doesn't make economic sense to sit with people you know.
- Many people come to events and walk around with a friend never separating. They walk together, laugh together, sit together, leave together, go through bankruptcy together, don't allow each other to meet other people, nor gather new information and rarely network. This is silly and the loss of future business is incredible.
- Never sit at an empty table. Let others choose a table first, and then you go to that person and ask, *"Is this seat taken?"*
- Never sit by someone from your office.
- Raise the self-esteem of a stranger at an event; your own self-esteem will thank you.
- Reach out to people you *don't* know.
- Sit between two people you don't know.
- Sit by a stranger:
    - A stranger at an event can open up unlimited possibilities.
    - Do you want comfort or a new contact?
    - Fill an empty chair beside someone. Allow no space between you and your dreams.
- Sitting by an empty chair has no value. A chair does not answer questions, does not have business cards, and does not make purchases.
- They don't buy from you. They don't sell to you; you don't need their business card.

Tardy Tales:
Being late for events is unprofessional. When people see you rushing in at the last possible moment that says a lot about who you are, your organizational habits and your procrastination habits. It shouts that the meeting is of low priority to you and shows your lack of sincere interest in the meeting. Those who are latecomers are rarely invited to be presenters. Whatever your excuse, the Champions don't believe your excuse or expect you ever to be on time.

If you were offered $50,000 to be an hour early at the next event, would you arrive an hour early? Probably so. You might stay all night so you would not miss the deadline.

If you arrive at an event and there are groups of people standing around, you are late, shame! Professionals enter events normally two at a time. Two is not a group. If you are early, you can get to meet some remarkable people. Arrive early. Leaders know this!

Learn to say: *"May I have your business card? I believe I know people you might want to know and you have people I might like to know. I'll give you a call tomorrow and let's determine if we should get together and help each other develop some new business, I have enjoyed meeting you…"* Spend no longer than five minutes with each stranger you meet. Be smooth, be subtle, and at the end of 300 seconds, no matter what…move on.

Questions to Avoid Asking at Events:
- •How is your family?
- •How is your golf game?
- •Where did you go on your vacation?

Know Your Outcome:
This is what you want people to say about your presentations after they are over:
- •Bravo! You made complicated subjects seem elementary!
- •Brilliant!
- •Excellent, and I heard nothing but compliments about the presentation!
- •Greatly contributed to the success of the conference!
- •Is one of the most entertaining speakers I have heard!
- •Please accept our thanks!
- •Spectacular!
- •It was excellent in terms of both presentation and content!
- •It was the best we have had in a long time!
- •Without a doubt the program you presented here!
- •You added greatly to my knowledge!

John Wesley's Thoughts:
At all the times you can,
Do all the good you can,
By all the means you can,
In all the ways you can,
In all the places you can,
To all the people you can,
As long as you ever can.

Cavett Robert, founder of the National Speakers Association and the 1949 winner of the Toastmasters International World Championship of Public Speaking, used to say, *"80% of the people don't care about your problems and the other 20% think you deserve them!"*

> *"March on. Fear not the thorns*
> *or the sharp stones on life's path."*
> **Kahil Gibran**

Go over the 5 "W's":

Who? Will be:

Presenters-trainers or facilitators.

Participants-all who will be receiving the presentation.

Others-anyone whose views or input will influence the presentation.

What? The topic to be covered in the presentation. What does the audience expect from the presentation? What resources are available for use in the presentation?

Why? What is the outcome of the presentation to be? Have reasonable objectives been set?

Where? Location.

When? Date and time, stay within your allotted time.

Lisa Combs shares: *"Prior to a presentation give serious thought to the order in which your speakers present. A serious, straight to the point kind of speaker presents early in the day. A lively speaker should speak after lunch in order to liven up for the next presenter. By being aware of your speaker's personality type and presenting style, you are able to structure your presentations to give your audience maximum benefit."*

Kathy Roland Smith shares: *"When you are prepared to present, stop and put on your presentation face! Let your face show that you are excited and passionate about what you are going to say and your message will penetrate others!"*

"Don't be afraid to give your best to what seemingly are small jobs. Every time you conquer one it makes you that much stronger. If you do the little jobs well, the big ones tend to take care of themselves."

Dale Carnegie

Would You Buy From You?
Test Yourself and See Prior to Your Presentation.

Plato, the Greek Philosopher wrote: *"The life that is unexamined is not worth living."* One of the most effective ways to assess your effectiveness in giving a presentation is by asking the question: *"If you were the customer, would you buy from yourself after your presentation?"*

You would if you scored well on the following quiz:
(Answer each question below by selecting either Yes or No.)

	Yes	No
•Based on your experience with customers over the past year, from the customers' point of view, would you be referred to as reliable?	☐	☐
•Can you honestly say most of your company's customers think of you as a friend as well as a business associate?	☐	☐
•Do customers look to you as a reliable source of product and industry information?	☐	☐
•Do you think you come across as an expert in the opinions of your customers?	☐	☐
•Has doing business with you contributed positively to most of your customers?	☐	☐
•Have you been effective in helping to solve customer challenges?	☐	☐
•Is your image one of honest and straightforward sincerity?	☐	☐
•Outside your business dealings, do you think customers believe you have their personal welfare and well being at heart?	☐	☐
•Whenever possible, would you say you handle customer complaints to the customer's satisfaction?	☐	☐
•Would most of your company's customers continue dealing with you even if a competitor approached them with a price that's a little bit lower?	☐	☐

Total Number of Yes answers_____

Your rating. Multiply the sum of your *Yes* answers by 5. If you achieved a score of 50 or higher, it's a privilege to do business with you. 45 is well above average. 35-40, you need to work on your presentation and sales skills much more.

Presentations Are Everywhere

Present fun gifts, be a go-giver
as well as a go-getter.

Jan Ruhe's Millennium presentation shoes worn on
her worldwide speaking tour celebrating
the turn of the century!

Take pictures of presentations -
they keep memories alive!

Presentations Are Everywhere

Be the one to create the wonderful
memories for others. These are stars in
Jan Ruhe's organization in the USA
Kathy Roland Smith, Pam Evans & Melynda Lilly

Long time friends
Laurie Butler & Jan Ruhe
Dog sledding together at Krabloonik
Snowmass, Colorado

Long time friends
Louise Adrian & Jan Ruhe
Vancouver, Canada

Chapter 3

Preparing
The Presentation

"Love presenting and leave out your personal drama."
Jan Ruhe

The Attitude of a Champion Presenter:

When you are a presenter your success depends on your attitude. From the minute you walk into the room until you are back home behind closed doors, you must maintain a positive mental attitude. People want you to give them a presentation that holds their attention. If you are negative or sarcastic, you are not going to get positive and powerful results. Prior to your presentation start by saying to yourself, *"I am happy, I am healthy and today's presentation is going to be my best one ever!"*

Presenter's Affirmations

- I am open to receiving huge sums of money from expected and unexpected sources *and I deserve it.*
- I deserve all that I need and want. All of my desires are good for me and for all concerned.
- In my career as a presenter, slumps are unheard of.
- My job is the pipeline by which I tap the infinite wealth of the universe for my own personal use.
- The slump is over and I am on a new and exciting upward trend, now.

Keep a Positive Attitude:

1. As a presenter you need to have a degree of boldness. You must be different. You are a messenger and must speak from authority, experience or wisdom. Be bold in your presentations. It's okay to stand out from the average.

2. It is essential to believe in your products and how they can help others. Use them yourself and teach others how to use them. Believe in your company and the opportunity you have to offer others.

3. Make a commitment to yourself of what you want to accomplish. Commitment means setting production goals of what you will do and this means a time commitment. Wishing will not make it so. Time and effort will.

4. Move on! Whatever your initial reaction to a situation, you must take action if you are ever going to move ahead. Don't let rejection get you down. People are not born optimists or pessimists; it is the attitude they assume that forms their outlook. You are the one who makes the determination.

5. Say to yourself: *"I am great! I believe in me."* Stick to your dreams. Do everything you can to realize them. The rest will take care of itself.

6. Some people sit back and say, : *"Boy, look at him/her. I'd love to be doing that sort of thing...(presenting)... but I just can't do that."* With that attitude nothing will ever happen. Give yourself a chance.

7. When you are giving a presentation, remember that the best presentation is filled with encouragement. Sprinkle encouragement throughout your presentation. People are magnetized to those who encourage them. They want to be around people who can encourage them to be better than they are. Be the one to encourage others.

8. Your attitude is basic to your success. Your positive attitude, your example to others sets their attitude for what they will do and accomplish.

9. Fire Up! Go for greatness!

10. Don't be average, be a Champion!

Have Courage:

What do most presenters have in common? They have courage. If you have courage, you can be a great presenter. You have to have courage. You have to have the courage to persevere. The danger in public speaking and making presentations is that you might fail. You have to have courage to take a risk every single time you make a presentation. Read everything you can on making presentations and have the courage to increase your presentation skills. Never be too proud to sit in an audience of a pro. Take notes on how they present their material. Have the courage to think success, develop a strong belief in yourself and visualize yourself being hugely successful. Great presenters encounter fear but they are able to overcome their fears. They call upon their inner self-confidence in their own abilities.

Non-Verbal Cues to Use in Your Presentation To Encourage the Audience to Like You:
- Keep eye contact for seven to ten seconds before looking away.
- Keep your body facing your audience.
- Lean forward.
- React to your audience by nodding and smiling.
- Use positive gestures.

The Benefits of An Enthusiastic Presentation:
- Attitudes are more important than facts. People would rather listen to an enthusiastic person than a know-it-all.
- Enthusiasm is contagious!
- When you are enthusiastic you will have more physical energy.
- You will attract amazing individuals into your life.
- You will make people feel better.

Presenter's Affirmations

- All my feelings of rejection have vanished into thin air!
- All the power of the universe is mine and I use it now to the advantage of all concerned.
- I am alive and well and I shall go forward to do my best and win!
- I am creative and have many ideas of how to increase my earnings.
- I create new and wonderful ideas at will.
- I forgive and release forever all who may have appeared to have hurt me.
- I know what I want in life and I will do whatever it takes to get it.
- I must seek self-awareness, self-approval and self-commitment in order to attain self-fulfillment.
- I will not follow where the path may lead. I will go instead where there is no path and leave a trail.
- Love to dream about what could be and involve others in my dreams.
- My creativity is a daily demonstration of my power.
- My income now far exceeds my expenses.
- My net worth increases daily whether I am at work, at play or asleep.
- These things that happen today only pave the way to success.

Get Enthusiastic:

Have you ever noticed how much more energy flows in groups of people instead of just one or two? Do you remember going to High School Pep Rallies? Everyone got very excited because they had a common goal, to cheer the team on to victory. The more people who came, the more fun it became! Plan your events to include at least three or more people at a time.

Enthusiasm is not jumping up and down, slapping people on the back and smiling at all times. It's more like totally bottled up excitement, energetic excitement. You can see it and feel it. Enthusiasm is a magnet, it attracts. Enter your presentations enthusiastically. The hardest part for many people is entering a room of strangers. Relax and enjoy the attention. If you are that special, people will make the first move and initiate contact with you. They will take care of you. Enter the room with a smile. That opens people up to talking with you. Don't walk into a room looking serious and forbidding so that you give out signals that say *"Don't talk to me!"* Let your body language be enthusiastic to show that you are glad to be there. The pace of your entry is important. Some people run up to the stage and think that it is a great way to enter a room. Others take their time and shake hands as they enter the room. Here are some tips on how to do it:

Be a *How* person!
Be a *Now* person!
Be a *Pow* person!
Be a *Vow* person!
Be a *Wow* person!

- Be proud of who you are, you are someone who can make a difference!
- Don't aim too low or move too slow!
- Don't knock it! Don't block it! Unlock it!
- Enthusiasm can wear out. There are limits to every person's emotional energy. When it runs out, refuel and revitalize.
    - *"Don't get angry and depressed"* power.
    - *"Hold on"* power.
    - *"Start over again"* power.
    - *"Stay with it"* power.
- Enthusiasm is a choice!
- Enthusiasm is power!
- Enthusiasm won't let you quit!
- Get a fresh color in your skin!
- Get consumed with enthusiasm!
- Go for your dream!
- Know that there is hope!

Using Enthusiasm:

Bob Webb shares: *"In your presentations people must feel you are enthusiastic about your company or products. If you are having a bad day/week, you have a few options, some of which may get you back to 'Fired Up!:' Talk to no one that day; find a motivator; or, play a good motivational, training or music audio."*

Carlos Gueits shares: *"Build the dream, because if you can help show them the "why" they will figure out the "how." "Your enthusiasm is more important than what you say because nobody is going to remember everything in your presentation the first time they see it, but your excitement they will remember."*

Cathy Barber shares: *"Be excited! Be excited! Be excited! People are not interested in hearing about the details but just that you are certain about your destiny and are committed to helping them get there also!"*

The last four letters of the word enthusiasm, *iasm,* stand for *"I am sold myself!"* If you are sold yourself and can articulate that for all of the personalities in your audience, you will have an outstanding presentation, count on it! Raw enthusiasm puts life into your presentation, it distinguishes you as a person who is interested in what you do and you enjoy what you do. Audiences value this in a presenter and are influenced by it. Have a contagious enthusiasm so people can't resist your excitement!

How to Present With More Enthusiasm:

- •Be more sensitive to others.
- •Be with enthusiastic people.
- •Give enthusiasm away.
- •Practice, drill and rehearse! Make it a daily part of your life!
- •Start each day by saying this affirmation: *"I feel healthy, I feel terrific, today is going to be a great day, abundance and prosperity are coming my way!"*

 Tip ➜ •*Don't keep a poker face.*
•*Don't lean or move away from your audience.*
•*Move around, give them some animation.*
•*Smile!*

Red Socks:

Edward Ludbrook claims, while doing his presentation, that he often wears red socks as a visual symbol for *"enthusiasm."* The audience always remembers him.

Red socks are actually a very upper class British country trait: Tweed jacket, wool tie, corduroy trousers, brogue shoes and red socks. In the British countryside, you often hear: *"Off for a pint at the Duck and Dog after pheasant shooting, old boy?"*

Question: Is it time to get more enthusiastic?

Ten Steps to a Powerful Presentation:

A powerful presentation contains certain techniques that must be applied throughout the presentation:

1. **Be confident.** Confidence inspires credibility. If they believe you, they'll like you. If they like you, they'll buy from you.
2. **Be focused.** Stay on point. Nothing will lose your audience more than your wandering off on some irrelevant tangent.
3. **Be forceful with your enthusiasm and vitality.** This is where you get the audience saying their *"amens"* along with you.
4. **Be positive.** Negative cut-downs and satire will drive the audience out the door.
5. **Care about others**. It's not what you know but what you show.
6. **Learn your story**. Inject your personality into presenting. Your outline gives you complete and confident control of every presentation.
7. **Outline your presentation**. Make a blue-print of your presentation.
8. **Preliminary preparation**. Gather the *benefits* about your product, service, opportunity and competition.
9. **Put your presentation into words.** Make points you must cover in an outline, using tested techniques for achieving a sure-fire presentation. Make masterful use of all your *benefits* for explaining your products and opportunity.
10. **Start every day** saying, *"Prosperity and abundance are coming my way."*

 Tip ➔ *The audience wants you to succeed.*

The Master presenters have found that first you must make people hungry and thirsty for something you can give them and then give them more than they bargained for. It is unfair to eat a seven-course dinner at someone's home, and then invite them over for a box lunch!

What is an Outstanding Presentation?

An outstanding presentation:
- convincingly satisfies your customer's buying motives and so persuasively removes all buying obstacles, that they decide to place an order.
- explains a saleable item or opportunity to someone by a salesperson.
- keeps the emphasis on the customer's point of view—on how the customer stands to gain by making a purchase or joining you in your opportunity.
- is smooth and convincing such that it leads in a logical manner from the opening sentence to the close of the presentation.
- persuades the audience to your point of view.

The success of your presentation depends on how:
- closely your presentation anticipates the audience's desires.
- much you have learned about your audience, and how well you fit the two together.
- thoroughly you know your product, subject matter or opportunity.

Jerry Clark shares: *"Try to understand their challenges, hurts, pains, dreams, aspirations, desires, wants and needs...know why they showed up to see and hear you...and be sure to leave them feeling that they got what they came for and more...make them want to come back and hear you again and bring other people."*

 Tip → *To sell Jane Smith what Jane Smith buys, you must see Jane Smith through Jane Smith's eyes.*

Geralynn Johnson shares: *"I have yet to see or hear what I believe to be the best presentation. Every presentation has been a great learning experience for me and I always take notes and learn something new from everyone. Each person has their own unique style and I try to incorporate some of these new techniques into my own presentation while maintaining my own style."*

 Tip → *Public speaking is the second biggest fear in the world next to death. Conquer it!*

> *"All the world's a stage, and all the men and women merely players. They have their exits and their entrances; and one man in his time plays many parts."*
>
> **William Shakespeare**

Use the *Engage* Formula:

E = *establish eye contact!*

N = *nod!*

G = *get happy!*

A = *aim your attention!*

G = *gesture appropriately!*

E = *effect an easy posture!*

Use the *Present* Formula:

P = *present with enthusiasm!*

R = *repeat key points!*

E = *enthusiastically present information!*

S = *sell the benefits!*

E = *use emotion!*

N = *nod your head up and down!*

T = *tell them again!*

Tip ➔ *When the people in the audience start looking at their watches, you are in trouble.*

A Successful Presentation has:

P = *strong product!*

P = *a plan!*

P = *passion!*

E = *energy!*

A = *action!*

Tip ➔ *Go for greatness, do not hold back.*

The one thing that builds fine presenters is the experience of doing presentations again and again. People can make outstanding presentations adequately by learning from books and tapes. Many have done fine not going to seminars or listening to presentations... so many people are just too busy to study great presenters and presentations and won't spend the money. The champions know more than just one presentation. Learn how to listen so as to find what people need. When we find out what the audience wants, all we have to do is present the benefits that will fit their needs. Over and over again. Stack your successes upon your successes and learn to love being a presenter!

Rod Nichols shares: *"Be a good story teller. People love to hear good stories. They will help maintain the audience's attention, making it easier for you to present your business."*

Andy Hummel shares: *"Presenting is learning to ask the correct questions, listening to what people say, and then showing them how what you have will allow them to accomplish what they want."*

Master Flexibility in a One-on-One Presentation:
- Flexibility means being able to switch your emphasis to appeal to an audience's buying motives.
- Flexibility means being able to meet unexpected challenges and interruptions and still control the presentation.
- If your presentation has been thoroughly prepared, it has anticipated what would otherwise be "unforeseen" challenges.
- Unexpected changes of direction will be kept to a minimum.

Benefits of Following a Prepared Presentation Word-for-Word:
- A planned and orderly presentation is the most efficient kind; it moves logically and convincingly from one point to the next.
- An organized presentation enables you to control the interview and smoothly guide the customer toward the close.
- If you master your presentation completely, you won't leave out or forget vital parts.
- In the process of preparing, you learn all about what you're selling and how it should be sold.
- People are impressed by presenters who show that they have taken the trouble to prepare and organize their material.
- You are sure of covering the important *benefits* in every presentation.
- You make the best use of your presentation minutes.
- Your words, carefully chosen, are the ones with maximum impact and persuasiveness.
- You have the confidence that comes from being well prepared.

Make Your Presentation Outline a Blueprint:
- A detailed outline simplifies the actual writing of a word for word presentation.
- Make your outline as complete as you can to help you develop your presentation.
- The best way to organize your material into a logical, orderly, and convincing presentation is to make an outline. This organizes your thoughts and enables you to make the best use of the facts and *benefits* that your want to present to your customer.
- Though an outline you can see how all of your information is going to go into an orderly presentation.
- Whether your outline is simple or detailed will depend on your product and your opportunity.

Tip ➔ *Take pains to make each step connect smoothly with the next. This will be of particular importance when you put your presentation into words, following your outline.*

Take Pride In:
- The contribution you make.
- Your ability to help other people improve their lives.
- Your ability to sell.
- Your appearance.
- Your honesty.
- Your knowledge.
- Your punctuality.
- Your reliability.
- Your reputation.
- Your skills.

Tip ➔ *Don't be satisfied with your presentation only. Be satisfied when you have achieved 100% customer satisfaction.*

Lena Akerman shares: *"Let your passion radiate the audience because passion is the most important tool to spur people to make quantum leaps in life. Let your heart conduct the presentation instead of your script."* Her favorite presentation is: *"The presentation that is interactive with the audience and filled with laughter."*

Tip ➔ *Look for the "New" in your product. Find something new in design, construction, service, enjoyment, fashion, and benefits. When you find it, build your presentation on it.*

John Milton Fogg shares: *"A great presentation comes down to one and only one thing. Where is the presenter's attention - on the audience, or on themselves? It's all a conversation, whether from the stage or across the table over coffee.*

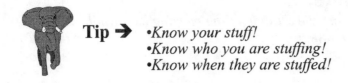

Tip → •*Know your stuff!*
•*Know who you are stuffing!*
•*Know when they are stuffed!*

Tom Schreiter shares: *"Make your presentations short. If I come to your door and had a little salesman hat on and I said, 'I have a long presentation and I have a short presentation, which one would you prefer?' You'd say, 'The short presentation.' Give them what they want."*

Presentation Time:

Watch your timing. Anytime you go over thirty minutes you stand to lose a portion of the audience. Some in your audience will want you to start and end on time because by going over you are now cutting into "*their time.*"

•Include enough information to accomplish every step of the sales process and do a superb selling job. Brevity must never overshadow the purpose of the presentation.
•Keep your presentations clear and brief. Keep it as short as it can be and still be complete.
•Some of the time consumed in a presentation is devoted to listening to what the customer has to say or answering questions asked, and sometimes to waiting out interruptions.
•Start the presentation at the most advantageous time.
•The actual length of a presentation in minutes will depend on what you sell, but it should normally be no more than fifteen minutes or less. Some products can be effectively presented in a minute and a half, using in that time perhaps two hundred well-chosen words.

Tip → *Don't be a chain talker!*

David Stewart shares: *"Set the audience up for success. A presentation really begins with your pre-meeting conduct. Arrive at least thirty minutes earlier than the scheduled time. Everything that takes place before the meeting will color the newcomer's perception of the presentation. Design your pre-meeting conduct and the presentation itself, so that it has the maximum effect of helping people understand the opportunity. When people witness a presentation, they have only a short time to see and understand a success story that has taken years to develop."*

Music and Your Attitude:

Gavin Scott shares: *"Your attitude and the attitude of the meeting as a whole are so very important for doing a great presentation."*

The meeting attitude:

Have you ever been in a lift, or a doctor's or dentist's waiting room, with no music? You can cut the atmosphere with a knife, everybody is hesitant to speak. Some meetings are like that and people really feel uncomfortable. The last thing you want is to have guests feeling uncomfortable. Have you ever been driving your car being a bit down, when a positive record comes on the radio. Wow! Three minutes later you are on the top of the world, your attitude back to 100%. Make sure your meeting has positive attitude music; and raise the volume as people arrive. When the meeting starts, your room will have a mega positive attitude. At one meeting we did not have the right music, people said the presentation was ok, but was not quite as good. We knew what was wrong. It's nice to give people a lift with positive music.

Your attitude:

If your attitude is negative, you might as well just cancel the presentation or let somebody else do it. I've done presentations for almost nine years now and only once did I do a presentation when I was negative, it was my third presentation. Two minutes before it started, someone accused me of stealing £25 and demanded the money right then and there in front of new people. I got him out of the room and cleared up the matter with him. I then started the presentation. At the end, I had a line of people asking what was wrong. He took the focus off the presentation. I have never put anything negative out to the audience, but I learned that if my attitude was not right, I should let someone else do the presentation. That person has never made it with our company, I wonder why? He's lost millions in bonuses so far. So a tip! Always have your favorite uplifting music playing, to keep your attitude up. And just to prove it works, tape three songs you hate and play them in a row and see how you feel. But, remember to have your positive tape ready to put you on track.

The Power of Music:

Music is a most important part of any presentation. To your audience, music speaks to the auditory side of their personality the most but it gives a good feeling to the kinesthetic side as well, and we all have a kino side, don't we? Music intervals during your presentation will have the effect of changing the state of your audience. You can control the tempo of your presentation with music. With music, you can get them to laugh with you or cry with you. You can get them high and you can get them low. Become a collector of great presentation music. With the new CD burners on the market today you can have a music collection for your speeches in no time. When preparing your presentation choose your music. There is a sample listing of music in the Appendix.

"Canned" Presentations Can be *"Great:"*

Don't let anyone discourage you from using what you have prepared as a great presentation because it is "canned." Some of the greatest presentations have been canned. Let's see what some people find objectionable about a canned presentation and how their arguments break down, if the presentation is impelling.

Myth #1: A "canned" sales talk sounds dead and lacks spontaneity.
Truth: Actors in long-run plays find meaning for lines they have said perhaps a thousand times. So do most really successful presenters, who stick to a perfected and memorized presentation that for them has proved its effectiveness. Having found the best way to tell their story, they continue to use it in its best form and are not in the least mechanical, judging by their success. Even presenters who would discredit using the standardized presentation admit that any kind of presentation, if given often enough, tends to settle into a fixed pattern.

Myth #2: Some presenters complain that interruptions throw them off when they are in the midst of a memorized presentation.
Truth: Actually any presentation can be disrupted by questions and interruptions unless you maintain control over the presentation and your thoughts. Using a well-prepared presentation minimizes interruptions by making one point flow smoothly into the next.

Myth #3: Another objection says that since no two prospects are alike, you must be flexible in your presentation.
Truth: Most sales people, however, call on people for whom their product or service is suited, and whose wants and needs therefore tend to be at least somewhat similar.

For some products or opportunities a completely memorized, standardized presentation may not be useful. For example, when presenting a specialized product, designed to meet individual customer needs, like big pieces of equipment, vary your selling presentations from customer to customer. Although you should not have to write out a complete sales presentation, you should mentally plan what you are going to say in each presentation.

 Tip ➜ *Even if the use of a standardized presentation is not for you, you will gain by standardizing the elements that are common to all of your presentations. You will reduce the time necessary to prepare for each new presentation, and you will arrive at the most effective way in which to present the benefits that are covered in most of your presentations.*

You Are a Performer:

There are many ways to do a presentation. The great ones, the Masters, find out as much as possible about what is expected of them prior to planning their presentation. They deliver what is expected of them. To just stand in the front of the room and talk to whomever will listen does not make you a Master at presenting. Athletes, dancers and actors prepare for their *"performances."* As a presenter you want to be the best you can be and that takes practice ahead of time. Refer to this guide often. Change how you begin your presentations…make it so much fun to be a presenter that people in your audience don't want your presentation to be over! They will want to come to hear you again and again!

 Tip ➜ *Read, listen, discuss, observe, think and then present!*

Presenter's Quick Checklist

- Complete the image with the next logical step as you see it, with both you and the customer shaking hands in total agreement. Warm feelings are present.
- Now allow yourself to think of nothing for a moment - then write down the results which you intend to produce at this presentation.
- Now letting go of all your images, wishes, and hopes just go and do your best.
- Repeat this affirmation: *I will succeed and all of the parties to this presentation will receive a just exchange of values.*
- Say a little prayer of thanks now. You have you, you have a job, you have an opportunity, and you have a customer.
- See yourself approaching the meeting with absolute and total confidence.
- See yourself field each question with the correct response and see each response receive a nod of approval from your audience.
- See yourself making recommendations to your customer and doing it with more self-confidence and panache than you knew you had.
- Visualize the client saying *"yes"* to everything and a customer/salesperson team forming to serve this customer and his needs.
- Watch yourself make the perfect presentation from start to finish.

This should take about 10 minutes.

28

Master Check List For Preparing a Presentation:

Refer to this list when making plans for a dazzling presentation!

☐ Analyze Your Audience:

Your audience has expectations. It's important to know who you are speaking to; what age group; what is the level of understanding; what the climate in the company is like; what three key ideas do you want them to go away with that will be of value to them. Do you need to be overly enthusiastic, calm, enlightening, entertaining, exciting, serious, informative? Start your analysis with the thought, *"If at the end of my presentation I ask for an evaluation form, what do I need to do to get an outstanding evaluation from this audience?"* Start with the outcome you have in mind for your presentation.

☐ Connect with Your Audience:

Use people's names in the room, look and smile at someone you know. Use words like, *"I am glad to be back again with all of you." "You might remember last time we talked about." "You are a special group here today." "You are the real stars, if you weren't here I would have no one to make my presentation to!"*

☐ Determine Your Purpose:

Gather information from those who have invited you to make the presentation. Come from contribution. Keep a journal and take notes about what is expected. Find out important information such as the date, time, location, and audience. If you have spoken before to this audience, do they want the same presentation or are they looking for more or different information from you?

☐ Gesture with a Purpose:

You don't want to stand still in one place with your arms hanging by your side, in and out of your pockets, leaning on the podium. To get your nervous energy focused in an appropriate direction, just make purposeful gestures. Move around and do not stand in one place. Take two or three steps at the same time; do not take one step at a time. When you take several steps at one time you look confident.

☐ Get Over the Lights:

Bill Gove was the speaking coach for Jack Benny and Bob Hope for many years. During those early years of live stage presentations there were huge lights beaming right on the presenter's face. All the presenter could see was darkness. The presenter could not see the faces in the audience as he was speaking to pure blackness. Bill Gove coached these giant presenter's to *get their message over the lights*. And it's still the same today. You must get your message across.

☐ **Go for Greatness:**

Expect nothing less than a terrific presentation. Prepare for abundance and prosperity. Be thrilled to be invited, not smug and exhausted. Get more enthusiastic on the inside and your presentation will ooze of confidence and excitement magnetizing people to you forever!

☐ **Make Eye Contact:**

Looking at the people in your audience for longer than one second is one of the keys for successfully engaging your audience. End your sentences looking at a person, not your notes. Show your audience you are interested in them.

☐ **Market Your Magic:**

When you get to the front of the room, or on the platform, smile, think big thoughts, you know what the message is that is coming to your audience. Market you, market that you are fun, you have valuable information, you are important, and you have a powerful message. Tell the audience with your body language and your words. Step out into your magnificence.

☐ **Move from Ordinary to Extraordinary:**

Ordinary people talk at people, the pros talk in conversation form. Talk to your audience as if you are having a conversation with them. It's not what you know, it's what you show!

☐ **Outline Your Points:**

Give yourself key words or phrases to use. You can do this from having the total speech typed out, double-spaced or triple-spaced in front of you, written on a power point presentation, teleprompter. Or you can simply put key words on a piece of paper or in your mind. Make sure you have your points clearly in order. It's too hard for a listener to hear, *"Oh I forgot this point, let me go back to it."*

☐ **Pause Between Points:**

Most speakers are in a hurry to get the presentation over. They ramble from one point to the next, never allowing a moment of silence in the room. You must pause between your sentences. Let the audience digest what you have said. When you are making a key point, say it slower, look right at the audience and pause at the end of the point.

> *"It's not what you know, it's what you show!"*
>
> **Jan Ruhe**

☐ Practice Out Loud:

Practice in front of the mirror. Practice with someone you will let critique you. Practice phrases, the timing and the words you will emphasize during your talk. There are lists of words and phrases to use in the Appendix. When you practice out loud, your confidence and your poise will increase. If you are doing a PowerPoint presentation, go through all of your screens and make sure you have them in order and that you understand each one. If you are presenting from a fill in the blank workbook, make certain you have the answers correct, go over them out loud and make sure they make sense.

☐ Present Like a Pro:

Be prepared. Be enthusiastic. Care about your message. Care about your audience. Give them your best. Give them you. Be real, don't be a phony. Deliver your message and when you finish it, end it like you are slamming a car door shut!

☐ Present to all of the Personality Types:

Auditories = *need to hear*
Digitals = *need statistics*
Kenos = *need to feel*
Visuals = *need to see*

☐ Present Your Speech:

Be prepared. Come from contribution to others. Control your nervousness by focusing on the fact that what you have to say has value. You are making a difference. Stop and put your invisible arms around the audience before you utter your first word. Smile, be prepared to have fun, the time will go fast. Preparation is everything. Think it all through. Get a good nights rest prior to the presentation. Know that you are going to be great and that audiences are excited to hear a powerful message. There are many many presentation ideas just in this one guide. Use them as a spring board for your future presentations.

☐ Research Your Topic:

Have you looked for and discovered interesting information that you can share during your presentation. Is the information you will be presenting accurate, up-to-date and interesting for your audience?

"PDR = Practice, Drill, Rehearse."

Tom Hopkins

☐ Select Your Topic:

Take a walk, think your presentation through, and take some time to think about your topic. Pass your topic by other presenters to make sure that you are not going to overlap what another presenter of the day is talking about. Make your presentation different. Think of all the alternative ways to present. Look for visuals as you go through shopping malls, magazines or online to help you make your point visually. Focus on your audience's interests. A Topic List is in the Appendix. FAYC= Forget about yourself completely!

☐ Support Your Points:

Use humor, statistics and stories. Be careful to not just use declarative statement after statement. Look the audience in the eyes, especially when you make your main points. Use pauses between points. Ask the audience, *"Are you with me?"* before saying *"good, then moving right along."*

☐ Use Visual Aids:

Many people cannot just sit and listen to a speaker, no matter how great their story or presentation is, people must move. You can change people's states of being by using visual aids. Pictures say a thousand words. Use words that paint the picture of what you are presenting. Have fliers to pass out, or a flip chart or a chalkboard to make points on.

☐ Visualize your Presentation Being Wildly Successful:

Over and over again, see yourself getting up in front of your audience and doing a fantastic job. See yourself being calm and enthusiastic being in front of your audience. See yourself energetically walking around. After all, you are the ticket!

☐ Watch Your Words:

If you want people to:
- *feel* better about themselves and you are giving a presentation about self-esteem you will use words like: feel, felt, found…
- *learn* a new skill you will use words like: here's how, next do this, the next step is…
- *take* your information and take action, then present using action words: go, do, be, move onward, upward, take action, urgent…

If you want to talk about statistics you will use words like: the bottom line, the numbers don't lie, our statistics are looking great, let's increase sales…

As you look through this guide, you will find all kinds of tips to help you succeed in giving your presentation better and brighter than you ever dreamed possible. A list of words and phrases to use is in the Appendix.

Sell The Benefits:

When discussing only a product's feature, imagine that the audience is thinking: *"So what! Your product has this shape or quality: how does it benefit me?"* If something is about you, your business, it is a feature. If something is about the person, it is a *benefit*. If it's a *benefit*, you should be able to place the words *"You get..."* in front of it.

All products have features or physical characteristics, such as :

- Color
- Delivery
- Packaging
- Price

- Quality
- Quantity
- Size
- Shape

 Tip ➔ *Don't focus on the product features.*

Debbie Gabinet shares: *"People don't care how much you know until they know how much you care."* She is passionate about the *benefits* her products provide and builds rapport with her audience by focusing on listening so she can match the appropriate *benefit* to their need, what ever it may be.

Listing Your Selling *Benefit* Points:

- Ask other people in your company (choose successful ones) what *benefits* they have the most success with.
- Ask for opinions. People who actually use a product can shed valuable light on its advantages and draw-backs.
- If you sell a product, study it physically as if you had never seen it before. Take it apart, if possible. Try to get a look at it in action, where you can watch it and listen to it.
- Review carefully all company literature and bulletins for *benefits* that you have forgotten or have overlooked.
- Search your mind for every single *benefit* that might be a selling *benefit*, including ones that you are aware of but aren't using now in your presentation.
- Write down all the *benefits* you can think of from memory.
- You may believe that you already know all you have to about what you are selling, remember that it is the salesperson who *knows the most* about the *benefits* who reaches the top.

> *"F.A.Y.C. Forget About Yourself Completely!"*
> **Louise Adrian**

How To Select the Selling *Benefit* For Your Presentation:

- Build your presentation around the best selling **benefits** on your list.
- Choose the **benefits** that suit the largest class in your audience when developing your presentation.
- It is the **benefits** that people want and will pay for.
- Naturally the **benefits** that help most to make your product or service stand out are its **exclusive benefits**.
- Whatever they are, emphasize any **benefit** that competitors can't offer. Even a small point carries weight when it has distinctive, only-one-in-its-field authority.
- Remember that the customer is the judge and will buy only what promises to provide the customer a **benefit**.
- The **benefits** that are not included in your prepared presentation bolster your confidence and serve as reserve ammunition when the going gets rough.
- To select the most **exciting benefits**, put yourself in the audience's place. Look carefully at every point and ask yourself these questions,
  - *Is that something I especially want or need in this kind of a product or service?*
  - *Is that what would satisfy my buying motives, if I were the customer?*
  - *Would that **benefit** make my offer look any better than, or different from, other opportunities the customer will hear?*
- You can't cover every **benefit** on your list in a normal sales presentation. Your presentation would take too much time.
- You have to change the customer's state of attention into favorable interest. Do this by telling the customer what **benefits** will be gained from the purchase of your product or by getting involved in your opportunity.

How a Company-Prepared List of Sales *Benefits* Helps:

- Be sure the company list has not become outdated by fast-moving conditions in the industry, by changes in the design of the product, or changes in competitors' products.
- In designing its products, your company tries to make them better than those its competitors have to offer.
- Enlarge the company list from your own knowledge of the product and its **benefits**.
- Since the company is in on the development of the product from the beginning, the engineers and sales promotion people usually have a thorough understanding of what the product can actually do.
- The company probably uses market research to discover the **benefits** that customers are likely to want in such a product.
- The lists of sales **benefits** that your company prepares are a wonderful source of information for building your great presentation.

34

Turning Facts Into *Benefits*:

- A customer does not buy:
  - **beauty**; but buys the *pleasure and pride that possession of a beautiful object will mean.*
  - **speed**; but *buys the time saving, or the greater production, or the excitement that speed provides.*
  - **strength**; a customer buys the *durability that strength provides.*
- Behind everything the customer wants, there is the more important reason why ownership is important.
- Buying motives are satisfied not by lists of impressive features, but by the **benefits** that those features will give. There is a clear distinction between the two.
- Draw up a list of product **benefits** and **benefits** of joining your organization or investing in your products, put down everything that you can think of that is good about the product or opportunity.
- Your presentation must satisfy the customer's buying motives.

 Tip ➜ *It is crucial to stress **benefits**. As you select the selling **benefits** from which to develop your presentation, visualize each point in terms of the **benefits** that it can bring to the prospect. You've got to show the customer what **benefits** they get from buying the product or the opportunity. Ask yourself 'So what?' on each point you used, and then list the corresponding **benefit** to the prospect. You'll see a huge difference.*

Outstanding Presenter's Benefits

- Being healthy, vigorous and vibrant.
- Being proud of your work and your family.
- Feeling happy all of the time.
- Giving and receiving love.
- Having it all!
- Having rewarding relationships with friends and associates.
- Having self-esteem.
- Having time to work and time to play.
- Looking forward to each new day.
- Never having to worry about money.
- Sharing your abundance with others.

How to Use the *Benefits* in Your Presentation:
•Use examples.
•Use these words:
  • *"Say, for example, that you..."*
  • *"Suppose you had the chance to travel..."*
  • *"That means that if for some reason you need to be home with your children..."*

Prepare a simple chart to help present your product facts vs benefits:

Opportunity/Product Facts	Benefit to Customer

The Ultimate Benefit:

Everybody says in making presentations, to sell the **benefits**— but many times it just doesn't seem to work. Here it is: Stop talking features. Start talking **benefits**. Most of the time people say:

*"Here is another catalog, sales letter or pre-approach packet with features and **benefits**."* or *"Here is yet another brochure touting the **benefits** of another opportunity or product."*

Here is what happens in real life after you have made your best presentation:

You write down all the wonderful features of your business opportunity. You present a whole list of **benefits** by talking about or writing about the wonderful features in opportunity meetings, person-to-person presentations, in your sales letters, emails and in your ads.

Your results? Almost none. Your customers ignore you and almost always throw out those expensive pre-approach packets. Next, you go to an expert in marketing and ask, *"How can I make my products or opportunity more attractive? I need people to want what I am presenting and it's going too slow, what can I do to speed up this process?"*

The expert replies, *"It's clear, you are just presenting features. It's more important to stress the **benefits**. Every feature has a **benefit**. Don't make your customer figure this out. Do it for them. Stress the **benefit** your customer will receive when they join your business or invest in your product."*

So, off you go, selling and selling and selling the **benefits**. All of them! Once again, little to no results, and disappointment and doubts creep in that you should not really be in sales, right? If you have done what the Masters and experts say to do, then why aren't people lined up down your street, knocking on your door to get your product or join you in your opportunity? Then you pour on more exciting **benefits**. You tell them as many **benefits** as you can think. You do everything you can . . . and your customer then goes into objections: *"I want to think it over, I need to talk it over with my spouse, I don't have any time, money, contacts, etc."* and ignores your products or opportunity. Instead of continuing to work hard with minimal to pathetic results, wouldn't it be great to get massive results like the champions have figured out how to do? Ask yourself:

"What separates the professional presenters from the overworked, unsuccessful, struggling presenters who get little to no results after their presentations?"

*"If features and **benefits** aren't the whole answer, what is the key that gets customers or your audience intensely interested?"*

Do you know the answer? It's so simple; it's the **Ultimate Benefit**. It's as easy as that. What is an **Ultimate Benefit**? It is the objective of all presenters. It's the goals we strive for in life, a better lifestyle. It's how we spend our time and resources. It's what we all really want. The products that help people achieve these **Ultimate Benefits** are really of secondary importance. Don't base your business on products alone, but on an **Ultimate Benefit**, or several **Ultimate Benefits** that you can let your customers or audience know they *will get* from you. It's the real **benefit**, it's what they are going to love about working with you, listening to you, using your products over and over again. It's like the church you choose to worship in, it's the feeling you get when you attend that church service, it's not that the sermon is the best every time. It's why you attend a certain team event where you cheer your team on, it's not that the team wins every game.

The **Ultimate Benefit** is the theme that links all your information and activity to what you are presenting. It's what you truly sell and you must become known for. It's why customers will do business with you over and over again, *to get* that **Ultimate Benefit**.

Truth: People don't really want your product. If you are product centered, you care less about what the customer wishes to achieve than about the great by-products of what your product can do for them. Customers are not motivated by your products, but by getting the **Ultimate Benefit** from your products. People want to live well and to have prestige, financial security, salvation, good health, a lifestyle, and smart children. If you can help them achieve that, then they will listen to your presentation.

Truth: **Ultimate Benefits** endure. They are the reason a customer buys once and why, if it works, a customer will buy over and over again.

Truth: Products come and go. Sell the **benefits** of doing business *with you, you are the ticket*. People will remember the name of the product or company, but if you are a presenter, they quickly will forget you. You must sell yourself. Build a relationship, follow up, take an interest in the customer. If you are dedicated to a product, you are going to be very disappointed when it goes. And it will go. Sooner or later, it will most likely be updated or replaced.

Truth: Sell the **Ultimate Benefit** to your customer. It is far more important than any individual product.

Adapted from Tom Schreiter

Present the
Ultimate Benefit

Here is a list of some **Ultimate Benefits**:
- •Achieving inner serenity.
- •Being attractive sexually.
- •Cutting expenses.
- •Gaining acceptance from one's peers.
- •Getting an edge in life.
- •Getting or staying financially secure.
- •Getting or staying healthy.
- •Giving your children an edge in the classroom.
- •Having adventure.
- •Having excitement.
- •Having prestige and arousing envy.
- •Living well.
- •Making the world a better place.
- •Protecting home.
- •Protecting our family.
- •Saving money.

 Tip ➔ •*Define your product or opportunity so that it embodies the* ***Ultimate Benefit.***
- •*Direct your product to the broadest possible market.*
- •*Get busy talking about the **Ultimate Benefit** of working with you, your product and/or your opportunity.*
- •*Make sure you can reach many people.*
- •*Make sure you find broad markets.*
- •*Select an **Ultimate Benefit** that your products will give the customer.*

Focus only on an **Ultimate Benefit** for which you are going to become known for when you make a presentation. Your products will be secondary to the one **Ultimate Benefit** which is the backbone not the wishbone of your future business. You will become known for delivering that **Ultimate Benefit** and you are going to focus on that from now on. What will the customer really get by using your product or joining your opportunity? Tune into the Station **WIIFM**, *What's in it for me?*

Present the
Ultimate Benefit

Study Your Competition:

- After you have compiled a list of the *benefits* you can offer, take a good look at what your competition has to offer.
- Be aware of all local factors that make competitive conditions in your area different. It has a direct bearing on the *benefits* to be emphasized and your preparation to meet objections.
- Knowledge of competing products enables you to evaluate your list of selling *benefits*.
- Stress *benefits* that are better than competitors can offer, or exclusive with your line.
- Studying competitors enables you to find out what their *benefits* are.
- The better you know your competition, the better you can select and utilize the *benefits* that are yours alone.
- The presentation should stress the superior or exclusive *benefits* of your product or opportunity.
- Your two biggest competitors, for example, might offer low initial kit costs, just as you can. You must still use this *benefit* in your presentation, because it is an important point, even though it is not exclusive with you.
- Your list of *benefits* must not omit other important advantages and *benefits* just because they are shared by competitors.

The Presenter's Creed:

- To serve every family as if it were my own.
- To treat every woman as if she were my own mother or sister.
- To treat every man as if he were my father or brother.

Be Prepared!
(Sung to the Boy Scouts song)

Be prepared, that's the speaker's marching song,
Be prepared, as through a speech you march along,
Be prepared to hold your temper pretty well,
Don't present to any customers you cannot sell.
Looking forward to each new day.
Be prepared to hide your pack of self-regrets.
Be prepared and never let them see you sweat.
If you fail to talk them into
All the good that you can do,
And your boss says, *"So what happened?"*
And you haven't got a clue,
You can always say, *"I left them with some things on which to chew,
But I prepared. I was just scared!"*

Patricia Fripp shares: *Anticipate your presentation mentally, physically and logistically.*"
Here's how:

Mentally:
Start by understanding that you will spend a lot more time preparing than you will speaking. As a general rule, invest three hours of preparation for a half-hour speech. When you have become a highly experienced speaker, you may be able to cut this time considerably in some cases, but until then, don't skimp. Part of your preparation will be to memorize your opening and closing - three or four sentences each. Even if you cover your key points from notes, knowing your opening and closing by heart lets you start and end fluently, connecting with your audience when you are the most nervous.

Logistically:
Go to the room where you will be speaking as early as possible so you can get comfortable in the environment. If you will be speaking from a stage, go early in the morning when no one is there and make friends with the stage. Then, during your presentation, you can concentrate on your audience, not your environment.

Physically:
A wonderful preparation technique for small meetings is to go around shaking hands and making eye contact with everybody beforehand. For larger meetings, meet and shake hands with people in the front row at least, and some of the people as they are coming in the door. Connect with them personally, so they will be rooting for your success. We as speakers usually become nervous when faced with the thought of an audience. Once you have met the audience, or at least some of them, they become less scary.

John Fuhrman shares: *"Get the audience to participate in some way. Get them all to shout an answer, invite a few up on stage to demonstrate something, give away a book, tape or other prize. By keeping them involved, you stand a better chance of getting your message across."*

 Tip ➜ *There is a lot of "sell" in a puppy dog's tail!*

Presenter's Affirmations

- I always tell the truth and keep my word.
- I attract only the best things and only the best things attract me.
- I forgive myself for all my past mistakes.
- I have all that I need and desire on this earth.

Elements of Communication:

Real communication happens when people listen with understanding. When beginning a presentation, you will automatically lose 30% of your audience. Within the next few minutes, you will lose another 30% of the audience. This means that within the first ten minutes, six out of ten don't like the presentation. The key to a successful presenter is how much of the audience they have brought back by the conclusion of the presentation. When you make a presentation, remember:

People learn approximately:
1% though taste.
2% through touch.
4% though smell.
10% through hearing.
83% through sight.

People generally remember:
10% of what they read.
20% of what they hear.
30% of what they see.
50% of what they hear and see.
70% of what they say or write.
90% of what they say as they are doing or saying something.
You are a successful communicator, if your audience retains 50%.

People make decisions about presentations in three key areas:
7% will be based on your words.
38% will be based on your voice quality.
55% will be based on your body language.
This means that it's not what you say it's how you say it that counts!

Great Presentations:

Have a:
- •Challenge.
- •Promise.
- •Payoff.
- •Tell a story, make a point!
- •Tell a story, make a point!
- •Tell a story, make a point!

Make Your Presentations From:

Acceptance.................people want to feel that the speaker is not going to talk down to them.

Achievement...............make sure you talk about achievement, awards.

Affection.....................everyone wants to be loved, cherished and emotionally wanted for his or her own sake. Do not hold this emotion back. Tell people that you are thrilled that they are there.

Approval.....................people are desperate for approval.

Belonging...................use the word *"belong"* over and over again.

Conformity.................people like to think they fit in.

Dependence................people want to be dependent while learning new skills and then become independent. Know when to let go.

Independence.............people want to be free to find their own path, let them take the best and leave the rest from you.

Recognition................people want to be noticed, appreciated, respected, valued and to become known. Use names in your presentations.

Sense of control..........how and where people fit in, family tree, organizational chart.

Sense of openness.......how well they feel they fit in.

Sense of significance..how much people feel a part of your event.

How People Listen to You:

People process information differently. Present your information with this one question in mind, *"how do my listeners think?"*

Adaptive......................listens and responds to any styles.

Affective.....................reactive, responsive, flexible and is open to anything.

Auditory.....................needs to hear, tell this person about what you have to say.

Hypothetical...............listens for the big picture. Asks questions and sorts through data which is listened for.

Kinesthetic..................needs to feel, be touched, makes decisions based on their emotions.

Digital........................connects based on experience. Moves from details to the big picture. Listens for logic. Needs stats and figures for a decision.

Rational......................makes abstract connections. Plans carefully, up for new ideas.

Visual.........................makes decisions based upon what they see.

"Get a Presentation Attitude."

Cathy Barber

How People Listen to What You are Saying at Different Levels:

•I never said it would be easy.
•I *never* said it would be easy.
•I never *said* it would be easy.
•I never said *it* would be easy.
•I never said it *would* be easy.
•I never said it would *be* easy.
•I never said it would be *easy*.

What to Do So People Come to Listen to You:

•Accept differences of opinions without becoming angry or upset.
•Appreciate them.
•Be an inspiration to others.
•Be enthusiastic.
•Be respectful.
•Don't be bossy.
•Don't swear.
•Don't take things personally.
•Don't talk while others are talking.
•Don't use sarcasm.
•Get them involved in decision-making.
•Give private and public recognition.
•Give them a sense of belonging and teamwork.
•Give them information that will help them advance, meeting their dreams and goals.
•Instead of handing out edicts and orders, present your thoughts as questions and let the audience ponder them. Most people can't be *sold*, you have to let them *buy*.
•Let them know that the fact that they are there is significant.
•Let them hear that their presence does make a difference.
•Make everyone feel appreciated.
•Make them feel capable of handling what you are offering.
•Meet their personal needs.
•Provide an opportunity for personal growth.
•Set the stage for enthusiasm.
•Tell them something significant is happening because the meeting exists.

> *"Work on Your Image."*
>
> **Bob Mega Webb**

Needs of Leaders Listening to Your Presentation:

Confidence:
- •To feel trusted in the work assigned to you.
- •To be told results desired by *"How to do it."*

To be given *Recognition* and *Appreciation* when earned:
- •To be acknowledged for efforts, ideas and work.
- •To be known, understood and to have concern shown for them as individuals.

To be *Involved:*
- •To be allowed to share in decisions that affect them.
- •To be kept *"in"* on all appropriate information.
- •To have a personal Sense of Belonging.
- •To have opportunities to be heard.
- •To feel free to ask questions without intimidation.

To be *Challenged:*
- •To create, discover, compete.
- •To have changes in new opportunities.

People With High Achievement Needs Want to Hear:
- •Assurances of success as long as they are doing their best.
- •Immediate, concrete feedback.
- •There is an opportunity to develop positive relationships.
- •There is an opportunity to make decisions about the process of the work.
- •They are valued as someone who has helped build the company, team, organization or contributed to something.
- •They take personal responsibility for their own success or failure.

Cathy Walker shares: *"I always make it a point, after asking questions of my audience, to stress that in my business we develop positive relationships and that I will not let you fail if you join my business."*

Feelings People Have About Groups:
Here is a list of universally accepted feelings people have about groups. People want:
- •To be effective.
- •To be free.
- •To find diversity more than conformity
- •To grow in a feeling of value.
- •To work through a group democracy.

Make Your Presentations Memorable:
- Ask a question every five sentences.
- Avoid lengthy sentences.
- Avoid unnecessary words.
- Don't just rattle off sentence after sentence, ask questions.
- Don't quote from someone when you have something worthwhile to say.
- If you are tempted to insert words such as *and, but, however, consequently* into the middle of a sentence, consider ending the sentence instead. Do not say, *"Do you know what I mean."* And then keep going.
- Organize your thoughts, keep the listener in mind.
- Short sentences are easiest to understand.
- Smile.
- Who is the listener, what is the listener listening for?

Key Points in Your Presentation:
- Acknowledge that your words represent your opinion.
- It doesn't matter how your message sounds to you.
- How does it sound to your listener?
- Keep your emotions in check.
- Look at your listener.
- Put yourself into the listener's position.
- Speak clearly and loud enough; project your voice.
- Speak from assurance.
- Speak from your diaphragm.
- Speak in an organized manner.
- Use precise words.

 Tip ➜ *Don't leave a mess, leave a message.*

Presenter's Affirmations

- Everything I give is returned to me tenfold.
- I am a money magnet. My purse, my wallet, and my pocket attract all the money that I need and want.
- I am now open to receive large sums of money from expected and unexpected sources and I deserve it.
- I am living the life of increase. The more I give, the more I receive.

Presentation Irritants:

•Being insistent that people do things only your way.
•Changing the subject midstream.
•Digging in your handbag.
•Doing all the talking, dominating.
•Giving people the runaround instead of straight answers.
•Interrupting.
•Not delegating, trying to do it all yourself.
•Not speaking up when appropriate, but complaining later.
•Pushing your glasses up onto your nose.
•Putting someone down, especially in front of others.
•Rustling papers, candy wrappers.
•Talking while the speaker is talking, leave the room if you need to talk.
•Tapping your pen.
•Telling people, *"Don't worry."*
•Trying to make someone make a decision in a short time frame.

Charlie "Tremendous" Jones shares: *"Help your audience listen less and think more. Encourage them to read, read, read and share, share, share. They will remember you forever if you get them to read a life-changing book. Every good thing in my life I owe to someone who got me to read a book that became a part of my life. You are the same person today as you'll be in five years except for two things, the people you meet and the books you read."*

How to Decide What Topic Would be Great for You:

•Are my ideas of interest to others?
•Do I have a tried system that works that would work for others?
•How can I be different from everyone else who has spoken on this particular topic?
•If I were a meeting planner, would I ask someone like me to give a speech?
•What is of interest to me?
•What could I get excited about?
•What would I like to become an expert on?
•What do I do for a living that would make me an expert on a subject?
•Who are experts on this particular topic? What can I learn from them first?

Next:

•Become an expert on your topic. Walk your walk.
•Clip out articles you are interested in from magazines, newspapers and other sources.
•Collect information about your subject, keep files, scan onto discs.
•Collect funny sayings (like there are in this guide).
•Collect stories to use.
•Search the Internet for ideas on your subject.
•Seek out those who are experts about your subject.
•Use your local library; find books on your topic.

Asking Questions:

Asbjørn Ølnes shares: *"Make certain in your presentation to ask questions to find the dream of the prospect and to show the pathway to fulfill this dream."*

- A question serves as a form of brief summary.
- As the presentation proceeds, ask questions to be sure that the customer understands and to get the customer thinking about how the product fits in with their needs.
- By asking a question you can be sure that the customer understands one point before you proceed to the next.
- If the customer can be *"yes"* conditioned during the presentation, the resistance to committing at the close is reduced.
- Nod your head up and down. If you nod the customer will nod, if the customer nods, they are with you, listening and going forward.
- The answers to your questions help you judge the progress you are making toward closing the sale.
- The more often the customer agrees with you, the more unreasonable a turn-down will seem at the end.

Encourage Participation:

If you have people participating in your presentation, decide what you will be including in your presentation:

Brainstorming... controlled process to stimulate creativity.

Buzz groups....... discussion groups reach consensus.

Case Study......... hypothetical situation.

Discussion.......... presenter as facilitator.

Dyads, Triads.... groups of two to three people who perform tasks.

PowerPods......... when several people take small groups around the room and there are presenter's who move from pod to pod. The people stay in their small groups, only the *PowerPod* presenters move around the room.

Role Playing....... participants act out a given situation.

 Tip →   •*Ask questions as you go.*
•*Get the audience into the act.*
•*Keep your presentation short.*
• *Make your presentation as dramatic as you can.*

Ways to Present When Looking For Something New:

Adapt................. What else is near this? What ideas does this suggest? What could I duplicate? Whom can I duplicate?

Combination...... Combine ideas? Combine teams? Combine purposes?

Magnify.............. Extra value? Greater frequency? Happier? Healthier? Higher? Longer? More products? Multiply? Stronger? Thicker? What to add?

Minify................. Condense? Lighter? Lower? Omit? Smaller? Shorter? Split up? Streamline? Subtract? Take away?

Modify................ New twist? Change: color, form, meaning, motion, odor, and shape. Other changes?

Rearrange.......... Another way to look at it? Change pace? Change schedule?

Reverse............... Opposites? Reverse roles? Turn it backward? Turn the other cheek? Turn upside down?

Substitute........... Other ingredient, process? Other location? Other tone of voice? What else instead?

Speaking:

•allows you to have a flexible work schedule.

•allows you to control your life.

•allows you to help others achieve their goals.

•allows you to travel.

•brings you friends.

•brings you more than monetary gain.

•is a great career.

•is continually challenging.

•is fun.

•it's creative.

•it's rewarding.

•keeps you in the world of people. You cannot hide.

•makes you accountable for your results.

•requires fortitude and persistence.

•requires a sense of humor.

•requires a supportive family.

•requires self-discipline.

•requires you to consider the other person before you consider yourself.

•teaches you to overcome guilt and doubt.

The Room Set Up!

- All side doors should be locked with signs on the outside that say, *"no entry."*
- Bathrooms need to be accessed outside the meeting room.
- Be organized.
- Chairs should be set up so the attendees have adequate room to write notes.
- Don't have round tables, use long straight tables set up classroom style.
- Have:
    - a bar stool up on the stage to lean on.
    - a flip chart.
    - a hand held microphone.
    - an evaluation sheet.
    - an overhead projector.
    - a registration table.
    - a slide screen available.
    - a table for you to put things on, on the platform.
    - a table set up to sell your books and tapes.
    - a table to present your products.
    - food prepared for you in your room, eat prior to the presentation.
    - good lighting.
    - people enter from back of room only.
    - plenty of water at your fingertips.
    - someone be responsible for the doors. Call them "door guards."
- Know where the light switches are.
- Know where all the exits are.
- Make sure:
    - that the room has the entry doors at the back.
    - you have a secure place to put money and orders you collect.
    - you have an order form.
    - you have several calculators.
- Move people around every 20-30 minutes. Stretch breaks are important.
- Music should be organized, checked with sound level desired.
- Never throw candy into an audience, place it at the end of the tables.
- No candy with wrappers, when people unwrap candy the sound is distracting.
- No columns in the room. They will block someone's view.
- Prior to the presentation, determine who will be speaking on either side of your room. You don't want to have a fired up meeting with lots of pumped up music with a Sunday School class of elderly people next door trying to sing together!
- Set up fewer chairs than people registered; never have empty chairs in the room; stack them in the back to add to the room as people come in.
- Use a classroom set up as often as you can with a center isle.
- Water pitchers on tables.
- Windows must have curtains that only let a little or no light in.

Using Words With Care:
The world would be a better place with kinder words. By using good words, the world would be a changed place with less criticism and more praise. The following words that move people should be taken to heart and then passed on to others. Delete the vicious, mean spirited and unkind words from your vocabulary and replace them with kindness. Trying to think of a clever, concise and memorable way to make your presentation? Chances are, someone somewhere has already said it. Use this guide. Get books of quotations and memorize several quotes. Your words you choose make all the difference. They make the difference between whether your audience laughs, cries or buys.

 Tip ➔ *There is a massive words list to use at the end of this Chapter.*

But = **B**ehold **U**nderlying **T**houghts.

Use Words That Get Massive Results:
- Be sure you understand the meaning of every word you use in your presentation.
- Learn some of your company terms.
- Make sure you pronounce every word correctly.
- Make your sentences short. Don't be complex. Keep it simple.
- No matter how many visual aids and products you use in a presentation, your chief communication with the prospect will be by the words you use.
- Once you get your prospect answering *"yes,"* the sale is just a question or two away.
- Prepare a series of words that describe the benefits of your product.
- Select simple and clear words.
- Select words with care.
- Techniques, words and great presentation skills work and are necessary to become a champion in selling.
- The right few words at the right time will get you a sale or a recruit.
- The words you select for telling your sales story must be chosen with care.
- Use words that are vivid and expressive.
- With the right words you can effectively transfer to your prospect the image of the sale that you make in his mind.
- You must take the time necessary to develop a vocabulary of selling words that make what you are selling become alive in the imagination of the prospect.
- Your vocabulary must be made up of vital, living words-picture building words.
- Your words must carry conviction.

Develop Important Words For Your Presentation:

•*I feel...*
•*I feel that you are...*
•*I see...*
•*I see that you are ...*
•*I think...*
•*I think that you are...*
•*I want...*
•*I want you to know that...*

Take it a step further

•*I feel you may have some great communication skills you could use...*
•*I see that you have looked over our catalog...*
•*I think we need to talk about your joining us...*
•*I want you to consider being part of our team...*

 Tip → *Guard against being too technical. Watch your words, you can turn off a customer by being too wordy. Remember that your purpose is to show what the product can do for the customer, details might be too much.*

Pedestal Words:

Use them and watch your popularity and bank account grow! These pedestal words raise the prospect to a level above the ordinary.

•*A person of your standing*........................ people want special standing.
•*As you of course know*............................ implies vast knowledge.
•*Because of your specialized knowledge*...implies skill, professionalism.
•*I'd like your advice*................................suggests superior wisdom.
•*I'd like your considered opinion*..............people like giving opinions.
•*I'd sure appreciate it if*...........................there is an implication here that the customer has the power to refuse or grant.
•*May I?*...asking authority implies authority.
•*Please*...a great word in human relations.
•*Spare time from your busy life*................implies prospect an important busy person.
•*You are so right*......................................a pat on the back.

Words to Use in An Executive Presentation:

When speaking to corporate executives, try using these words in your presentations:

- Attracts talent.
- Bottom line.
- Concept-oriented.
- Decides.
- Directs.
- Effective
- Goal-oriented.
- Increase profits.
- Long-term planners.
- Manages resources.
- Mediates.
- Mission oriented.
- Operates in internal and external politics.
- Represents organization.
- Sees whole.
- Studies environment.
- Synthesizes.
- Thoughtful.
- Uses staff work.
- Works in future.

When presenting to credit union executives you always talk in terms of their *"members"*, *not "customers"*. When talking to Network Marketers you talk in terms of *"agents"*, *"distributors"*, *"team"*, *"consultant"*, *"members"*, *"associates"* and *"customers."*

Presenter's Affirmations

- I am a winner!
- I am healthy, wealthy and successful!
- I am fit and trim!
- I am relaxed and at peace!
- I approve of myself!
- I completely and freely release all these things and thank them for the service they have given me.
- I completely forgive and fully release all those persons who are not good for me anymore.
- I deserve all that's good!
- I have no need to hold on to things that are not good for me. I release them for my greater good.
- I have total abundance in my life!
- I have decided to create the life I want and deserve, today!
- I let go of all old illnesses and make room for excellent health.
- I let go of old, negative relationships and make room for new positive ones.
- I'm a wonderful and loving person!
- I now allow the new things that are wanted and needed to come into my life.

Use *You-Ability* and *We-Ability* Words:

- Approach people from the *we* and *you* angle. Give people a position to play on *your* team. Use *we* and *our* and *us* and *you* to get them on your side. Let others look through their end of the telescope; let them see how large a life they will get!
- Magnify the "*you*", and minimize the "*I*".
- Make it a big "*you*" and a little "*I*".
- Put the spotlight on what the other person, not you, *will get.*
- Spotlight what the other person will get if he/she does the things you'd like them to do. Stock your mental shelves with desirable "*products*" to make the prospect thirsty and hungry for what you are presenting.
- The great presenters in history were persuaders and knew how to say or imply the little word "*we*" and got big results.
- Think "*you*", not "*I.*"
- *You* and *we* together become more powerful than either one by itself.
- *You* and *we* together can go places.
- *You* is the most powerful word in our language. *We* is the next most powerful. "*I*" is the smallest and weakest.
- *You* are more important than "*I.*"
- *You-ability* and *we-ability* will get you farther in life with other people than *I-ability.* What you will receive isn't half as important to others as what will happen to them!

Here is a great example. President Lincoln's Gettysburg Address; it's full of "*we's.*"

> "*Fourscore and seven years ago our Fathers brought forth
> on this continent a new nation. . . . now **we** are engaged
> in a great civil war. . . .**We** are met on a great battle
> field of that war. **We** have come to dedicate a portion of
> that field. . . .it is altogether fitting and proper that **we**
> should do this. . . .the world will little note more long
> remember what **we** say here. . . .*"

Altogether he uses the word **we** ten time's; **our** twice; **us** twice. Not once did he use the word **I**. Imagine, all this **we** and **our** and **us** in a presentation that took just four minutes.

Arabic Proverb: "*If I listen I have the advantage; if I speak others have it.*"
Arabic Proverb: "*When the mind becomes large, speech becomes little.*"
Spanish Proverb: "*A fish dies by an open mouth!*"

"*A helping word to one in trouble is often like a switch on a railroad track,
but one inch between a wreck and smooth rolling prosperity.*"
Keith & Polly Blythe

54

The Basic Needs of Those to Whom You are Presenting:

People crave these four basic principles. They steal, invest, murder, love, die, save, strive, work hard, scheme, and gamble just to get these four basic principles. Then along you come and show them how they can get these things easily, at little cost, without murder or death, and these people will follow you anywhere. Arouse these desires in others by being a trader instead of a beggar. Don't approach people in the attitude of begging. Trade them one of these four basic commodities in exchange for what you want, and watch them do business with you gladly. There are many other desires such as making money, security, imitating others, love, romance, travel, but these four basic desires will cover 85% of your daily contacts in the world. The market is wide open!

Make people thirsty with these four basic principles:

1. **To feel important:**
   So sell others the feeling of importance!
2. **To feel appreciated:**
   So sell others appreciation!
3. **To feel liked by others:**
   So sell others that they are liked!
4. **People like to be lazy and get by.**
   So save people extra steps in life!

Words that Convince the Other Person They are Really the One Who Thought of It:

- *A few days ago you said...*
- *As you have implied...*
- *As you say...*
- *I agree with you that...*
- *I see your point...*
- *Last time you remarked...*
- *Something you said the other day impressed me...*
- *You are certainly right...*
- *You once said...*

The day of Ali Baba and his *"open sesame"* is over and no pinch of smoke or words produces a friend. You do have a greater power, the power in words; words that make people do things for you faster and with greater willingness.

Presentations Are Everywhere

Role model success
if you want your children
to be successful!

Take pictures of your children
in all different scenes!
Aspen, Colorado

There is nothing quite like a view from the top!
Sarah, Clayton & Ashley
Top of Snowmass, Colorado

Chapter 4

Presentations

Accept Your Role Presentation:
Not every player on a football team can be the number one quarterback. In order for the team to succeed, everyone from the water boy to the coach is important to success.

Acres of Diamonds Presentation:
There once was a farmer in Africa who was told of diamond discoveries in another part of Africa. He sold his farm and died never finding a diamond. The person who bought the farm had a beautiful curio on his mantle over his fireplace. One day a friend of his asked him what it was and he said, *"oh, those are all over my farm."* It just so happens that the curio actually was a diamond. The first farmer made the mistake of not examining what he had before running off to something he had hoped was better.

A Father's Presentation:
There are those who work all day, those who dream all day, and those who spend an hour dreaming before setting to work to fulfill those dreams. *"Go into the third category"*, the father said, *"because there's virtually no competition."*

A Fishing Expedition Presentation:
Go to the massive word list we have provided you in this guide in the Appendix. Choose your top five favorite words. Pretend that you have been fishing all day. You have caught five fish that you had hoped to catch. Check the words list and choose five words you value the most. Now, while you doze off on the riverbank, two get away. Mark out these two that you caught from your list. Then, along comes your best buddy and he's hungry and you give him one of your fish (cross it off). And, while you talk, an animal creeps up and runs off with another fish, leaving you with just one. Which word is it? It's probably what you value most...what are you doing to see that your lifetime is spent in activities that will provide you with this top one value?

An *American Indian* Presentation:

The following beautiful and prophetic presentation statement made on behalf of the environment has been attributed to Chief Sealth (Seattle) and has caused him to become the folkloric hero of the environmental movement, speaking both the mind and the conscience of all concerned about the earth. It was said to have been Chief Sealth's (Seattle's) reply to President Franklin Pierce in December of 1854, upon the United States Government's offer to buy two million acres of Native American land in the Pacific Northwest.

How Can You Buy or Sell the Earth?

"The Great Chief in Washington sends word that he wishes to buy our land. The Great Chief also sends us words of friendship and good will. This is kind of him, since we know he has little need of our friendship in return. But we will consider his offer.

How can you buy or sell the sky, the warmth of the land? The idea is strange to us. If we do not own the freshness of the air and the sparkle of the water, how can you buy them? Every part of this earth is sacred to my people. Every shining pine needle, every sandy shore, every mist in the dark woods, every clearing, and every humming insect is holy in the memory and experience of my people. The sap, which courses through the trees, carries the memories of the red man. So, when the Great Chief in Washington sends word that he wishes to buy our land, he asks much of us…

This we know: All things are connected. Whatever befalls the earth befalls the sons of the earth. Man did not weave the web of life; he is merely a strand in it. Whatever he does to the web, he does to himself. But we will consider your offer to go to the reservation you have for my people. We will live apart, and in peace.

One thing we know, which the white man may one day discover—our God is the same God. You may think now that you own Him as you wish to own our land' but you cannot. He is the God of man; and his compassion is equal for the red man and the white. This earth is precious to Him and to harm the earth is to heap contempt on its Creator. The whites too shall pass; perhaps sooner than all other tribes. Continue to contaminate your bed and you will one night suffocate in your own waste.

But in your perishing you will shine brightly, fired by the strength of God who brought you to this land and for some special purpose gave you dominion over this land and over the red man. That destiny is a mystery to us, for we do not understand when the buffalo are all slaughtered, the wild horses are tamed and the view of the ripe hills blotted by talking wires. Where is the thicket? Gone. Where is the eagle? Gone. And what is it to say goodbye to the swift pony and the hunt? The end of living and the beginning of survival. So we will consider your offer to buy the land.

58

If we agree, it will be to secure the reservation you have promised. There, perhaps, we may live out our brief days as we wish. When the last red man has vanished from the earth, and his memory is only the shadow of a cloud moving across the prairie, these shores and forests will still hold the spirits of my people. For they love this earth as a newborn loves its mother's heartbeat. So, if we sell our land, love it as we've loved it. Care for it as we've cared for it. Hold in your mind the memory of the land, as it is when you take it. And preserve it for your children, and love it…as God loves us all. One thing we know. Our God is the same God. This earth is precious to Him. Even the white man cannot be exempt from the common destiny. We may be brothers after all.
We shall see…"

A framed copy of this presentation can be found in the home of Jan Ruhe in Aspen, Colorado and in the homes of all three of her children.

A *P.I.E.* Presentation:

Here is the approach I would like us to take….

    P = *preserved ("It was perfect!")*
    I = *improved ("Good, but next time I'd…")*
    E = *eliminated ("Waste of time, let's not ever do this again!")*

Attitude of Gratitude Presentation:

•If you woke up this morning with more health than illness…
    you are more blessed than the million who will not survive this week.
•If you have never experienced the danger of battle, the loneliness of imprisonment, the agony of torture, or the pangs of starvation…
    you are ahead of 500 million people in the world.
•If you can attend a church meeting without fear of harassment, arrest, torture, or death…
    you are more blessed than three billion people in the world.
•If you have food in the refrigerator, clothes on your back, a roof overhead and a place to sleep…
    you are richer than 75% of this world.
•If you have money in the bank, in your wallet, and spare change in a dish someplace…
    you are among the top 8% of the world's wealthy.
•If your parent's are still alive and still married…
    you are very rare.
•If you can read this:
    you are more blessed that over two billion in the world who cannot read at all.

Be a Champion! Presentation:

Champions work on excellence and on inspiring others to be the best that they can be every day. You can't leave this to chance. Being a champion doesn't just happen on it's own. You must desire it, go after it and achieve it. Go for greatness! It starts today! Here are eight tips to start you on your path to being a Champion!

1. Love and embrace Change. Nothing stays the same forever, prepare for change. Do not resist change. When you have something change in your life, look for the opportunity and lesson. Remember, you control your reaction to change. As a champion, your team will look to you for how to react to change. You can either resist or embrace it.

2. Take Risks. Try to embrace change quickly. If you can do that, you probably can take risks easily. Ask yourself these questions: *What is the worst thing that could happen? What is likely to happen? What's the best that could happen?* It's okay to stray from the herd. It's okay to try new things, to not hold back but to flat out go for greatness. The future belongs to the people who can celebrate failure and move on. If what you try doesn't work, get over it and move on.

3. Take Action. People who go for greatness take *massive* action. In today's world, people who take action are rewarded, avoid stagnation, and make a decision to lead your field. Massive action produces massive results.

4. Feed your Mind. Readers are leaders and leaders are readers. Develop your skills. Your attitude towards learning speaks volumes to your team. Work hard on increasing your skills so that you add value to your team. Turn your car into a classroom, listen to audiotapes. Join the Jan Ruhe Book of the Month Club at www.janruhe.com. Attend seminars taught by **only people who are living the lifestyle you want**. Do not listen to those who just want to talk at the front of the room, listen to those who are living the lifestyle you want. Attend a Jan Ruhe MLM Nuts $ Bolts training.

5. Get Feedback. Ask for feedback. After you do a presentation, make sure that you have an evaluation sheet so that you can get feedback. Then tackle areas of weaknesses. Find out where you are strong and where you are weak and really focus on your weaknesses. If you do, you will become the champion presenter you are meant to be.

6. Have Self Esteem. Be the person who can't be beat.

7. Be Sincerely Interested. Always be thinking of the *benefits* and the other person.

8. Why not you and why not now? Ask the question.

60

Be a Dream Merchant Presentation:
- •Be a dream merchant.
- •Dreamline your life.
- •Find someone with a dream and help them get it.
- •Give people something to dream about.
- •Use vivid words to stir dreams.

Dreams, needs, nightmares, are all interwoven throughout our lives. The combination of giving needs to people wrapped up in their dreams will immediately banish a nightmare.

Be a Friend Presentation:
A true friend is someone who believes in you after he/she has seen you at your worst. Act happy to see people, you never know who will become a real friend.

Be Great in Your Own Home Presentation:
Greatness consists not in the holding of some future office, but consists in doing great deeds with little means and the accomplishment of vast purposes from the private ranks of life. To be great at all one must be great at just being the best they can be. You who can give to this city better streets and better sidewalks, better schools and more colleges, more happiness and more civilization, more of God, you will be great anywhere. Let every man or woman here, if you never hear me again, remember this, that if you wish to be great at all, you must begin where you are and what you are, now. You who can give to your city any blessing, you who can be a good citizen while you live here, you who can make better homes, you who can be a blessing whether you work in a shop or sit behind the counter or keep house or a huge business, whatever be your life, you who would be great anywhere must first be great in you own home.

Believe in Yourself Presentation:
Desire a team of people who believe in themselves. You can't be a great coach, a great team player or a great entrepreneur if you don't have faith in yourself and others. Great pitchers need great catchers.

Care About People Presentation:
Teamwork is the foundation of success. The three universal questions that an individual asks of his boss, upline, coach, player, employee, employer, and distributor are these: Can I trust you? Are you committed to excellence? Do you care about me? If we don't care about one another, we don't stand a chance.

Closing Presentation:

I am planning my next tour and want to invite you to go with me. It's to a place I've never been before. It's a place called *"Tomorrow."* When we get there, they will ask us where we came from and we will say *"Yesterday."* Then they will give each of us a gift and we will call it, *"Today"*!

Columbus's Presentation:

Queen Isabella wasn't interested in proving that the earth was round. She didn't care anything about whether Columbus was a great discoverer or not. What sold her was Columbus's presentation. He promised wealth and fame. That made her mouth water. *"Here is something for me!"* She was sold.

Don't Flinch Presentation:

Believe you are going to succeed with all of your heart. You cannot flinch; you cannot let people think that you are seriously in jeopardy of failure. You must present full out and don't let anyone kill your dream.

Do Right Presentation:

You know what's right, you know what's wrong. Too many people talk about their personal rights. Instead, today let's talk about our obligations and responsibilities....

Do Your Best Presentation:

It is not enough just to have desire, you must take action. In order to succeed day in and day out, each of us must strive to do the best we can.

Embrace the Day Presentation:

When a bird sings it's first song, it is perfect. The bird does not improve the song. When the spider spins its web for the first time, it will never improve upon it. When the bee first creates its delicious honey, it will never improve the honey. However, you as a human being can change, improve, evaluate, measure, and grade your presentations and decide to make them better! You have great potential! You have more potential to create, communicate and relate than you ever dreamed possible! Pioneers and living legends have turned impossibilities into possibilities! Most people dream, set goals and then figure out how they will get what they want. Not me. I get up every day and stop and decide what I am going to get accomplished during the day. I have a blank slate in front of me and day that is waiting for me. I want to get up and *embrace the day*, whatever it may bring. I look at what I can do and what I can be.

Five Year Old Playing Mozart **Presentation:**

A Philadelphia, USA school, teaches children five years old to play the violin. Do you know what their first lesson is? To walk up on the stage without their violins and listen to the teacher say "*Bravo!*"

Foot in Mouth Disease **Presentation:**

An American businessman was attending an important banquet in Hong Kong and was seated next to the official of the Republic of China. The Chinese official said nothing and the American businessman racked his brain on how to start a conversation. When the soup arrived, he said, "*Likee soupee?*" and the official nodded in affirmation. That was the entire extent of their conversation. After coffee, the Chinese official was asked to make a presentation, which he did in perfect English. At the end of the speech he sat down, turned to the diplomat and asked, "*Likee speechee?*"

I Am Full **Presentation:**

"I have had a great sufficiency.
Any more would be a copious redundancy.
For gastronomical satiety admonishes me,
that I have arrived at a state of deglutition.
Consistent with dietetic integrity."
Edith Penniman Knowles

I Have a Premonition **Presentation:**

"I have a premonition that soars on silver wings.
I dream of your accomplishments and other wondrous things.
I do not know beneath what sky that you will conquer fate,
I only know that it will be high
and I only know that it will be great!"
Unknown

It's Up to Whom? **Presentation:**

- Being an actor or actress cannot give you joy and happiness!
- Business doesn't owe you a job!
- Going to church will not save your soul!
- Society won't give you moral and ethical character!
- The doctors can't give you good health!
- The new day does not promise to give you all that is good!
- The university doesn't give you an education!
- The world doesn't owe you a living!
- Your marriage is not up to the minister who marries you!

Let's Change Our Meetings Presentation:

Everyone hates a meeting when…
- The energy is low…
- The examples don't pertain to the audience…
- The important points don't stand out…
- The information is impractical…
- The material is old…
- The speaker is boring…
- The speaker is just standing up talking at the audience telling them what to do and how to do it when they have never done it themselves…
- The topic is old…

Magic Carpet Presentation:

Being successful takes a commitment to ride on that magic carpet! *Are you going to ride as fast as you can on that magic carpet and let it take you to places you have never been before, or are you going to buy some drapes to match it and put it on the floor?*

Mary Had A Little Lamb Presentation:

The two verses to the song goes like this, *"Mary had a little lamb, little lamb, little lamb, Mary had a little lamb whose fleece was white as snow. And everywhere that Mary went, Mary went, Mary went, and everywhere that Mary went the lamb was sure to go."* Children learn with repetition. They hear the same words over and over again and learn this way. Do you remember the third and fourth verse? *"Why does the lamb love Mary so, Mary so, Mary so? Why does the lamb love Mary so? The eager children cry!"* *"Because Mary loves the lamb, you know, the lamb you know, the lamb you know, the lamb loves Mary so so much, because Mary loves the lamb."*

On Making Excuses Presentation:

There is a man who is mowing his yard. He only has a few feet left to mow and his lawn mower completely quits. He works on it for several minutes and realizes it's of no use that he will have to get another lawnmower. However, he doesn't want to miss any more of the sporting event on TV to go invest in another lawnmower. So he goes across the street and knocks on his neighbor John's door to see if he can borrow his lawnmower for 15-20 minutes. Upon knocking on the door, John comes to the door with a beer in his hand and the TV blaring with the exciting sports event on TV. The man asks John if he can borrow his lawnmower and neighbor John says, *"No you cannot, my wife is scrambling eggs right now."* The man looks dazed and confused and says, *"John, help me understand, what does scrambling eggs have to do with me borrowing or not borrowing you lawnmower?"* John replies, *"It has nothing to do with borrowing my lawnmower, it's just an excuse, I don't want you to borrow my lawnmower and one good excuse is as good as another!"*

64

Opposites are Tricky Presentation:

Opposites are tricky…but opposites are fun.
Someday we will know them, we'll learn them one by one.
Happy faces smile, sad ones make a frown.
To use a slide go up, up, up…and then slide down, down down.
Clothes too big are loose…clothes too little are tight.
Rocks and bricks are heavy, feathers and kites are light.
A turtle's shell is hard; a bunny's fur is soft.
Something missing can be found, if it can't we say it's lost.
Many people are short…many people are tall.
A whale in the ocean is very large…a goldfish is very small.
When babies eat they're messy, when grown ups eat, they're neat.
A lemon is a sour fruit, but oranges can be sweet.
Opposites are tricky…but opposites are fun.
Someday we will know them, we'll learn them one by one.
Barb Milne dedicated her book, *Opposites are Tricky* to Ashley, Jan's daughter.

Overcome Adversity Presentation:

There is one thing in life that is universal. You are going to have life challenges and adversity, so be prepared for them.

Practice Fundamentals Presentation:

Our team is based on doing little things the right way. Let little things slide and the whole foundation of your organization will collapse. Sweat the small stuff.

Set Goals Presentation:

You have to have something that you wish to obtain. Everyone here has to understand what we are trying to accomplish. Why are we here? There are a lot of reasons why you are here…

S.O.S. Presentation:

Isn't it interesting that even with the computer age, it's still difficult to communicate in the world fast? It's amazing that there is one universal phrase…It started in 1906, and the letters S.O.S., spelled out in wireless code, have been the international distress signal. Why is that we can have a universal code for disaster and not a code to spread happy news as well? Today, I am going to only give you happy, upbeat, fired up and safe signals.

> *"Give Safe Signals."*
>
> **Kathy Roland Smith**

Success Principles Presentation:

It's the little things that make the big difference. The opportunity for greatness will never come down like Victoria Falls in Zimbabwe, but rather it comes slowly, one drop at a time. Be prepared for set backs and times that are difficult, navigate through them. Keep in control of your attitude so that you can be effective and productive. With the right mental attitude you can obtain the winning edge. In Network Marketing you are paid very little in the beginning for doing a lot, in the end you get paid a lot for doing very little. You can have everything in life you want if you will just help enough other people get what they want. Take a daily Check up from the Neck Up. If you are tough on yourself, life will be easier on you. Eight hundred million Chinese are not worried about what you are worrying about. Stop the Stinkin Thinkin, you don't want hardening of the attitudes! Take time for yourself. Delegate. Don't try to stuff fifteen hours of work into a ten hour day. Develop better organizational skills to help you manage your time.

Survey The Audience Presentation:

Say *"By a show of hands"* or *"By your applause."* The popular show, *"Who wants to be a Millionaire"* has the audience primed to be a lifeline answering puzzling questions for the contestants. When polled, the audience gets to work helping the contestant!

Take Yourself to a New Level? Presentation:

- Your beliefs determine your convictions.
- Your character determines your future.
- Your convictions determine your satisfactions.
- Your habits make you predictable.
- Your thoughts determine your actions.
- Your work defines your legacy.

The *Anxiety* Presentation:

It's surprising how much wé worry about things we can do nothing about. Here is how the anxiety of the average person is divided:

40% -things that will never happen.
30% -things about the past that can't be changed.
12% -criticism from others, mostly untrue.
10% -health, which gets worse with stress.
8% -real challenges that will be faced.

> *"Unless you are willing to drench yourself in your work beyond the capacity of the average person, you are just not cut out for positions at the top."*
>
> **J.C. Penny**

The *Automobile* Presentation:

Take a tip from the automobile manufacturers. When designing a new model, they first send it out to be tested. If anything is wrong with the automobile, they don't try to fool the public about it. Instead, they go to work perfecting the car. They keep working at it until it becomes the car which will do what the advertisements say it will do. You don't want to tell people how to do something in your presentations that might sound good but is not a proven method. Compare yourself with other presenters to see how you measure with them. If you fall short, go to work and perfect your performance. Don't try to trick others.

The *Before School-Kiss in the Hand* Presentation:

Every morning, right before your children go to school, get on their same eye level and ask them to present their hand to you, palm up. Now kiss the little hand. Then say, *"I want you to hide that kiss someplace on you, in your pocket, your sock, lunch sack, dress, hair band, etc."* And watch them find a place to hide it. *"Today, while you are at school, if the other children say something mean to you, or your teacher for whatever sad reason makes you feel silly or inadequate, I want you to reach to find your hidden kiss from (Mommy or Daddy). I love you and that will never change, no matter what. I can't wait to hear all about your day after school. When you go to school today, spread some sunshine. After all, there are children coming to school today who don't feel loved like you do, they need you to be kind to them. Do your best today, have a happy day at school."*
This presentation was provided by Sarah, Clayton and Ashley. Jan Ruhe's children.

The *Big Picture* Presentation:

Take a camera with you to the podium. Then say, *"Normally if any picture is taken at a gathering like this, it's a photo of the speaker. But I think it should be the other way around. Without an audience to give a presentation to, there would be no speaker. You are the important ones here today. So let me pause and take your picture for my scrapbook. It will remind me of this day."* Once you have snapped the picture you can then launch into *"the big picture"* of your presentation.

The *Bus Driver* Presentation:

Start by telling everyone that you hope they are listening to you, that you are going to have some fun by telling them a story and asking them for information about the story. Now you say, *"You are a bus driver. The bus goes six miles north and stops at a bus stop. At the stop, the bus driver gets off the bus and stretches his legs for a few minutes while three people get on. The bus goes four miles East and stops at another bus stop. Two people get off the bus and three more people get on the bus. The bus goes one mile south and stops again. Six people get off the bus here. The bus driver is really nice and they all love to ride the bus, especially when this bus driver is the driver. What is the age of the bus driver?"* People will look at you like you are crazy. They will think it is impossible to tell you the exact age. So start again…and say, *"**You** are the bus driver....."*

The Catch the Wave Presentation:
Something exciting is happening at this very moment - more people than ever before are fired up to get happily involved with our product and opportunity - hurry, join in the fun today - catch the wave.

The *Change Your Approach* Presentation:
An ad was printed in the local paper asking young boys to apply for summer jobs. There was a young man who decided to get up early so he could go and apply for the job, but when he got there **400** other boys were already in line. Remember if your plan doesn't work you need to **change your approach,** and continue to take **action.** When the boy stood behind all of those other boys he knew that he **MUST** change his approach. Getting up early had not worked very well. The boy took a piece of paper, and wrote a note. He then went to the head of the line and asked someone to give the note to the person that was hiring. On the note were these words:

"I am the 400th boy in line. Don't hire anyone until you talk to me!"

Do you think he got the job? I would be willing to bet that he did. Most of us would have quit after seeing all of those kids in front of us in line, but he just changed his **approach,** and continued to take **action.**

The *College Quiz* Presentation:
Two guys were taking chemistry at the University of Arkansas. They were so confident going into the final that two days before, they decided to go up to the University of Tennessee and party with some friends. They had a great time. However, they overslept and didn't make it back to Arkansas until the morning of the exam. Rather than take the final, they found their professor afterward to explain why they missed the final. They told him that they drove to the University of Tennessee for the weekend, and had planned to come back in time to study, but that they had a flat tire on the way back, and didn't have a spare, and couldn't get help for a long time, so they were late in getting back to campus. The professor thought this over and told them they could make up the final on the following day. The two guys were relieved. They studied that night and went in the next day for the final. The professor placed them in separate rooms, and handed each of them a test booklet and told them to begin. They looked at the first problem, which was worth 5 points. It was something simple. *"Cool,"* they thought. *"This is going to be easy."* They did that problem and then turned the page. Question #2 said: *"Which tire?"* (95 Points). *This presentation was provided by Lois Penniman Kelley.*

"Catch the Wave!"

Gavin Scott

The *Colonel Sanders* Story:

Every successful person you meet will tell you that if you want to become successful in anything, you must **take action.** As a great example, the founder of Kentucky Fried Chicken, Colonel Sanders knew the meaning of taking action. He had a good recipe for fried chicken, and he wanted to make money from it. Colonel Sanders decided to take his recipe, and try and get owners of restaurants to give him a percentage of their profits just to use his famous recipe. Colonel Sanders **took action,** and made presentations to many owners of restaurants, but it seemed that no one wanted his opportunity. Well, the story goes that Colonel Sanders called on 1009 owners before one person said *"yes, I am interested."*

How many people would have quit after the first 100 or 500 *"no's"*?
How many people would have quit after the first 1000 negative responses?

The real key for Colonel Sanders was that he had learned from his mistakes, changed his approach, and continued to **take action!**

The *Courage of Convictions* Presentation:

Be your own person. If you don't want to drink, don't drink, if you don't want to smoke, don't smoke. The same goes for using drugs, lying, cheating, criticizing and other negative things. Make your decision right now. Will drugs, alcohol and cigarettes help you in reaching you goals in your life? The simple answer is no. They can only do you a great harm, so eliminate them from your life. Have the courage of your convictions. Commit to excellence and avoid anything and anyone who stands in your way. If you don't you are only fooling yourself, hurting yourself and cheating yourself. Associate with people of good qualities; it's better to be alone than in bad company or with gossips, hypocrites or critics. If your friends have lower standards than you do, pull them up to your level; don't stoop to theirs. Have the courage to be different, to take a stand and dare to be great!

The *David and Goliath* Presentation:

David was a small shepherd boy who faced the greatest warrior of all time - Goliath. Goliath was huge, a giant who struck fear in everyone. No one would dare fight Goliath. They all said, *"He's so huge, there is no chance to win."* David thought, *"He's so huge, I can't miss."* But, David prevailed defeating Goliath with merely his sling, a few stones his belief and faith.

"Refuse to be average, be a champion."

Jan Ruhe

The *Echo* Presentation:

On a one-on-one presentation just repeat what the other person says:

> *"I am on my way to Nigeria."*
> *"To Nigeria?"*
> *"Yes, I am going there to speak on building a new business."*
> *"A new business?"*
> *"Yes, I am actually meeting with twenty very interested people who want to get involved?"*
> *"Twenty people?"*

This way you can keep the other person talking and gather great information that will help you discover their values. Be a great listener, see how long you can keep them talking!

The *If the Earth Was Round* Presentation:

If the earth were only a few feet in diameter, floating a few feet above a field somewhere, people would come from everywhere to marvel at it. People would walk around it, marveling at its big pools of water, it's little pools and the water flowing between the pools. People would marvel at the bumps on it and the holes in it and they would marvel at the very thin layer of gas surrounding it and the water suspended in the gas. The people would marvel at all the creatures walking around the surface of the ball and the creatures in the water. The people would declare it as sacred because it was the only one. And they would protect it so that it would no be hurt. The ball would be the greatest wonder known, and people would come and pray to it to be held, to gain knowledge, to know beauty and to wonder how it could be. People would love it and defend it with their lives because they would somehow know that their lives, their own roundness could be nothing without it. If the earth were only a few feet in diameter.

This presentation was provided by Sue and Robin Bell.

The *Elephant* Presentation:

Massive elephants roam free in parts of the world. In Thailand, however, elephants are captured and tamed. An iron band at the end of a very heavy chain is put around each elephant's foot and the elephant is chained to a large tree. The elephant struggles and pulls, trying to break the chain or uproot the tree until it gives up and realizes that it can't be done. This powerful animal tries to lift its leg and can't so it just gives up. The elephant, as strong as it is, cannot win. It loses and totally gives up. Then the elephant is unchained and taken out to work and is tied to a small stake in the ground. The elephant believes that it is chained to the tree and doesn't want the pain that the heavy chain brings it. The elephant has no idea that with the slightest effort that it could break free. So, today, are you letting what happened in the past be so painful that you won't break free and go for greatness?

The *Fire Up* Presentation:
- •Allow a light to go on in your mind!
- •Assume leadership over your dreams and your destiny!
- •Become a sudden expert as a challenge solver!
- •Cast the deciding vote!
- •Dare to think bigger than you ever have before!
- •Dare to try!
- •Don't surrender leadership to foes, fears and fences!
- •Face impossible situations!
- •Get turned on to your new dream!
- •Give tickets away!
- •Grab hold of your personal power!
- •Rearrange and reestablish your priorities!
- •Reject, expel and get rid of the word *"impossible!"*
- •Seize the potential!
- •Show the courage to make a commitment!
- •Turn every challenge into a decision!

The *Fool Gives His Life* Presentation:
Get money, but stop once in a while to figure what it is costing you to get it. No person gets money without giving something in return. The wise man gives his labor and ability. The fool gives his life.

The *Football Huddle* Presentation:
Football plays get called from the sideline. So, why the huddle? Why do the players need to come together? Do you know why? Because out on the field where they line up, it's lonely. They get humiliated in front of thousands of people. In the huddle, they regain their self-esteem and they line up again and forget the last play and go forward again.

The *Four Boxes* Presentation:
"Decisions have to be made box"	= Put every challenge you have into a box labeled this way.
"I believe it box"	= Write on a box, *"I believe it."* Put your challenge in the box, close the lid and work on something else. Leave it for weeks at a time or take it out the next day.
"I can box."	= Cut photos of eyes out of magazines and glue them onto a can or box.
"The invisible box."	= Have an invisible box in your mind before you go to sleep. Put all your worries, cares, ideas and plans for tomorrow in that box and slip it under your bed for the night.

The *Four Fuels* Presentation:

Here are the four forms of fuel for achieving lasting ongoing success:

Fuel #1 *Visualization* = a picture is worth a thousand words, use mental pictures of mountains, and beaches. While making your presentation, put your invisible arms around the audience and visualize a famous person in history standing behind you cheering you on. Try treasure mapping. Take some magazines and flip through them, cut out pictures of what you want to do, have and be. Carefully choose the pictures of what you want to create in your lifetime. Any shape, size, huge portion and put them on a poster board. View them daily. Look at it the first thing every morning and every night before you go to bed.

Fuel #2 *Unshakable faith* = SWSWSWNextSW....*Some will want what you present. Some won't. So what? Who's next? Someone is waiting!* You must not let anyone kill your dream! When it comes down to it, there is only one person who matters where trust is concerned, you know who.

Fuel #3 *Education and knowledge* = People spend $500+ a year on the outside of their head (haircuts, sprays, shampoos, hats). What is the cost of ignorance? One idea alone from a book, an audio tape, a seminar can make you major money. Knowledge is power. Ben Franklin said, *"Take everything you own and put it in your mind, that way no one can steal it!"* Ask for books, tapes and seminar tickets for your holiday gifts, feed your mind.

Fuel #4 *Environment of support* = It's impossible to fly like an eagle if you surround yourself with turkeys. Surround yourself with success. Immerse yourself in excellence. Seek out excellence, have a passion for excellence. Surround yourself with people with like goals, dare to be great, read great books, see fine films, eat at fine restaurants, seek out the acknowledged leaders and learn from them and from their mentors. Surround yourself with positive high-energy successful people. Don't participate in negative talk, seek out quality, it will rub off. Focus on making every moment of your presentation the best it can be.

The *Four Seasons* Presentation:

- •Winter..........It is time for the 5-5-5 Rule: Call 5, acknowledge 5, email 5.
- •Spring..........It is the time to plant your ideas in the minds of others.
- •Summer.......It is the time to plan for the fall.
- •Fall...............It is the time to harvest that which you have sown. Close em!

---

5 - 5 - 5 Rule
"Call 5, Acknowledge 5, Email 5"

Jodi Carville

The *Froggies* Presentation:

After a torrential rain in Ireland there were a group of froggies hopping along one day together as a group. All of a sudden a part of the group of froggies dropped down into a deep bog filled with water. They began to madly jump to get out of the bog but it was too deep. The froggies that did not fall in gathered around the bog and began to watch with horror how hard each of their froggie friends were trying to survive and jump out of the bog! It was a horrible scene to witness and finally when the froggies saw that it was of no use for their froggie friends to keep trying, they leaned over the bog and began to scream *"Give Up! You are going to die, there is no way out, you can't jump high enough to get out, give in, we love you and will miss you!"* And sure enough, one by one each little froggie turned upside down and floated in the water, exhausted from jumping and died. Except one little froggie. He continued to jump! His friends yelled at him, *"Give up! There is no way out, look at all of your friends and family froggies, they have all given up, everyone of them, you might as well do the same, give up!"* But the little froggie kept jumping and jumping until one of the times he made a huge effort; he jumped right out of that cold and scary bog! He lay on the ground panting for a breath and all of his froggie friends surrounded him astonished at his accomplishment. They said *"Didn't you hear us screaming to you to give up? Why didn't you give up?"* And with that the little froggie said *"Ey? I am hard of hearing! I thought you were cheering me on!"*

 Tip ➔ *Never encourage others to give up on their dreams.*

The *Goldmine* Presentation:

I own a gold mine and I am going to share it with you. I am going to let you go into my fabulous gold mine but there is one catch, you can only go in and out once. So what are going to do first?

    1. Rush in and take everything with your hands and raw enthusiasm?

    2. Go and get some tools and make a fortune?

The *Golden Handcuff* Presentation:

In the fall, plan a contest or a special for January or February - this way you'll hold on to your customers through the holidays. Smart business!

 Tip ➔ *Desire sleeps, it can be awakened by using stories, in words to songs and in your presentation.*

The *Gotta Wanna* Presentation:

One warm summer evening, a Master presenter of information was practicing his speech in a huge auditorium. He wanted to get a feel for the platform, look at the room from all angles, sort out his notes, make sure the equipment worked and decided to make a run through of his entire presentation. The markers worked fine on the easel, the lighting was perfect and so he began to speak. He varied his tone of voice, smiled at the audience and gave an incredibly moving speech about going for greatness. What he didn't realize was that in the shadows, a janitor had been watching and listening to the speech, as he made his way up to the front of the auditorium. All of a sudden the Master presenter looked down from the platform and saw the janitor and asked him if he was having a nice evening. He shared with him that he was practicing for a massive event the following day. The janitor listened and then told the Master presenter that although what he had to say was awesome, powerful, exciting and bold; he thought that he could sum up the entire presentation in two little words! The Master presenter said, *"Of course you can't! I have years of experience, I am an expert, I have sold more books and tapes in this country than any other presenter, I have the best connections, the best knowledge, the most wisdom of anyone else in this industry. How can you possibly sum up what I have just said in the last hour into two words, it just can't be done?"* And the janitor looked him right in the eyes and said, *"Gotta Wanna. You see, if you don't wanna do what I am teaching you to do today, you won't do it, no matter how long I talk or what I say!"*

 Tip ➔ *The point of this presentation is to have people realize they must have desire before any action will be taken on the information you present.*

> *"You see, if you don't wanna do what I am teaching you to do today, you won't do it, no matter how long I talk or what I say! You Gotta Wanna!"*
>
> **John Curtis**

The *Hats* Presentation:

For this presentation you will need: a hard hat, a fire fighter's hat, a baseball cap and whistle for props. This is for a presentation on leadership and personality styles. Bring up three or more peak performers in the audience and have them each one take one of the hats (you might want to have a couple of each hat).

The take-charge person wears the hard hat, which is needed to get through tough times as a project manager. It's easy to find the people who have pressed on to become leaders in an audience. The person wearing the hard hat does not need a script or to even know about this ahead of time. When they are onstage with you, you say, *"It's my way or...*and let them say ...*the highway!"* Or you might say, *"It's my way or else..."* or *"It's my way or no way..."* Always make them the star of the show, do not be afraid to involve them.

The person wearing the fire fighter hat does not need a script or to even know about this ahead of time. When they are on stage with you, you say, *"There are those of you in the room who have put a lot of fire's out, or who are fired up, or who are going to spread the wildfire, remember that we are counting on you. This person is a great example of someone who is fired up!"* Always make them the star of the show, do not be afraid to involve them.

The person wearing the baseball cap and whistle does not need a script or to even know about this ahead of time. When they are on the stage with you, you say, *"There is a great need for people to be coaches in our business. Don't be afraid to step up to bat. Just say, 'Put me in Coach, I'm ready to play!'"* Always make them the star of the show, do not be afraid to involve them.

The *"I'm 100% Behind You"* Presentation:

Check with the meeting planner before you do this to make sure it's okay with them. Have everyone stand up and get behind someone else and face a wall.

Then say, *"Now put your hands on the person in front of your shoulders and give them a nice massage. While massaging them lean over their right or left shoulder and say "I'm 100% behind you!"*

The *It Isn't Entirely Education* Presentation:

- Many successful people have little formal education.
- Abraham Lincoln was self-educated.
- Benjamin Franklin never attended school at all.
- H. G. Wells was born in poverty and fought ill health.
- Jan Ruhe started working with a college degree in Dallas, Texas for Merrill Lynch in 1971 for $75 a week, paid for parking and a one-bedroom apartment, without a kitchen.
- The Wright Brothers weren't scientists but bicycle mechanics by trade.
- Thomas Edison had only three month's education.

The *Johnny Appleseed* Presentation:

John Chapman was known as Johnny Appleseed. He slung a sack of apple seeds over his shoulder and took off from his home in New York. He headed west, planting seeds, which would not bear fruit for his own benefit but for those who might happen upon them in the future. He gave saplings to the natives and all the settlers. Not only did he plant apple seeds, he also planted seeds of another kind. He would sit under the shade of a tree and invite those who came across his path to join him while he read from his special books. Be like Johnny Appleseed, plant away. Who knows what can happen when you sow good thoughts. The hope is that they might take root and grow into giant trees someday that will bear fruit for someone you will never know.

The *Know How* Presentation:

Know how:
- to get along with people.
- to get people to do things you want done.
- to sell your ideas.
- to sell yourself to your employees—to your employers—get co-operation and loyalty.
- to sell yourself to your friends, families, and neighbors—everyone with whom you come in daily contact.

The *Lighthouse* Presentation:

The following is an actual radio conversation released by the US Chief of Naval Operations, October 10, 1995:

Hail: Please divert your course 15 degrees to the North to avoid a collision.

Reply: Recommend you divert YOUR course 15 degrees to South to avoid a collision.

Hail: This is the Captain of a U.S. Navy ship. I say again, divert YOUR course.

Reply: No, I say again, you divert YOUR course.

Hail: This is the aircraft carrier Enterprise, we are a large warship of the US Navy. Divert your course now!

Reply: This is a lighthouse....your call.

The *Laws of Prosperity*

- Clear your mind of negativity.
- Forgive yourself for not having faith.
- Set new goals.
- Work as if it will all turn out a you planned.

76

The *Make Them Thirsty* Presentation:

You can get a dog to do tricks, you can get even get a mule to move if you are persistent. But, when it comes to humans, you very rarely can get them to do anything they don't want to do. Today, I want to share with you how to get people to do things because they want to do what you want done. Be careful, watch for the people who try to trick you into thinking they are loyal to you…they are the ones who will turn against you in an evil way.

When people are hungry enough, they will eat.
When people are thirsty enough, they will drink.

Here's how to get people to do that which you want done. Appeal to a need of the other person or to their daydream. Their hopes, desires, wishes, faults, challenges, all must be appealed to.

If people aren't thirsty for your companionship, they will go elsewhere. Remember, in life, you will find that there are some who you don't thirst for their companionship either.

The *Old Donkey* Presentation:

There once was a farmer who was getting tired of farming. He had lost his wife and all of his children were grown and gone. It was hot and he was tired of taking care of the old donkey who was growing older also. All of a sudden, the farmer heard a crash and ran outside to find the poor old donkey had fallen in a well. The farmer couldn't bear to hear it braying with pain and anguish! He ran back into his house and called some neighbor farmers to hurry over to his farm and to bring their shovels. There was no way they could get the donkey out of the well, he was doomed! The poor old mule was hoping that all the farmers could get him out of the well. However, he was so wrong; what was actually happening is that they decided to bury him alive to put him out of his misery. The farmers all gathered round and one by one began to throw dirt into the well! The donkey became frantic, what was happening? *How could they do this? How could he be treated like this? Did they think he had no more value? Did they not care about him or how he felt? After all he had contributed to farmer's life? How could he be dismissed so easily? What did he do to deserve treatment like this? Does my old farmer really not appreciate me after all I have done?* When all of a sudden, the donkey started thinking. Wait a minute, I am smart. I have wisdom. I have experience. Think, think, think! And with that he had an idea. Every single time dirt would be thrown on him; he would shake it off his back and step up. Shake it off and step up. This became his mantra, shake it off and step up. And he said those words to himself over and over for hours until voila, they had given him so much dirt to step up on, that he stepped right out of that well. The farmers were amazed. The donkey survived and left us all a very valuable lesson.

The Moso Bamboo Tree Presentation:

Have you ever seen a Moso Bamboo Tree? What an awesome sight to see, soaring over one hundred feet straight up. Do you know how this bamboo tree grows?

First, get a moso bamboo stock, about 18 inches long. Next, dig a hole 3 feet deep, and bury the stock completely in the ground. For the next 5 years, that stock must be watered every single day, 365 days a year. If one day is missed, the tree will never appear. But, if meticulous care is taken for that 5 years, it is said that on that 1,825th day, the ground will break open and the tree will appear out of the ground.

Next is the phenomenon of the Moso Bamboo Tree. The tree will grow to over 90 feet in a matter of 6 weeks! It grows at a rate of three feet every 24 hours. You could practically sit back and watch it grow. Some people say it takes 6 weeks for a bamboo tree to grow, while others say it takes 5 years and 6 weeks to grow. I guess it depends on if you were the one watering it for 5 years.

Imagine if you were to plant a bamboo tree in your back yard, and went out every day to water it, rain or shine. Suppose one of your neighbors sees you doing this for several days and asks, *"What are you watering the same spot of ground for every day?"* You reply, *"I'm growing a bamboo tree. You water it every day for 5 years, then it grows to 90 feet in 6 weeks. You ought to try it."* He ponders the idea, then replies, *"No thanks, I think I'll wait and see if yours works."*

The next year, that same neighbor sees that you are still watering the spot of ground. He asks, *"Why are you still watering the spot and nothing happens?"* You tell the man, *"It takes time to grow a bamboo tree, but once it comes out of the ground, it is the most awesome sight to see. You ought to grow one too!"* The neighbor just laughs and replies, *"No thanks, I'll just wait to see how yours turns out."*

The third year, the neighbor isn't talking to you any more, doesn't want anything to do with you. The whole neighborhood has heard about the crazy lady on the block that keeps watering this same spot in her yard, hoping to grow a bamboo tree. The fourth year, they're sizing you up for a straight jacket, and none of the children are allowed to play near your home. But in that fifth year, the ground breaks open, and that stick that you had planted catches it's first rays of sunshine, and away it goes!

Six weeks later the neighbors are admiring this awesome sight that you now have, wishing they had a bamboo tree. But they would have to wait 5 years for theirs to grow! Boy, do they wish they would have listened to you 5 years ago.

If you had planted your stock in your business, it would be much like a bamboo tree. It takes watering every day. You don't see anything happen for some time, but you keep watering it. Many people will ask you, *"How's your business going? Have you made your fortune yet? I'll wait to see how you do."* Then one day, your organization will open up, catch it's first rays of sunshine, and away it goes! You could practically sit back and watch it grow, faster and faster, higher and higher. While you're sitting on the top of your bamboo tree enjoying the view, others will be thinking, *"I wish I had listened, and planted my stock."*

The *Mix-It-Up* Presentation:

As people get seated, they like to sit with their friends. However, in meetings it's lots of fun and it keeps people awake to move them around. Every twenty minutes, have people get up and move to a new location in the room. Or have people count off, one, two, three and four and all the ones go to table one, all the twos go to table two and so forth.

The *Money* Presentation:

Managing money is a matter of education. Saving money is a matter of discipline. Discussing money and what you will do with it is fun. There is more than enough money to go around and you do deserve it.

 Tip ➔ *Remember the mantra of the old donkey...Step up and shake it off!*

The *One Word* Presentation:

Here is the way it goes:

"You like this product, don't you?"

"Yes," responds the prospect.

"This product would benefit you or someone you love, don't you think?"

"Yes," answers the prospect.

"Now you can see how our product is unique, can't you?"

"Yes," replies the prospect.

The next step is...

The *Pat on the Back* Presentation:

Do this while you tell others to do this:

"Reach way over your shoulder and give yourself a pat on the back for coming."

The *Partner* Presentation:

You can do this in a small or large group. Make sure they understand the rules. Say, *"Here is something you can do in your meetings. It only takes a moment to do. But for it to work, please be perfectly silent. Without saying a word or making a noise, stand up. Okay, now, stay quiet, face a person you don't know, but stay quiet. Okay, here is what we are going to do. I am going to count to three. When I say three I want you to look at your partner and then at the top of your lungs yell these four words, 'What do you want?' One, two, three!* Everyone will scream these words and then laugh. Next you say, *'Okay, that was sort of okay, but I bet you can do better. The next time I want you to scream will be a little bit harder. This time I will count to three and when I say three, I want you to look at your partner and with your utmost sincere smile and with your most sincere voice, scream 'Hi there, how can I be of service to you?' One, two, three!"* This may take a few tries!

The *Personal Sizzlemanship* Presentation:

Successful people always know how to sell themselves to other people. We are all *"salespeople,"* morning, noon and far into the night! We are selling our ideas, our plans, our energies, our enthusiasms to those with whom we come in contact. The person of genial personality is bound to accomplish more than the person without it. So be an unabashed self–promoter.

Just think of all the questions we ask each other:

"What is a great movie to see?"

"Who is the best doctor in town?"

"Who is the best lawyer in town?"

The *P.R.A.M.* Presentation:

> **P** = *praise!*
> **R** = *recognition!*
> **A** = *appreciate!*
> **M** = *motivate!*

The *Secret of Success* Presentation:

- Find a challenge and solve it!
- Find a hurt and heal it!
- Find a need and fill it!
- Find a person and help them!
- If it works, improve it!

The *70's Sitcoms Music* Presentation:

Get a CD of the 70 Sitcoms and play them in your presentation. Many people can tell you the name of the sitcoms now decades later! It brings so much fun into the presentation!

The *Sex vs. Education* Presentation:

You say, *"In just a moment, I am going to illustrate to you the meanings that our words have. When you are making presentations and having conversations, your words take on different meanings sometimes than you intended. I want you to break into groups of five to ten people and pull your chairs around together and select a chairperson who will take notes. Everyone with me? After I give you the two words you must, as a group decide what word you will choose and write down all the descriptive words you can think of as a team. This should take no longer than three minutes from the start to the end. At the end, your Chairperson will stand and read the word you as a team chose and the descriptive words you associate with that word. You are not going to believe the end result of this three to five minutes! Now, listen carefully, the two words you have to choose from are: "Sex" or "Education." Go!"*

The Sable Presentation:

Sable stands for:

S = *success attitudes!*
A = *action speaks louder than words!*
B = *be accountable!*
L = *love others!*
E = *enthusiastically present!*

> *"Improve your presentation skills and within a year you will find yourself setting and meeting high goals. Just remember that the mastery of presentations requires that you work on your skills."*
>
> **Melynda Lilly**

The *Shadab Weather Bulletin* Presentation:

Sherry Shadab sent this email out the morning after Jan Ruhe spoke in Alabama.

!WEATHER BULLETIN!! TORNADO STRUCK TOWN!!
BIRMINGHAM NEVER THE SAME AGAIN
HOT S-T-E-A-M (Y) CLIMATE! NO RELIEF (WANTED) IN SIGHT!

Last night the whipping whirling winds of the life-altering, yet uncalibrated Ruhe Tornado hit Birmingham and left massive amounts of devastating Whirlwinds, Floods, Power Surges, Fires and Successes in it's wake! It began innocently enough and yet you could begin to feel something different in the air. The slow steady hum began to rise and build the thunder(ous) claps forewarned all of incredible raw Power they were about to experience but no one yet knew the full extent of it's strength!

As the Whirlwinds of Wisdom and Wit were unleashed on the crowd they were whipped into a never before felt frenzy of simultaneous tears, laughter, delight, self-recognition and discovery! Everyone was rocked with unrelenting bolts of lightening that tore through their psyche's and set them on Fire! Torrents of Passion pelted the night like never before! Howling winds were screaming .... *"I can do it better!"* Currents of electricity ripped through the Lodge and set all in their path on Fire!!!!! The Mighty Ruhe Tornado made history!...breaking all records for Size, Speed and Burning Desire! All of those in it's path were ignited and set ABLAZE! These inextinguishable FIRES swept through Birmingham and beyond into, Georgia, Mississippi, Tennessee, Florida and as far as Indiana, flooding the streets with electrical charges that will be setting more people and places on FIRE! All day long reports of these blazing Fires and their laser like movements have been coming into Command Central via email, fax and telephone lines!
FIRED UP!: Andrea and Amy flew back to Tennessee to heat up Ole Hickory's turf!
   Gail ignited strangers resulting in two recruits and several party bookings!
   Janice flew back to Indiana jet-propelled and on Fire!
   JoAnn and Stephanie seriously plotted and strategized, and set new goals!
   Kimberly cell-phoned prospects on her drive back to Pensacola, arrived, faxed
      paperwork for her newest recruit.
   Linda zoomed back to Georgia to get her new leads hot off the presses!
   Michelle has two new hot prospects flaming over to Monday's meeting!
   Tzena started making a Smokin' list of her lost schoolmates, scattered across the
      country on her quest to... BREAK-A-STATE!!
Stay tuned to this station for more incredible developments as reports of raging Fires out of control are still flooding in from all around the globe! Although already one for the history books, the extent of last night's Ruhe Tornado's astounding effects are yet to be measured...as casualties seem to be unique in their unabashed determination to...
STAY......FIRED UP!!!!!!!!!!!!

The *Short Sentence* Presentation:

"*I am,*" is the shortest complete sentence in the English language. "*I am finished*" is the phrase every audience loves to hear. So today, "*I promise I will keep my remarks brief.*"

The *Sincere* Presentation:

Concentrate on developing the kind of genuine personality that attracts others naturally. Sincerity is the magic touchstone that makes your presentation sizzle instead of fizzle. The biggest success secret of the Master presenters is to present with sincerity. When you are sincere, people will tell others. You will soon find you are in the big business of making friends. You can't pretend to like people. You must like them. You must develop a genuine interest in them.

The *Skeptics* Presentation:

In 1807, Robert Fulton attracted a large crowd to witness the first full scale demonstration of the steamboat on the Hudson River. When he tried to get the engine started, the crowd shouted, "*It will never start! It will never start!*" When the engine finally did start and the steamboat took off with a flurry of sparks and heavy smoke, the crowd was silent for a moment, but only for a moment and then they began screaming, "*It will never stop! It will never stop!*" Despite the skeptics, press on.

The *Smiling* Presentation:

"*Turn the corners of your lips up! Now raise your cheeks!*"
- Smile after you smile!
- Smile all the way!
- Smile any way!
- Smile even when you do not feel like smiling!
- Smile every day!
- Smiling is a sign of good health!
- Smiling is great for you; it's a healthy exercise!
- Smiling is the universal sign of happiness!

The Stating of Goals Presentation:

Do you set goals? Setting goals is essential. Many people are afraid to set goals because they think they can't reach them. They shrink their income to match their goals, instead of expanding their income to reach their dreams. Here's how to set goals. Start with the end result you are seeking, then just sort out the best way of achieving it. "*As I share with you my goals, think of whether they match yours or not. If we are not going in the same direction, how we choose to travel there is of no value. I hope you agree with my goals and that we have a match; then we can proceed to examine the specific ideas to make these goals possible. I am going for greatness and will not be denied the fabulous lifestyle I desire.*"

The *S.T.E.A.M.* Presentation:
During your presentation formulate your questions using this acronym:

S = *Sales*
Who do you know in sales?

T = *Teacher*
Who's your child's favorite teacher?

E = *Enthusiasm*
Who's the most enthusiastic person you know?

A = *Attitude*
Who do you know with a positive attitude?

M = *Money*
Who do you know who needs extra money?

The *"Take the Chair"* Presentation:
Would you like to be on a committee? How about the Chairperson on a committee? Have you ever thought of where the word *"Chairman"* came from? It comes from the custom during the Middle Ages when the master of the house and his lady were the only ones who owned and sat on chairs. The rest of the household, although it shared a communal dining table, sat on stools or cushions at a lower level. Being invited to *"take the chair"* honored guests of great importance.

The *That Will Work* Presentation:
"That will work, I aspire to change myself in a way that when I present I will inspire others to be more positive."

"Awake the giant within"
Tony Robbins

The *Vienna* Presentation:

Jan and Bill Ruhe, Jan's daughter Sarah, Bonnie and David Arypes and Gavin Scott were having dinner in the private dining room of the Tower Restaurant in Snowmass, Colorado, in May 2001. Doc Eason, one of the top magicians in the world, came upstairs and regaled them with a private magic show. During this show he shared this story…

"What could be better for a magician than being invited to perform at the creme de la creme of the magic world, the Ball of Magicians in Vienna, Austria? Being invited back, of course. That is what happened to me this last March, 2001. Still riding the wave of euphoria from last year's gala event, I sent an e-mail to the organizers of this year's Ball de Magier, wishing them well. Almost immediately, I received a reply from the committee asking me if I would consent to return. I, of course, jumped at the chance. For over two decades, I have been the predominant fixture at the Tower Comedy Magic Bar in Snowmass, Colorado. My job, every night, is to present memorable experiences to the patrons of this unique venue. While I have garnered international recognition before, this one is a real feather for my cap. The Ball of Magicians (or "Ball de Magier") in Austria is an annual affair coinciding with "Fasching Season" in Austria (roughly the equivalent of Carnival in other parts of the world). Many different balls are held during this season, the most notable of which is the Opernball, which is attended by many political and social celebrities. Other occupations, such as physicians and confectioners, also hold their own gala events, but the magician's ball is special. Not all of Vienna's finest enjoy dancing. So this event has the added sparkle of having the best magicians from all over the world performing in various venues. I performed the close up act that I have been doing for the last 24 years in a setting not unlike the intimate surroundings of the Tower Bar. What a treat it was to do what I do for such a prestigious and appreciative crowd.

One of the high points for me was to be in the Grand Ballroom of the Vienna Hilton watching the satin and velvet adorned women and their tuxedoed and tailed partners enjoying the evening. The four piece combo was able to produce nearly any kind of music but, when the band broke into a Strauss waltz, something truly wonderful happened. So engrained is this type of dancing in the Viennese culture, that at the first strains of the waltz, the mood in the room palpably changed and everyone grabbed their partners and rushed to the floor and began dancing, swirling, waltzing around the floor. To add to the moment, billowing smoke was pumped from under the stage, filling the dance floor so it appeared that the whirling dancers were floating on a cloud. In the enchantment of the moment, I was transported to a place where I saw these dancer's parents and their parents, swirling and dancing down through the years. At that instant, I felt truly blessed to be where I was. A high point of my life, this was truly magical moment for me."

The "*What if?*" Presentation:

Play the game, "*What if?*"

"*What if I can get out of debt? Get a new car? Go to college? Learn to play a musical instrument? Build a large organization?*"

Answer these three questions; write them down, no conditions, no limitations:
   1. If I didn't have to work for a living, what would I love to do?
   2. If I was just given $1 million tax-free what would I do with it?
   3. If I learned that I had six healthy months left to live, what would I do?

Who Gets the Credit? Presentation:

> '*A great deal of good can be done in the world*
> *if one is not too careful who gets the credit.*'

If your object in life is to get credit, you'll probably get it, if you work hard enough. But don't be too much surprised and disappointed when some person who just went ahead and did the thing, without thinking of the credit, winds up with more recognition than you, with all your striving, the person who really achieves the most credit, is the one who does it and does not expect recognition. You can accomplish a lot in your life if you are not concerned about who gets the credit for it. Be so busy giving recognition that you don't need any yourself.

Who is Worthy of Loyalty? Presentation:

Loyalty is never automatic. It must be earned. How do you earn loyalty?

1) Be accessible.
2) Be a master trainer or teacher.
3) Be objective.
4) Bless and release easily, those who are not like minded.
5) Give praise freely.
6) Handle criticism.
7) Have a personal growth & development program.
8) High expectations of themselves and whom they work with.
9) Initiate change.
10) Lead the field.
11) Preparation.
12) Prevent challenges, but when they come make a decision.
13) Promote leaders and make them successful.
14) Recognize value in people.

The *Wizard of OZ* Presentation:

L. Frank Baum, author of The Wizard of Oz had finished the outline to the story, but had not come up with the name of the enchanted land where Dorothy, the Tin Man, the Scarecrow and the Cowardly Lion sought the help of the Wizard. As he gathered up his files, Baum's eyes fell upon a drawer in his filing cabinet marked. "*O-Z.*" You never know where your inspiration will come from.

The *Write and Speak to Help People* Presentation:

"I hope I may never be guilty of writing anything intended to make poor people contented with their lot. I would rather be known as one who sought to inspire his readers with a divine discontent, bad health, and to show them how, by hard work, they can have better health. To make them discontented with their intelligence and to stimulate them to continued study. To urge them on to better jobs, better homes, more money in the bank. But it does not harm, in our striving after these worth-while things to pause once in a while and count our blessings." – Bruce Barton

You are a Millionaire Presentation:

You might not think of it today, but you are a millionaire. Let me tell you how. First of all, I would like to buy your right arm, how much would you sell it for? Next, I would like to buy your left foot. Then what about your lungs, your liver, your spleen, your nose, your ears? And then there is more, your skin, your nails, your eyes, and more, your faith, your loved ones, your dreams, your goals and your personal power…Tally all those up, approximately how much do you think you are worth now??? Millions!!!!!

You are Like a Computer Presentation:

Turn your real computer on! Does it work if it is turned off? Not likely! Now turn on the computer in your brain. On the screen in your mind appears a set of instructions. Click on the icon that says success! Watch the messages come across your imagination screen. Potential! Prioritize! Probe the Possibilities! Internalize! Organize! Revitalize! Search! Send orders! Transmit messages! Connect with others! Communicate! Catch the passion! Increase the enthusiasm! Get excited! Get that energy flowing! Your mind is a computer that can: **Choose! Decide! Feel! Judge! Think!** Turn it on and keep it on!!!!!!!!!!!

> *"A Chieftan who doesn't plan for himself is always reacting to the plans of others. You lose if reaction becomes your only option."*
>
> **Atilla the Hun**

What Kind of Person Are You? Presentation:
Are you an I-I person?
When faced with decisions, this person asks these questions:

"Does it fit in with my plans?"
"What's in it for me?"
"What will I get out of it?"

It doesn't matter if others don't like it; no matter if others would be helped or not; no matter if others are hurting.

These people say:

"I am a non-sharing, non-caring, non-burden bearing person."
"I've got enough challenges of my own."

Instead say:

"How can I help you?"
"What can I do to help you?"
"I love you because I want you."

Are you an I-It person?
Do you find emotional fulfillment in things?
Want happiness? Go shopping, buy something.
Are you bored? Go to a movie.
Guilty? Buy someone something.
Fearful? Buy a gun.
Insecure? Hoard money.
Need to impress people? Buy things that are unimportant to you but important to others.
Lonely? Go to a bar.
I-it people are trapped with things: Paint me, plaster me, patch me, repair me, replace me, dust me, rearrange me and take care of me.

These people say:

"What are the income possibilities?"
"What are the benefits to me and my family?"
"What will it cost me?"
"I love you because I need you."

Are you an I-You person?
I-you people relate to other people who have dreams, desires, hurts and needs. These people love people. They are the real success stories. They are filled with goodness, kindness and helpfulness. They are energetic, constructive and dynamic, really priceless friends.

These people say:
"I love you because you need me." = Real love.

You Can Take Yourself Farther **Presentation:**

Say to the audience: *"You know that you can take yourself farther than you ever dreamed. It's just visualization and focus."*

Ask everyone to stand up:
Next, say, *"Stand where you can stretch out your arms on both sides of you, and then stretch out your arms and make sure you are not touching another person or a wall or an obstruction of any kind."*

Next, say, *"Turn and face me."*

Next, say, *"This is not going to be a contest where you have to compete with each other. If you have a bad back do not participate."*

Next say, *"Now with your arms out on either side of you and keeping both feet on the floor, in the same location. Loosen up and rotate from side to side while I tell you what we are gong to do next. On the count of three, I want you to rotate with both feet on the floor facing me, and stop. Rotate as far as you can possibly go. Stretch as far as you can. Point to and remember a spot on the wall and hold that position for further instructions."*

Pause and then say, *"Okay, One, two, three, rotate, stop, point and hold that position!"*
Next say, *"Now, I want you to mentally focus on your point. Got it? Now, gently, put your arms down and once again face me."*

Keep talking, *"Now I am going to show you some magic. And you are part of my magic show. Close your eyes, visualize your point that you stopped at the first time you did this exercise. Do you have that place in your mind? Well, I believe that you can go farther than you just did the first time...I now want you to visualize another foot beyond your first point. Open your eyes and on the count of three, I want you to rotate and point one foot farther than your first time. Ready?"*

Pause and then say, *"Okay, One, two, three, rotate, stop, point and hold that position!"*
Next say: *"Wow, you did it! You went farther than you thought you could! It's magic!"*

You can continue this several more times...this amazes audiences and they love it!

"Life's a dance."

Dorothy Wood

89

The *10 Worst Excuses For Not Making* Presentations:

• I am feeling stress and need to rest.
• I am hoping that people will send me orders so that I will get reenergized to make more presentations.
• I broke a finger nail and can't leave the house.
• I expect a lot of people to call me back today.
• I had a big order this morning but they canceled it and I am depressed.
• I had car problems this morning.
• I thought I had enough prospects.
• I won the top recruiting award last month and I wanted to give somebody else a chance to win something.
• My computer malfunctioned and I can't make calls without it.

Now Commit to
Improve your Presentations!

I, _____, fully intend to improve my presentation skills so that I can reach the lifestyle I so richly deserve. I am not just going to acquire things, instead I am going to plan a lifestyle that nurtures and reinforces and lets me reach out to people who will benefit from my information and wisdom.

_____
(your signature)

_____
(Date)

Chapter 5

Sayings & Stories

"Following are sayings & stories that I have found useful for including in a presentation. Their use greatly helps in bringing the lessons across to the audience."

Jan Ruhe

A Thousand Marbles

"Well, Tom, it sure sounds like you're busy with your job. I'm sure they pay you well but it's a shame you have to be away from home and your family so much. Hard to believe a young fellow should have to work sixty or more hours a week to make ends meet. Too bad you missed your daughter's dance recital. I want to share with you something that has helped me keep a good perspective on my own priorities......Do the arithmetic. The average person lives about 75 years. Some live more and some live less, but on average, folks live about 75 years. Now, multiplied 75 times 52 and I came up with 3,900, which is the number of Saturdays that the average person has in their entire lifetime. It takes most people to the age of 55 years old to think about all this in any detail; by that time you have had lived over 2,800 hundred Saturdays. I got to thinking that if I lived to be 75 years old, I only had about a *1,000 Saturdays left to enjoy.*

So I went to a toy store and bought every single marble they had I ended up having to visit three toy stores to round up 1,000 marbles. I took them home and put them inside of a large, clear plastic container right next to where I spend every Saturday morning. Each Saturday since then, I have taken one marble out and thrown it away. I found that by watching the marbles diminish, I focus more on the really important things in life. There is nothing like watching your time here on this earth run out to help get your priorities straight. Now let me tell you one last thing before I sign-off with you and take my lovely wife out for breakfast. This morning I took the very last marble out of the container. I figure that if I make it until next Saturday then I have been given a little extra time. And the one thing we can all use is a little extra time. It was nice to meet you Tom, I hope you spend more time with your family, and I hope to meet you again here on the band.

"75 year Old Man, this is K9NZQ, clear and going QRT, good morning!"

You could have heard a pin drop on the band when this fellow signed off. I guess he gave us all a lot to think about. I had planned to work on the antenna that morning, and then I was going to meet up with a few hams to work on the next club newsletter. Instead, I went upstairs and woke my wife up with a kiss. *"C'mon honey, I'm taking you and the kids to breakfast." "What brought this on?"* she asked with a smile. *"Oh, nothing special, it's just been a long time since we spent a Saturday together with the kids. Hey, can we stop at a toy store while we're out? I need to buy some marbles."*

Winnie the Pooh said:
*"If you live to be a hundred, I want to live to be a hundred
minus one day, so I never have to live without you."*

This presentation was provided by Sue duPreez.

Abraham Lincoln Didn't Quit

Abraham Lincoln could have quit many times—but he didn't and because he didn't quit, he became one of the Greatest Presidents in the history of the United States.

"The sense of obligation to continue is present in all of us.
A duty to strive is the duty of us all.
I felt a call to that duty."

If you want to learn about somebody who didn't quit,
look no further than Abraham Lincoln.

Born into poverty, Lincoln was faced with defeat through out his life. He lost eight elections, twice failed in business and suffered a nervous breakdown. But Lincoln was a champion and he never gave up. Here is a sketch of Lincoln's road to the White House:

1831-Failed in business
1832-Defeated for Legislature.
1833-Second failure in business.
1836-Suffered a nervous breakdown.
1838-Defeated for Speaker.
1840-Defeated for Elector.
1843-Defeated for Congress.
1848-Defeated for Congress.
1855-Defeated for Vice President
1858-Defeated for Senate.
1860-Elected President of the United States

"The path was worn and slippery. My foot slipped from under me, knocking the other out of the way," Lincoln said, after losing a Senate race. *"But, I recovered and said to myself, 'It's a slip and not a fall.'"*

The Acres Of Diamonds

Pastor Russell Conwell

There once lived not far from the River Indus an ancient Persian farmer by the name of Ali Hafed. It was said that Ali Hafed owned a very large farm, that he had orchards, grain-fields, and gardens; that he had money, and was a wealthy and contented man. He was contented because he was wealthy, and wealthy because he was contented. One day there visited the old Persian farmer, a Buddhist priest, one of the wise men of the East.

The priest sat down by the fire and told the old farmer how this world of ours was made. He said that this world was once a mere bank of fog, and that the Almighty thrust His finger into this bank of fog, and began slowly to move His finger around, increasing the speed until at last He whirled this bank of fog into a solid ball of fire. Then it went rolling through the universe, burning its way through other banks of fog, and condensed the moisture without, until it fell in floods of rain upon its hot surface, and cooled the outward crust. Then the internal fires bursting outward through the crust threw up the mountains and hills, the valleys, the plains and prairies of this wonderful world of ours. If this internal molten mass came bursting out and cooled very quickly it became granite; less quickly copper, less quickly silver, less quickly gold, and then, diamonds were made.

The old priest said, *"A diamond is a congealed drop of sunlight."* Now that is literally scientifically true, that a diamond is an actual deposit of carbon from the sun. The old priest told Ali Hafed that if he had one diamond the size of his thumb he could purchase the county, and if he had a mine of diamonds he could place his children upon thrones through the influence of their great wealth. Ali Hafed heard all about diamonds, how much they were worth, and went to his bed that night a poor man. He had lost nothing, but he was poor because he was discontented, and discontented because he feared he was poor.

Ali Hafed said, *"I want a mine of diamonds,"* Early in the morning he sought out the priest and said to him: *"Will you tell me where I can find diamonds?'"*

The priest said, *"Diamonds! What do you want with diamonds?"*

Ali Hafed said, *"Why, I wish to be immensely rich!"*

The priest said, *"Well, then, go along and find them. That is all you have to do; go and find them, and then you have them."*

Ali Hafed said, *"But I don't know where to go."*

The priest said, *"Well, if you will find a river that runs through white sands, between high mountains, in those white sands you will always find diamonds."*

Ali Hafed said, *"I don't believe there is any such river."*

The priest said, *"Oh yes, there are plenty of them. All you have to do is to go and find them, and then you have them."*

Ali Hafed said, *"I will go."*

So he sold his farm, collected his money, left his family in charge of a neighbor, and away he went in search of diamonds. He wandered on to Europe, and at last when his money was all spent and he was in rags, wretchedness, and poverty, he stood on the shore of that bay at Barcelona, Spain, when a great tidal wave came rolling in between the pillars of Hercules. Unable to resist the awful temptation that poor, afflicted, suffering, dying man cast himself into that incoming tide, and he sank beneath its foaming crest, never to rise in this life again.

The man who purchased Ali Hafed's farm one day led his camel into the garden to drink, and as that camel put its nose into the shallow water of that garden brook, his successor noticed a curious flash of light from the white sands of the stream. He pulled out a black stone having an eye of light reflecting all the hues of the rainbow. He took the pebble into the house and put it on the mantel, which covers the central fires, and forgot all about it.

A few days later this same old priest came in to visit Ali Hafed's successor, and the moment he opened that drawing-room door he saw that flash of light on the mantel, and he rushed up to it, and shouted:

"Here is a diamond! Has Ali Hafed returned?"

The owner of the farm said: *"Oh no, Ali Hafed has not returned, and that is not a diamond. That is nothing but a stone we found right out here in our own garden."* The priest said; *"I tell you I know a diamond when I see it. I know positively that is a diamond!"*

Then together they rushed out into that old garden and stirred up the white sands with their fingers, and lo! there came up other more beautiful and valuable gems than the first.

It is historically true, there was discovered the diamond-mine of Golconda, the most magnificent diamond-mine in all the history of mankind, excelling the Kimberly itself. The Kohinoor, and the Orloff of the crown jewels of England and Russia, the largest on earth, came from that mine.

The moral of the story is that if Ali Hafed had remained at home and dug in his own cellar, or underneath his own wheat-fields, or in his own garden, instead of wretchedness, starvation, and death by suicide in a strange land, he would have had

'Acres of Diamonds.'

For every acre of that old farm, yes, every shovel full, afterward revealed gems which since have decorated the crowns of monarchs. They were on his property all of the time.

Across The Stage of Time

Bruce Barton
From a 1924 Radio Broadcast

Those of you who were brought up on the Bible will recall
the account of Joseph's very remarkable business career.
It tells how he left his country under difficulties and, coming into a strange country,
he rose, through his diligence, to become the principal person in the state,
second only to the King.

The Biblical narrative brings us to that point—
the point where Joseph had made a great success and was widely advertised throughout
the country—it brings us up to the climax of his career and then it hands us an awful
jolt. Without any words of preparation or explanation, it says bluntly:

"And Joseph died, and there arose a new King in Egypt
which knew not Joseph."

Now that sentence is one of the most staggering lines, which has ever been written in a
business biography. Here was a man so famous that everybody knew him and presto, a
few people die, a few new ones are born, and nobody knows him.

The tide of human life has moved on…

Apply that story to modern business.
An hour ago there were in this country sick, in bed, several thousand old folks.
It is perhaps indelicate for me to refer to that fact, but it is a fact…
in this single hour which has just passed, those old folks have died, and all the good-will
which advertising has built up in their minds has died with them—all the investment
made by that past advertising has gone on
into another world where the products are not for sale.

And in this same hour another thing—equally staggering—has happened.
There have been born into this country several thousand lusty boys and girls to whom
advertised products mean no more than the Einstein theory.
They do not know the difference between
a Mazda Lamp and a stick of Wrigley's chewing gum.
Nobody has ever told them that Ivory Soap floats or that children cry for Castoria…

The tramp of human feet is ceaseless across the stage of time…
for every day and every hour the King—which is the public—dies;
then there arises a new King
which knows not Joseph.

97

Around the Corner

Around the corner I have a friend
in this great city that has no end,
Yet the days go by and weeks rush on,
and before I know it, a year is gone.
And I never see my old friend's face,
for life is a swift and terrible race.
He knows I like him just as well,
as in the days when I rang his bell, and he rang mine.
If, we were younger then, and now we are busy, tired men.
Tired of playing a foolish game, tired of trying to make a name.

"Tomorrow" I say *"I will call on Jim"*,
"Just to show that I'm thinking of him."

But tomorrow comes and tomorrow goes,
and distance between us grows and grows.
Around the corner!- yet miles away,

"Here's a telegram sir-"
"Jim died today."

And that's what we get and deserve in the end.
Around the corner, a vanished friend.
If you love someone, tell them.
Remember always to say what you mean.
Never be afraid to express yourself.
Take this opportunity to tell someone what they mean to you.
Seize the day and have no regrets.
Most importantly, stay close to your friends and family,
for they have helped make you the person that you are today
and are what it's all about anyway.

A Reason- A Season- A Lifetime

What are you? Are you a Reason? A Season? Or a Lifetime?

People come into your life for a reason, a season or a lifetime. When you figure out which one it is, you will know what to do for each person.

A Reason?

When someone is in your life for a reason...It is usually to meet a need you have expressed. They come to assist you through a difficulty, to provide you with guidance and support, to aid you physically, emotionally or spiritually. They may seem like a godsend, and they are! They are there for the reason you need them to be. Then, without any wrong doing on your part, or at an inconvenient time, this person will say or do something to bring the relationship to an end. Sometimes they die. Sometimes they walk away. Sometimes they act up and force you to take a stand. What we must realize is that our need has been met, our desire fulfilled, their work is done. The prayer you sent up has been answered. And now it is time to move on!

A Season?

Then people come into your life for a season. Because your turn has come to share, grow or learn. They bring you an experience of peace, or make you laugh. They may teach you something you have never done. They usually give you an unbelievable amount of joy. Believe it! It is real! But, only for a season!

or A Lifetime?

Lifetime relationships teach you lifetime lessons; things you must build in order to have a solid emotional foundation. Your job is to accept the lesson, love the person, and put what you have learned to use in all other relationships and areas of your life. It is said that love is blind but friendship is clairvoyant.

Commitment to Excellence
Vince Lombardi

I owe almost everything to football,
which I spent the greater part of my life in.
I have never lost my respect,
my admiration
nor my love
for what I consider a great game.
Each Sunday after the battle,
one group savors victory;
another group wallows in the bitterness of defeat.
The many hurts seem a small price to pay for having won and
there is no reason at all which is adequate for having lost.

For the winner,
there is 100% elation,
100% laughter,
100% resolution and
100% determination.

The game I think, is a great deal like life.
Every man makes his own personal commitment
toward excellence and toward victory.
Although you know the ultimate victory can never be completely won,
it must be pursued with all of one's might
and each week there is a new encounter,
each year a new challenge.

All of the rings and all of the money and all of the color
and all of the display,
they linger only in a memory.
But **the spirit, the will to win, the will to excel,**
these are the things that endure
and these are the qualities, of course,
that are so much more important
than any of the events that occur.

I'd like to say that the quality of any man's life
is a full measure of that man's personal commitment
to excellence and to victory,
regardless of what field he may be in.

Consider the Rose

The first day of school our professor introduced himself and challenged us to get to know someone who we didn't already know. Right then, a gentle hand touched my shoulder. I turned around to find a wrinkled, little old lady beaming up at me with a big smile. She said, *"Hi handsome. My name is Rose. I'm eighty-seven years old. Can I give you a hug?"* I laughed and enthusiastically responded, *"Of course you may!"* and she gave me a giant squeeze. *"Why are you in college?"* I asked. She jokingly replied, *"I'm here to meet a rich husband, get married, have a couple of children, and then retire and travel."* *"No seriously,"* I asked. I was curious what may have motivated her to be taking on this challenge at her age.

"I always dreamed of having a college education and now I'm getting one!" she told me.

After class we shared a chocolate milkshake and became instant friends. Every day for the next three months we would leave class together and talk nonstop. I was always mesmerized listening to this *"time machine"* as she shared her wisdom and experience with me. Over the course of the year, Rose became a campus icon and easily made friends wherever she went. She loved to dress up and everyone loved her!

At the end of the semester we invited Rose to speak at our banquet. She was introduced and stepped up to the podium. As she began to deliver her prepared speech, she said in a quiet voice: *"My speech will be short, let me just tell you what I know."* And she began:

"We do not stop playing because we are old; we grow old because we stop playing."
There are only three secrets to staying young, being happy, and achieving success:
Secret #1: You have to laugh and find humor every day.
Secret #2: You've got to have a dream. When you lose your dreams, you die. We have so many people walking around who are dead and don't even know it! There is a huge difference between growing older and growing up. If you are nineteen years old and lie in bed for one full year and don't do one productive thing, you will turn twenty years old. If I am eighty-seven years old and stay in bed for a year and never do anything I will turn eighty-eight. Anybody can grow older; that doesn't take any talent or ability. The idea is to grow up by always finding the opportunity in change.
Secret #3: Have no regrets. The elderly usually don't have regrets for what we did, but rather for things we did not do. The only people who fear death are those with regrets. She concluded her speech by courageously singing, *"The Rose."* She challenged each of us to study the lyrics and live them out in our daily lives. At the end of the year, Rose finished the college degree she had begun all those years ago.

One week after graduation Rose died peacefully in her sleep. Over two thousand college students attended her funeral in tribute to the wonderful woman who taught by example that it's never too late to be all you can possibly be.

Dare Greatly Presentation

Jan Ruhe

Have you ever wondered what would happen if you really went all out for greatness in your business and in your life? What if you decided to *dare greatly* to take a risk? After all, it's risky not to take a risk!

Have you watched college and NFL football, NBA basketball, tennis matches, wrestling, rugby, pro golf tournaments, the Olympics and all kinds of sporting events? Many spectators go to the World Cup ski races in Aspen and watch the champion skiers from all over the world and the 24 Hours of Aspen ski event where the skiers ski 24 hours non-stop! The top pros are paid a lot of money, wouldn't you agree? They work out and stay in great shape for years, they retire, or some become announcers of their favorite sport, some coach, some play golf. Become a mega student of these pros. Keep notes and journals of what they say after winning and losing. Decide to be an expert, a pro!

Champions *dare greatly*! They play full out! They want to be on the playing field! They *want and desire* that Super Bowl ring! They don't want to be spectators. They are not interested in watching others succeed. They take pride in their name, their team name and what they are accomplishing! They envision themselves winning, achieving greatness! Have you watched great pros fumble, miss baskets, miss putts, etc? Do they give up or quit? No way, they make fast comebacks! They are pros! They work on their attitudes! They are in control of their destiny! They make big plays, little plays, smile, and love what they do! They are experts, the pros, and they play for lots of money! They go onto the field to win! They don't like to settle for anything less than winning! They *dare greatly*! We can learn so much from the pros, the experts of the past and the present! Pay attention, success leaves clues!

Casinos all over the world are filled with people who gamble thousands of dollars day and night. They walk in the door and have the look of hope and big dreams on their faces. Many spend hours at the nickel machines, many spend hours at the quarter machines, one dollar and five dollar slots or at the crap tables. Some win, most don't. Most leave a lot of money in the Casinos. The noise of the clanking of money coming out of the machines makes you hope that you can win! However, it's all *chance*. There is no going for greatness, there is simply hope. If you just go for the entertainment, it's fun. But if you get caught up in the hopelessness of it all, it can be devastating. Do the gamblers give up and quit?

Of course, time after time. Why? Because it's all chance, the gambler has no control. But, you can take risks and become a champion! Just make the decision to decide to focus on going for greatness and never give up! Just *dare greatly*! Have you jetted around your country? There are the sun seekers! The fun seekers! The jetsetters! And the globetrotters! And those who are busy spending most of their time on earth traveling! There are people up and down the rows on the airplanes working away on laptops, reading and pouring over reports, business suits, checking and picking up luggage, going through customs, hurrying through life! The minute the plane lands they are on their cell phones making plans to stay busy, to meet and greet others! However, many are just staying busy through life, many not *daring greatly*!

As time has gone by, have you thought about *daring greatly*? Here is what works: Study the pros! The champions! Study those people who are living the lifestyle you want to have! Do not be denied! Find out what the poor people read and what shows they go to and watch on TV, and pay attention to what they eat. Avoid their lifestyle! Big time! Watch and study those **daring greatly!** Those who get results! Those who are going for greatness! If you want to be rich, study the rich! If you want to be a pro, study the pros! You can be rich **and** you can be a pro! Just make the decision to decide. Come to the table of plenty, you are invited to come to the table and spend time with the pros, but only if you *dare greatly*. Play full out and go for greatness!

Why not you and why not now?

Who is someone you admire who has **dared greatly**? Is it your turn? I think so! There is nothing quite like a view from the top! *Dare greatly* my friends, play full out, be the one who says *"I am so glad I did"* instead of *"I wish I had!"*

> *"I cannot wait for*
> *the rugby match to begin.*
> *I get in the game and go for greatness."*
>
> **Marcus Leach**
> Wales National Under 19 Rugby team

Decide to Be Fired Up!

Jan Ruhe

Use every email and call you make,
every conversation you have,
every meeting you hold or attend
to let everyone know your dreams and desires!
Let people know of your vision of what you expect!

Fire Up! others around you!
Fire Up! and forgive those who have hurt you!
Fire Up! your vocabulary and choose your words carefully!

Believe in miracles, expect them, do not be surprised by them!
Believe in yourself!
Come to the table of plenty, there is a place set for you!
Concentrate on what you do right!
Focus on your goals, your dreams and your hopes!
No human is perfect, forgive yourself!
Radiate your passion!
Spread the fire of desire!
You are a powerful person!
You can't change the past!

Your success will be served on a silver platter!

Stay **Fired Up!** no matter what!
The day you decide is the day that your life will change for the better forever!
Decide to stay **Fired Up!** for life!

Why not you and why not now?
If not you, then who?

Desiderata

Max Ehrmann

Go placidly amid the noise and the haste,
and remember what peace there may be in silence.
As far as possible without surrender be on good terms with all persons.
Speak your truth quietly and clearly and listen to others,
even to the dull and the ignorant, they too have their story.
Avoid loud and aggressive persons they are vexatious to the spirit.
If you compare yourself with others, you may become vain or bitter,
for always there will be greater and lesser persons than yourself.
Enjoy your achievements as well as your plans.
Keep interested in your own career, however humble,
it is a real possession in the changing fortunes of time.
Exercise caution in your business affairs, for the world is full of trickery.
But let this not blind you to what virtue there is,
many persons strive for high ideals and everywhere life is full of heroism.
Be yourself.
Especially, do not feign affection.
Neither be cynical about love, for in the face of all aridity
and disenchantment it is as perennial as the grass.
Take kindly the counsel of the years gracefully surrendering the things of youth.
Nurture strength of spirit to shield you in sudden misfortune.
But do not distress yourself with dark imaginings.
Many fears are born of fatigue and loneliness.
Beyond a wholesome discipline be gentle with yourself.
You are a child of the universe, no less than the trees and the stars,
you have a right to be here.
And whether or not it is clear to you,
no doubt the universe is unfolding as it should.
Therefore, be at peace with God, whatever you conceive Him to be.
And whatever your labors and aspirations in the noisy confusion of life
keep peace in your soul.
With all it's sham, drudgery and broken dreams, it is still a beautiful world.
Be cheerful, strive to be happy.

Don't Miss The Boat

Edward Ludbrook

It had been pouring with rain for days and everyone knew
the valley was going to flood. Jim said to himself,
*"It will be O.K., I've prayed to God and I know
he'll send a sign and save me."*

Shortly, there was a knock on the door and Jim opened it to
find a **policeman**, who said,
*"Come on, I've got a truck, let's go!
The dam's busted; the whole valley will be flooded."*

Jim said,
"You go on, I'm O.K., I've prayed and I know God will save me."

Well, the waters came and rapidly flooded the ground floor,
so Jim moved to his first floor. There was a knock on the
window; a soldier poked his head in and said,
*"Come on Sir, the waters are rising but
I'm in a **boat**, so come on."*

Jim said,
"You go on, I'm O.K. I've prayed and I know God will save me."

Well, the waters kept rising and flooded the first floor
so Jim moved on to his roof. With a thud-thud of wings,
Jim looked up to see a **helicopter**, whose loadmaster called to say,
"Come on Sir, the waters are still rising, we can take you out."

Jim smiled and said,
"You go on, I'm O.K. I've prayed and I know God will save me."

Well, the waters kept rising and so Jim
got washed off and drowned. When Jim arrived in heaven,
he was furious and stormed up to God and said,

*"What is the story?
I prayed and prayed and
what help did you send?"*

"What help?" said God.
**"What about the policeman, boat and helicopter!
What more did you want?"**

Don't Quit

When things go wrong, as they sometimes will,
when the road you're trudging seems all-uphill.
When the funds are low and the debts are high,
and you want to smile, but have to sigh.
When care is pressing you down a bit—
rest if you must,

but don't you quit!

Life is queer with its twists and turns,
as every one of us sometimes learns,
and many a person turns about
when they might have won had they stuck it out.
Don't give up though the pace seems slow-
you may succeed with another blow.

Often the struggler has given up
when he might have captured the victor's cup;
and he learned too late when the night came down,
how close he was to the golden crown.

Success is failure turned inside out—
So stick to the fight when you are hardest hit—
It's when things seem worst that

you *must not quit*.

Don't Pre-Judge

Many many years ago, a lady in a faded gingham dress and her husband,
dressed in a homespun threadbare suit, stepped off the train in Boston,
and walked timidly without an appointment into the outer office of the President of
Harvard University. The secretary frowned, she could tell in a moment that such
backwoods, country hicks had no business at Harvard and
probably didn't even deserve to be in Cambridge.
"We want to see the president," the man said softly.
"He'll be busy all day," the secretary snapped.
"We'll wait," the lady replied
For hours, the secretary ignored them, hoping that the couple would
finally become discouraged and go away. They didn't.
The secretary grew frustrated and finally decided to disturb the president,
even though it was a chore she always regretted to do.
"Maybe if they just see you for a few minutes, they'll leave,"
she told him. And he sighed in exasperation and nodded.
Someone of his importance obviously didn't have the time to spend with them,
but he detested gingham dresses and homespun suits cluttering up his outer
office. The president, stern-faced with dignity, strutted toward the couple.
The lady told him, *"We had a son that attended Harvard for one year.
He loved Harvard. He was happy here. But about a year ago, he was
accidentally killed. And my husband and I would like to erect a
memorial to him, somewhere on campus."*
The president wasn't touched; he was shocked.
"Madam," he said gruffly, *"We can't put up a statue for every person
attended Harvard and died. If we did, this place would look like a cemetery."*
"Oh, no," the lady explained quickly, *"We don't want to erect a statue.
We thought we would like to give a building to Harvard."*
The president rolled his eyes. He glanced at
the gingham dress and homespun suit, and then exclaimed,
*"A building! Do you have any earthly idea how much a building costs?
We have over seven and a half million dollars in the physical plant at
Harvard"*. For a moment the lady was silent. The president was pleased.
He could get rid of them now.
And the lady turned to her husband and said quietly,
"Is that all it costs to start a University? Why don't we just start our own?"
Her husband nodded. The president's face wilted in confusion and bewilderment.
And Mr. and Mrs. Leland Stanford walked away, traveling to Palo Alto,
California where they established the University that bears their son's name.

108

Everybody, Somebody, Anybody, and Nobody

This is a story about four people named

Everybody

Somebody

Anybody

and *Nobody*.

There was an important job to be done and *Everybody* was sure that *Somebody* would do it.

Anybody could have done it, but *Nobody* did it.

Somebody got angry about that, because it was *Everybody's* job.

Everybody thought *Anybody* could do it, but *Nobody* realized that *Everybody* wouldn't do it.

It ended up that *Everybody* blamed *Somebody* when *Nobody* did what *Anybody* could have.

Faith

Roy Campanella, Catcher
Brooklyn Dodgers, World Series Champs

We're a rugged breed; us quads.
If we weren't we wouldn't be around today.
Yes, we're a rugged breed. In many ways, we've been blessed
with a savvy and spirit that isn't given to everybody.
And let me say that this refusal of total or full acceptance
of one's disability all hooks up with one thing-faith,
an almost divine faith.

Down in the reception room of the Institute of Physical Medicine and
Rehabilitation, over on the East River in New York City,
there is a bronze plaque that's riveted to the wall.
During the months of coming back to the Institute for treatment,
two and three times a week, I rolled through that reception room many times,
coming and going. But I never quite made the time to pull over to one side
and read the words on that plaque that were written,
it's said, by an unknown Confederate soldier.
Then one afternoon, I did. I read it, and then I read it again.
When I finished it the second time I was near to bursting, not in despair,
but with an inner glow that had me straining to grip the arms of my wheelchair.
I'd like to share it with you.

A Creed for Those Who Have Suffered

I asked God for strength, that I might achieve.
I was made weak, that I might learn humbly to obey…
I asked for health, that I might do greater things.
I was given infirmity, that I might do better things…
I asked for riches, that I might be happy.
I was given poverty, that I might be wise…
I asked for power, that I might have the praise of men.
I was given weakness, that I might feel the need of God…
I asked for all things, that I might enjoy life.
I was given life, that I might enjoy all things…
I got nothing I asked for, but everything I had hoped for.
Almost despite myself, my unspoken prayers were answered.
I am, among men, most richly blessed!

110

Fun Topics to Use In a Presentation

- Do you need a silencer if you are going to shoot a mime?
- How can someone '*draw a blank*'?
- How can there be '*self help groups*'?
- How does the guy who drives the snowplow get to work in the mornings?
- If a cow laughed real hard, would milk come out her nose?
- If nothing ever sticks to TEFLON, how do they make TEFLON stick to the pan?
- If pro is the opposite of con, is progress the opposite of congress?
- If someone invented instant water, what would they mix it with?
- If you can't drink and drive, why do bars have parking lots?
- What does Geronimo say when he jumps out of a plane?
- What is another word for '*thesaurus*'?
- When they ship Styrofoam, what do they pack it in?
- Why are there interstate highways in Hawaii?
- Why are we afraid of falling? Shouldn't we be afraid of the sudden stop?
- Why did kamikaze pilots wear helmets?
- Why does an alarm clock '*go off*' when it begins ringing?
- Why does *flammable* and *inflammable* mean the same thing?
- Why does '*slow down*' and '*slow up*' mean the same thing?
- Why does your nose run and your feet smell?
- Why do fat chance and slim chance mean the same thing?
- Why do they put Braille dots on the keypad of drive up ATM machines?
- Why do '*tugboats*' push their barges?
- Why do we drive on parkways and park on driveways?
- Why do we sing '*take me out to the ball game*' when we are already there?
- Why is it called '*after dark*', when it is really after light?
- Why is it called a TV '*set*' when you only get one?
- Why is it that when you transport something by car, its call a shipment, but when you transport something by ship, it's called cargo?
- Why is the word '*abbreviate*' so long?
- Why is there an expiration date on sour cream?

He Won Because He Never Quit
Coach Bear Bryant
The winningest coach in major college football history!

There is a lot to learn about presentation skills from Coach Bear Bryant.

"Coach Bear Bryant's halftime locker-room speeches were <u>never</u> impromptu. During the week leading up to the game, he would prepare something to say if we were ahead and something else if we were behind. Sometimes he would be emotional and some times he was very quiet and confident. He was a master at it. Coach Bryant would say something like, "These are the five things that we need to do," – boom, boom, boom, boom, boom, and then we'd go out and make things happen. He had a tremendous influence on me, just like he did with everyone. He always knew which guy needed a pat on the shoulder and which one needed a kick in the butt. Guys would be thinking about calling him names or how they didn't like football anymore, and twenty seconds later he'd have his hand on your shoulder, saying "I really know you can be a leader, Lee Roy, and that you won't let me down," and that was all it took for me. His timing was impeccable, every time. Listen to Coach Bryant, and savor what he says. I sure do."
Lee Roy Jordan

Coach Bryant passed away in 1983. His passing stunned his millions of fans throughout the world. He had coached his final game less than a month before when his Alabama team defeated Illinois, 21-15 in the Liberty Bowl. Tributes poured forth from all corners of the world, praising Bryant for his contributions to football and for his personal standards of excellence. Tears and banners and saddened faces said goodbye to a maker of miracles, a modest hero, a compassionate teacher, a challenging taskmaster and a winner.

In the late 1960's Jan Ruhe became a University of Alabama fan. She paid close attention and became a student of Coach Bear Bryant. He was more than a coach, he was a motivational speaker. He believed that hard work, dedication and self-confidence were the traits that are the keys to success. Two of Jan's children graduated from this grand University. Jan finally shares some of the quotes that kept her going for over twenty years. These are in her private quote book that she reviews almost daily. She paid attention to Coach Bear Bryant. When you ever visit her home, she has the flag of the University of Alabama waving outside her office to remind her of his presentation greatness, his love of the game, his winners attitude and to think often of her children's education.

112

"He had the ability to motivate everyone, even the secretaries. We'd work holidays, weekends, whatever was necessary. He did it and everybody else did it. His enthusiasm rubbed off on everyone."
Rebecca Christian, Bryant's personal secretary, 1967-82

"Coach Bryant didn't coach football; he coached people."
A.O. "Bum" Phillips, former NFL coach and Bryant assistant

"Coach Bryant was one of the toughest people to ever come across the face of this earth, but he was also kind, fair and tender hearted. He genuinely cared about people."
John David Crowe, Heisman Trophy winner

"Coach Bryant hated penalties and he was the first coach I ever heard of that used an official at practice every day to call any penalties. He started it in about 1959, and it was an every day thing. He wanted the officials to be picky about it, too. He worked at avoiding penalties and he wanted total discipline on the field. I remember New York Jets coach Weeb Ewbank coming to a practice in the mid-sixties and taking note of my officiating it at practice. He asked what I did and seemed to think it was a great idea. I don't know if anyone did it before Coach Bryant, but I doubt if anyone was a conscious of avoiding penalties as Coach Bryant was. It was just one of the, many things he worked on that helped his teams win."
Eddie Conyers, Alabama football practice official, 1960-82

"This is the beginning of a new day. God has given me this day to use, as I will. I can waste it or use it for good. What I do today is very important because I am exchanging a day of my life for it. When tomorrow comes, this day will be gone forever, leaving something in its place I have traded for it. I want it to be a gain, not loss—good, not evil. Success, not failure, in order that I shall not forget the price I paid for it."
W.W. Heartsill Wilson, (Tam Sessions, a former legislator from Birmingham, sent this quote to Bryant. It became one of his favorites and he kept a tattered copy in his wallet.)

> *"As long as someone has to be the winningest coach, heck, it might as well be me."*
> **Coach Bear Bryant**

Here are the Bear Bryant's quotes:

• *"Always be totally loyal to the organization for which you work. If you don't have the best interest of the organization at heart or if you can't be loyal, you are in the wrong place."*

• *"Beware of 'yes' men. Generally, they are losers. Surround yourself with winners. Never forget, people win."*

• *"Don't look back, don't lose your guts, and teach your team to go out on the field and make things happen."*

• *"Don't over coach them. Let them play some. If you're out there coaching them all the time, when are they going to practice?"*

• *"Don't talk too much. Don't pop off. Don't talk after the game until you cool off."*

• *"Don't talk too much or too soon."*

• *"Don't tolerate lazy people. They are losers. People who come to work and watch clocks and pass off responsibilities will only drag you and your organization down. I despise clock-watchers. They don't want to be part of a winning situation. They won't roll up their sleeves when you need them to. If you have lazy people, get rid of them. Remember, it is easy to develop the bad habits of lazy people."*

• *"Expect the unexpected."*

• *"Find your own picture, your own self in anything that goes bad. It's awfully easy to mouth off at your staff or chew out players, but if it's bad, and you're the head coach, you are responsible. If we have an intercepted pass, I threw it. I'm the head coach. If we get a punt blocked, I caused it. A bad practice, a bad game, it's up to the head coach to assume his responsibility."*

• *"Get people who work for your organization because it means something to them. Most organizations get people who are interested in drawing their paycheck for their forty-hour week. Don't forget, those folks usually don't work but about ten hours out of the forty they are paid for. To be the best, if you want to be the best, get people who care about your institution, people who are proud to be associated with your organization. Get winning people."*

• *"If anything goes bad, I did it.*
  If anything goes semi-good, we did it.
  If anything goes really good, then you did it.
  That's all it takes to get people to win football games for you."

• *"If you want to coach you have three rules to follow to win. One, surround yourself with people who can't live without football. I've had a lot of them. Two, be able to recognize winners. They come in all forms. And, three have a plan for everything. A plan for practice, a plan for the game. A plan for being ahead, and a plan for being behind 20-0 at the half, with your quarterback hurt and the phones dead, with it raining cats and dogs and no rain gear because the equipment man left it at home."*

• *"I tell my players they are special. They're someone everybody should be proud of. They are not like the other students I'd say, "If you were we'd have fifteen thousands out for football. You've got to take pride in being someone special."*

• *"Make something happen."*

114

- *"Mama wanted me to be a preacher. I told her coachin' and preachin' were a lot alike."*
- *"Many of our teams had only three, four or five great players. I had some with only one or two. Be we usually had a dozen or so guys in the fourth quarter who got to thinking they were great."*
- *"Over the years, I've learned a lot about coaching staffs, and the one piece of advice that I would pass on to a young head coach, or a corporation executive or even a bank president is this: Don't make them in your image. Don't even try. My assistants don't look alike, think alike, or have the same personalities. And I sure don't want them all thinking like I do."*
- *"The thing about recruiting is that you have to learn, and learn fast, that you can't make the chicken salad without the chicken."*
- *"When people ask me what do I want to be remembered for, I have one answer: I want the people to remember me as a winner, cause I ain't never been nothing but a winner."*
- *"You don't have to talk a lot to be a leader."*
- *"You learn to work. You have to work hard to succeed in anything."*

His teams won because he not only demanded discipline, class and excellence but also personally demonstrated it and expected it from each player. And they won because they never quit. And they never quit because he never quit.

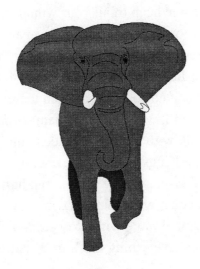

Roll Tide - Roll!

If
Rudyard Kipling

If you can keep your head when all about you
are losing theirs and blaming it on you,
If you can trust yourself when all men doubt you,
but make allowance for their doubting too;
If you can wait and not be tired by waiting, or being lied about,
don't deal in lies, or being hated don't give way to hating,
and yet don't look too good, nor talk too wise.
If you can dream and not make dreams your master;
If you can think and not make thoughts your aim;
if you can meet with Triumph and Disaster
and treat those two impostors just the same;
If you can bear to hear the truth you've spoken
twisted by knaves to make a trap for fools;
Or watch the things you gave your life to, broken,
and stoop and build 'em up with worn-out tools;
If you can make one heap of all your winnings and risk it
on one turn of pitch-and-toss, and lose, and start again at your beginnings
and never breathe a word about your loss;
If you can force your heart and nerve and sinew to serve your turn
long after they are gone, And so hold on when there; is nothing in you
except the will, which says to them: *Hold on!*
If you can talk with crowds and keep your virtue;
Or walk with Kings-nor lose the common touch;
If neither foes nor loving friends can hurt you;
If all men count with you, but none too much;
If you can fill their unforgiving minute with sixty second's worth of distance run,
yours is the Earth and everything that's in it, and which is more,

You'll be a man my son!

I Love to Make Presentations

I love to make presentations...

...like a dancer loves to dance.
...like a poet loves to write.
...like a singer loves to sing.
...like a swimmer loves to swim.
...like an artist likes to draw.
...like an eagle likes to soar.

I am passionate about making presentations!

...A life is changing for the better!
...Forget the applause and awards!
...Forget the compensation!
...I love being with positive people!
...I love the excitement of knowing that people are going to be inspired!
...I love to learn new ideas from people!
...I love to make new friends!
...I love to see people react to information that will benefit them!
...I love to share my wisdom and experiences with people!
...Making presentations revitalizes me! It builds my adrenaline, makes me excited because I am passionate!

Life Time

Imagine there is a bank that credits your account each morning with

$86,400.

It carries over no balance from day to day.
Every evening the bank deletes whatever part of the balance
you failed to use during the day.
What would you do?

Draw out all of it, of course!!!

Each of us has such a bank.

Its name is *time*.

Every morning, it credits you with
86,400 seconds.

Every night it writes off, as lost, whatever of this
you have failed to invest to good purpose.
It carries over no balance. It allows no overdraft.

Each day it opens a new account for you.
Each night it burns the remains of the day.
If you fail to use the day's deposits, the loss is yours.

There is no going back. There if no drawing against the *"tomorrow."*
You must live in the present on today's deposits.
Invest it so as to get from it the utmost in
health, wealth, happiness and success!
The clock is running. Make the most of today.

Treasure every moment that you have!
And treasure it more because you shared it with someone special,
special enough to spend your time.

Yesterday is history.

Tomorrow is a mystery.

Today is a gift.

That's why it's called the present!!!

Little Eyes Upon You

There are little eyes upon you
and they're watching night and day.
There are little ears that quickly
take in every word you say.
There are little hands all eager
to do anything you do;
and a little boy who's dreaming

of the day he'll be like you.

You're the little fellow's idol,
you're the wisest of the wise.
In his little mind about you
no suspicions ever rise.
He believes in you devoutly,
holds all that you say and do;
He will say and do, in your way,

when he's grown up like you.

There's a wide eyed little fellow
who believes you're always right;
and his eyes are always opened,
and he watched day and night.
You are setting an example
every day in all you do,
For the little boy who's waiting

to grow up to be like you.

Nelson Mandela
1994 Inaugural Presentation

Our deepest fear is not that we are inadequate.

Our deepest fear is that we are powerful beyond measure.

It is our light, not our darkness that most frightens us.

We ask ourselves, who am I to be brilliant, gorgeous, talented and fabulous?

Actually, who are you not to be?
You are a child of God.

Your playing small does not serve the world.
There's nothing enlightened
about shrinking so that other people
won't feel insecure around you.

We are born to make manifest
the glory of God that is within us.
It's not just in some of us; it's in everyone.

And as we let our own light shine, we unconsciously give
other people permission to do the same.

As we are liberated from our own fear, our presence
automatically liberates others.

Never Give Up

Jan Ruhe

It's always great to have a presentation about someone who did not give up and pressed on to finish the task. This is a true story.

In the late 1990's there once was a football player who played on an iron-man football team for his High School. This means that each player had to play more than one position, and during most of the game. During his Junior year in High School, this incredible football player broke three State Football Records, which is no small feat. In fact, he scored eight touchdowns in one football game! And that record has stood for years. His coach, friends and family was so proud of him. By his Senior year, there were not enough football players to field a team. So instead of quitting the game, he went to play for another local team; and his coach became the coach for that football team. The coach changed his attitude and began to tell this football player that he was *"Not working hard enough; that he was no good; that he was going to fail, that he would never make college football, that he might as well give up."* He tried to motivate the player with this negative talk. And he told the football player those negative declarative statements every day at practice. Day after day. The young man came home after practice one evening and put his head down on the kitchen table and told his mother that he wanted to turn in his football pads and quit football. He didn't want to play anymore and be criticized by the coach. His mother encouraged him to finish his last season in High School and to not give up. It was a hard decision. The young football player decided to continue playing the rest of the season and he did not give in or give up..

Day after day he tried to show his coach that he was not lazy, that he was not a loser, after all, he had broken and held three State Champion records only the year before!

The last game of the season, the final game of his Senior year came and the night was very very cold. All the parents and fans were in the stands ready to cheer for their team as the game began! The young football player came out for the first quarter and on one of the plays he fumbled the ball and the other team recovered the ball. The coach began to scream horrible words right in the young man's face and yelled at him to sit on the bench, that he was out of the game for good. The young football star walked quietly over to the sidelines and motioned for his mother to come down close to the field. This was unusual because never in his career had he wanted to talk with his mother during a game. The mother walked down the bleachers and walked to where she could see her son. Under the big football helmet she could see his big brown eyes full of tears. It was so painful to see her son hurting. The young man said to his mother, *"Mom, it's almost half-time, when I go in to the locker room at half time, I am going to quit and not come out the second half, my coach told me I am through, it's cold, I don't need to sit on the bench, I am out of here!"* With every bit of strength that the mother could muster up, she looked right in those big chocolate brown eyes and said *"You must not quit, you go in at half time and you get in your coach's face and you let him know that you plan to play. That this is your last football game of your entire High School years! Don't you dare quit, your team needs you. You must not give up, never give up!"*

Half time came and that mother could barely make it through, you see, she had tears streaming down her face. How could her son have such a mean coach? What were the lessons her son was learning? What if the coach didn't let him play? Should she have supported his desire or should she have encouraged him? How much more could this young man take before this effected him for the rest of his life?

As the second half got ready to start, out on the field ran the team, led by the young football player who had decided not to quit! The third quarter came and went and there was no score. Not one score, still 0-0. On the final play of the game, the young football player, carried the football into the end zone! Touchdown!!!! The only touchdown scored in the entire football game and they won the game!!!! As everyone jumped and shouted, the mother watched the young football star get down on one knee and looked up to the heavens above.

After the game, when the football star got home, his mother asked him about his decision to not give up. He shared that at half time, he had told his coach that he wanted to play and that he could be counted on to make something happen, to give him another chance. Fortunately, the mean old coach changed his attitude and let him play. Then the mother asked the young football star about the end of the game. The young man told his mother that he got down on one knee and thanked God that he had a mother who encouraged him

to never give up.

He still, today, holds those three football records and not only that, the last time he touched a football in High School, and he scored a touchdown. He went out a winner. He didn't give up. And by the way, the mean old coach was fired immediately after the game for the way he talked to the young football star when he fumbled. *(You can hear the football star tell this story on the MLM Nuts $ Bolts tapes, this is a true story, it happened to be Clayton, Jan Ruhe's only son who does hold three Colorado State Football Records, his football jersey is framed and is hanging in his room at home in Aspen to this day.) To order the tapes or the Never Give Up music that this young man inspired his mother to write, go to www.janruhe.com.)*

Presentations
That Were a Little Off
Kay Anderson

- *Airplanes are interesting toys but of no military value.*
  Marshall Foch, French Military strategist and future World War I commander, 1911
- *Computers in the future may, perhaps only weight 1.5 tons.*
  Popular Mechanics magazine, forecasting the development of computer technology, 1949
- *Everything that can be invented has been invented.*
  Charles Duell, US commissioner of patents, 1899
- *I have no political ambitions for myself or my children.*
  Joseph P. Kennedy, 1936
- *Television won't be able to hold on to any market it captures after the first six months. People will soon get tired of staring at a plywood box every night.*
  Darryl Zanuck, head of Twentieth Century Fox, 1946
- *The horse is here to stay, but the automobile is only a novelty, a fad.*
  a president of the Michigan Saving Bank advising Horace Rackham (Henry Ford's lawyer) not to invest in the Ford Motor Company, 1903 (Rackham ignored the advice, bought $5,000 worth of stock and sold it several years later for $12.5 million)
- *There is no reason for any individual to have a computer in their home.*
  Kenneth Olsen, president of Digital Equipment Corp., 1977
- *We don't like their sound. Groups of guitars are on the way out.*
  Decca Records, rejecting the Beatles, 1962
- *What use could this company make of an electrical toy?*
  Western Union president William Orton, rejecting Alexander Graham Bell's offer to sell his struggling telephone company to Western Union for $100,000.
- *Who the hell wants to hear actors talk?*
  Harry Warner, Warner Brothers, 1927

The RFM Presentation
Ashley

A Friend should be Radical, Fanatical, and Most of All, Mathematical

Radical

A Friend should be *Radical*;
They should love you when you're unlovable,
hug you when you're unhuggable,
and bear you when you're unbearable.

Fanatical

A Friend should be *Fanatical*;
They should cheer when the whole world boos,
dance when you get good news,
and cry when you cry too.

Mathematical

But most of all, a Friend should be *Mathematical*;
They should multiply the joy, divide the sorrow,
subtract the past, and add to tomorrow,
calculate the need deep in your heart,
and always be bigger than the sum of all their parts.

Road Map
to Presentation Greatness

Act professional.

Attend the right meetings.

Be coachable and learn from the best. Learn from those living the lifestyle you want.

Be like Teflon.

Be visible.

Develop a real-world marketing strategy.

Don't listen to dream thieves.

Do your homework.

Follow-up promptly.

Have a professional telephone image.

Have fun!

Identify your own A,B,C prospect list.

If you have a niche, become a leader in that niche within that industry.

Keep your word.

Practice, drill and rehearse your presentation.

Prospect.

Really know your stuff.

Research ... Research ... Research.

Understand that your selling skills are the key to your success.

Use stories and quotes.

Work diligently on your platform skills.

Seize the Moment... the Present is a Gift

Jayne Leach

I have a friend who lives by a three-word philosophy: *Seize the Moment*. Just possibly, she may be the wisest woman on this planet. Too many people put off something that brings them joy just because they haven't thought about it, don't have it on their schedule, didn't know it was coming or are too rigid to depart from their routine. I got to thinking one day about all those women on the Titanic who passed up dessert at dinner that fateful night in an effort to cut back. From then on, I've tried to be a little more flexible. How many women out there will eat at home because their husband didn't suggest going out to dinner until after something had been thawed? Does the word *"refrigeration"* mean nothing to you? I cannot count the times I called my sister and said,

"How about going to lunch in a half hour?" She would gasp and stammer, *"I can't. I have clothes on the line. My hair is dirty. I wish I had known yesterday, I had a late breakfast, It looks like rain."* And my personal favorite: *"It's Monday."* She died a few years ago. We never did have lunch together. We live on a sparse diet of promises we make to ourselves when all the conditions are perfect. We'll go back and visit the grandparents when we get Stevie toilet-trained. We'll entertain when we replace the living-room carpet. We'll go on a second honeymoon when we get two more kids out of college.

Life has a way of accelerating, as we get older. The days get shorter, and the list of promises to ourselves gets longer. One morning, we awaken, and all we have to show for our lives is a litany of *"I'm going to,"* *"I plan on"* and *"Someday, when things are settled down a bit."*

When anyone calls my 'seize the moment' friend, she is open to adventure and available for trips. She keeps an open mind on new ideas. Her enthusiasm for life is contagious. You talk with her for five minutes, and you're ready to trade in your bad feet for a pair of roller blades. My lips have not touched ice cream in ten years. I love ice cream. It's just that I might as well apply it directly to my hips with a spatula and eliminate the digestive process. The other day, I stopped the car and bought a triple-decker cone. If my car had hit an iceberg on the way home, I would have died happy.

Now...go on and have a nice day. Do something you want to do...not something on your Should Do list. If you were going to die soon and had only one phone call you could make, who would you call and what would you say? And why are you waiting?

126

Sayings to Spice Up Your Presentation

- A man spends the first half of his life learning habits that shorten the other half of his life.
- A truly happy person is one who can enjoy the scenery on a detour.
- Birthdays are good for you - the more you have the longer you live.
- Don't cry because its over, smile because it happened.
- Everything should be made as simple as possible, but no simpler.
- Happiness comes through doors you didn't even know you left open.
- How long a minute is depends on what side of the bathroom door you're on.
- If ignorance is bliss, why aren't more people happy?
- If Wal-Mart is lowering prices every day, how come nothing in the store is free yet?
- If we'd stop trying to be happy we could have a pretty good time.
- I have noticed that the people who are late are often so much jollier than the people who have to wait for them.
- I wish the buck stopped here. I could use a few.
- Living on Earth is expensive, but it does include a free trip around the sun.
- Laughter is the shortest distance between two people.
- Most of us go to our grave with our music still inside us.
- People are like stained-glass windows. They sparkle and shine when the sun is out but when the darkness sets in, their true beauty is revealed only if there is a light within.
- Some mistakes are too much fun to only make once.
- *"Stewardesses"* is the longest word that is typed with only the left hand.
- The average person falls asleep in seven minutes.
- There are 336 dimples on a regulation golf ball.
- We could learn a lot from crayons: some are sharp, some are pretty, some are dull, some have weird names, and all are different colors, but they all have to learn to live in the same box.
- You may be only one person in the world, but you may also be the world to one person.

Ten Little Indian Boys
Sarah, Clayton, Ashley

One little, two little, three little Indians, four little, five little,
six little Indians, seven little, eight little, nine little Indians,
ten little Indian boys!

They climbed in a boat and the rowed to the Island,
They climbed in a boat and the rowed to the Island,
They climbed in a boat and the rowed to the Island,
ten little Indian boys!

They rowed and they rowed and they rowed to the Island,
They rowed and they rowed and they rowed to the Island,
They rowed and they rowed and they rowed to the Island,
ten little Indian boys!

The boat tipped over and they splashed in the water,
The boat tipped over and they splashed in the water,
The boat tipped over and they splashed in the water,
ten little Indian boys!

They swam and they swam and they swam to the Island,
They swam and they swam and they swam to the Island,
They swam and they swam and they swam to the Island,
ten little Indian boys!

They ran and they ran and they ran to their Mommies,
They ran and they ran and they ran to their Mommies,
They ran and they ran and they ran to their Mommies,
ten little Indian boys!

Mommy hugged and hugged them and put them to bed,
Mommy hugged and hugged them and put them to bed,
Mommy hugged and hugged them and put them to bed,
ten little Indian boys!

The ABC's of Presentations
Sarah

Are you:

Action packed?

Booking presentations?

Committed to your goals?

Dedicated, determined, driven?

Enthusiastic?

Fired Up? Following up? Fun? Friendly?

Goal-oriented?

Hungry? Happy?

Inspired?

Jet-setting? Joyful? A joiner?

Kind?

Leading?

Making a living or designing a life?

No matter what?

Organized?

Powerful?

Queen or King of 3-foot rule?

Reading?

Sharing your opportunity?

Team oriented?

Unstoppable?

Visioning a successful future?

Where you want to be?

Yearning?

Zestful?

The "Big Rocks" of Life
A Time Management Presentation

Many people want to know how they can manage and balance their time better. Here is a great presentation to use. Stand in front of the audience you are presenting to, and say:

"Okay, time for a quiz."

Pull out a one-gallon, wide-mouthed mason jar and set it on a table in front of yourself. Next, pull out about a dozen fist-sized rocks or golf balls and carefully placed them, one at a time, into the jar until the jar is filled to the top and no more rocks can fit inside.
Then you say:

"Is this jar full?"

Most say, *"Yes."*
Then you say, *"Really?"*
Next, pull out a bucket of gravel. Dump some gravel in the jar and shake the jar causing pieces of gravel to work themselves down into the spaces between the big rocks.
Then you say:

"Is this jar full?

By this time the audience will be on to you and will think more carefully.
"Probably not," they will most likely respond.
Then you say: *"Good!"*
Next pull out a bucket of sand. Dump the sand in the jar and it will go into the space between the rocks and the gravel.
Then you say:

"Is this jar full?"

"No!" will be the reply!
Then you say: *"Good!"*
Next, get a pitcher of water and began to pour the water in until the jar is filled to the brim.
Then you say:

"What is the point of this presentation?"

You will most likely get this answer: *"If you think your time is all filled up, there is probably more time that you have and didn't think about having."*
Then you say: *"That's a good answer, but that's not the point."* Pause.
Then you say: *The truth this presentation teaches is:*

"If you don't put the big rocks in first, you'll never get them in at all."

What are the big rocks in your life? A project that you want to accomplish, time with your loved ones? Your faith, your education, your finances, a cause, achieving your dreams, teaching or mentoring others?

Remember to put these big rocks in first or you'll never get started.

130

The Dangerous People

The dangerous people are not the ones who hit you
with clubs and rob you with guns!
The thief won't attack your character traits or belittle
your abilities to your face.
It likely will be a well-meaning friend who merely
crushes your will to win!
No, he doesn't rob you at the point of a gun,

He simply says,
"It can't be done!"

When pointed to thousands who already are done.
He then smiles and says,
"Oh, they're superior, personality wise and in ability too!
They're way ahead of what others can do!"

It matters not that his words are untrue for you feel others
must know you. So you're robbed of your dreams,
your hopes to succeed, robbed of material blessings received,
robbed of the faith that says,

"I can!"

And robbed by an ignorant gunless friend!
So the deadliest of men is not 'He with a gun'
but, the one who tells you,

"It can't be done!"

For that taken by burglars can be gotten again
but who can replace –

Your Will to Win!

The Easy Roads are Crowded

Edgar Guest

The easy roads are crowded
and the level roads are jammed;
The pleasant little rivers
with drifting folks are crammed.
But off yonder where it's rocky,
where you get the better view,
You will find the ranks are thinning
and the travelers are few.
Where the going's smooth and pleasant
you will always find the throng,
for the many—more's the pity,
seem to like to drift along.
But the steps that call for courage
and the task that's hard to do,
in the end result in glory
for the never-wavering few.

---

*"It's a pretty good rule to remember that if the road is difficult,
the end will be easy, whereas if the road is easy, the end may be difficult.
If your pathway is filled with excellence,
the future will be filled with comfort, peace of mind and satisfaction.
Life was never intended to be merely a pleasure trip.
It's a struggle, a testing and a training."*

Bob Holker

The John Jacob Astor Story

How did John Jacob Astor make the money of the Astor family when he lived in New York? Did you know he came across the sea in debt for his fare. But that poor boy with nothing in his pocket made the fortune of the Astor family on one principle. He paid attention to what the customer wanted. Some will say, *"Well they could make those fortunes in New York but they could not do it in my state!"*

In a statistical account of the records taken in 1889 of 107 millionaires of New York, only seven made their money in New York City. Out of the 107 millionaires, 67 of them made their money in towns of less than 3,500 inhabitants, the others in other parts of New York. The richest man in this country never moved away from a town of 3,500 people. *It makes not so much difference where you are as who you are.*

John Jacob Astor illustrated what can be done anywhere. He once had a mortgage on a store, and they could not sell enough bonnets to pay the interest on his loan. He foreclosed the mortgage, took possession of the store, and went into partnership with the very same people, in the same store, with the same capital. He did not, however, give them a dollar more of capital. They had to sell goods to get any money. He left them alone in the store as they had been before, and he went out and sat down on a bench in the park in the shade. What was John Jacob Astor doing out there, and in partnership with people who had failed at his own hands? He had the most important, the most pleasant part of that partnership. For as John Jacob Astor sat on that bench he was watching the ladies as they went by. If a lady passed him with her shoulders back and head up, looking straight to the front, as if she did not care if all the world did gaze on her, he studied her bonnet, and by the time it was out of sight he knew the shape of the frame, the color of the trimmings, and the crinklings in the feather. Then he went into the store and said: *"Now put into the show window just such a bonnet as I describe to you, because I have already seen a lady who likes such a bonnet. Don't make up any more until I come back."*

Then he went out and sat down again, and another lady passed him with a different form, a different complexion, with a different shape and color of bonnet. He would then go into the store and say, *"Now, put such a bonnet as that in the show window."*

He did not fill his show window with a lot of hats and bonnets to drive people away, and then sit on the back stairs and bawl because people went elsewhere to buy a bonnet. He did not have a hat or a bonnet in that show window but what some lady liked before it was manufactured. The tide of custom began immediately to turn in, and that has been the foundation of the greatest store in New York in that line. John Jacob Astor made his fortune after others had failed in business, not by giving them any more money, but by finding out what the ladies liked for bonnets before they wasted any material in making them.

The Guy in the Glass

When you get what you want in your struggle for self
and the world makes you king for a day
go to the mirror and look at yourself,
and see what that guy has to say.

For it isn't your mother or father or wife,
whose judgment on whom you must pass.

The fellow whose verdict counts most in your life
is the guy staring back from the glass.
He's the one to please, never mind all the rest,
for he's with you clear to the end.
And you've passed your most dangerous and difficult test.
if the guy in the glass is your friend.

You might be like Jack Horner and chisel a plum and think
you're a wonderful guy;
but the guy in the glass says you're only a bum
if you can't look him straight in the eye.

You may fool the whole world down the pathway of years
and get pats on your back as you pass,
but the final reward will be heartache and pain

if you've *cheated the guy in the glass.*

The I Can Presentation

When you write these eight words over and over again your brain will believe it and you will begin to achieve your dreams: Fill in the Missing Words:

I Can Do What I Need To Do.
I Can ___ What I Need To Do.
I Can Do What _ Need To Do.
I ___ Do What I Need To Do.
I Can Do What I Need To ___.
I Can Do What I ____ To Do.
I Can Do What I Need To Do.
_ Can Do What I Need To Do.
I Can Do _____ I Need To Do.
I Can Do What I Need __ Do.
I Can Do What I Need To Do.
I Can ___ What I Need To ___.
I Can Do What I Need To Do.
I Can Do What I Need To Do.

The Lusitania Went Down

Well, so what?

"What of it?" you cry. *"The whole world was shocked.*
For days the newspapers talked of nothing else."

Well, but what of it? After all, it was a little thing.

How many Lusitanias would have to go down to carry all
the dead and missing soldiers and the dead civilians of the great World War?

One Lusitania a day.
For a year.
For 10 years.
For 25 years.
For 50 years.

One Lusitania a day for 70 years, or one a week;
beginning nearly a century before the discovery of America
by Columbus and continuing to the present hour.

That is the number of Luistanias that would be required to carry the dead.

The dead of all nations who died in the war.

136

The Midas Touch Presentation
Jodi Carville

Gold permeates our culture-and our language. There's the Golden Gate Bridge, and the golden rule. The golden age and the gold card. The Golden Gloves and Gold's Gym. High-quality goods are "good as gold". In the Olympics-as in so many other realms-gold is a symbol of excellence, wealth, and enduring value"....

King Midas and the Golden Touch:

King Midas' golden touch became dangerous and he had to learn the hard way that *gold* isn't everything in life! Lets explore the whole person, body mind and heart.

Body:

How you dress?…King Midas loved gold-he dressed in gold outfits everyday. He loved gold and dressed in it from head to toe. That's why I am wearing today a sequined hat, gold blouse, gold slippers. You must *see* yourself in gold!

Mind:

King Midas programmed his mind. He thought gold. He surrounded himself with **gold.** *Gold* cats, *"gold*ilocks", *gold*en retriever, a *gold*finch, *gold*fish and a daughter named "Mari*gold"*.

Golden Tips:

- Allow your mind to be fed, commit to being the ultimate student!
- Change your state of mind…here's how…Play Music!
- Don't miss an event to advance your skills.
- Feed your mind with CANI = *Constant and Never Ending Improvement*!
- Feed your mind so you are a smart business person....
- Focus on moving your skills forward.
- How many times do you hear:
    "Surround yourself with your goals," or
    "Paint a picture for yourself of your future and share it with others to see."
- Ideas: "*gold*en Retreat", "*gold*en girls", *gold* slippers, *gold* star nametags, *gold* wrapping paper, *gold*slager liquor, serve *gold* treats...*gold*fish crackers, *gold* nuggets, *gold* candy.
- Know how to *earn incentives.*
- Know how to *manage your money* and most of all......
- Know how to *maximize your tax benefits.*
- Know your *company promotions.*

137

- Know your *compensation plan.*
- Listen to people who are *accomplishing what you wish to accomplish,* who are *making it happen,* who are *practicing what they talk about*! and those who *are living a lifestyle that you want!*
- Read more books now, read them again, listen to tapes over and over.

Heart:

- King Midas realized his heart was more important than anything! His wish for a *"golden touch"* wasn't what really made him happy.
- Happiness: he felt happy and elated when achieved *"golden touch"* goal.
- Pain: felt pain, because he didn't like the person he had become.
- Revelation: realized *"golden touch"* wasn't the answer! It was a goal, a *stop* along the way, a vehicle to achieve the overall lifestyle...*rich surroundings, beautiful flowers, successful and happy family and on and on....*
- Come from contribution...here's how...Be concerned about others.
- Don't *"sell."* Give great customer service to people and they will buy from you.
- Find ways that will help stimulate your business to achievement.
- Find ways to serve others.
- Find ways to serve the community with your products.
- Have a heart of Gold! Set goals, dream big, have a vision.
- Have a heart with others and be the leader you always wanted.
- Help improve other's lives.
- Make being in business with you fun.
- Provide information.
- Recognize others constantly.
- Share your opportunity.
- If you know where your heart is, if you have a vision, then...stress turns into invigoration.
- *"Burn-Out"* is no longer in your vocabulary and there is no *"pressure"*...there is *"chaos"* and *"excitement!"*

Going Gold with *The Midas Touch* means:

G = *Going Gold and Beyond...*
O = *Ongoing Belief System...*
L = *Leading Leaders...*
D = *Develop People...*

There is Greatness All Around You

Bob Richards
Two Time Olympic Gold Medalist

There are many people who could be Olympic Champions,
All-Americans who *have never tried.*
I'd estimate five million people could have beaten me in the pole vault
the years I won it, at least five million.
Men that were stronger, bigger and faster than I was could have done it,
but they never picked up a pole, never made the feeble effort
to pick their legs off the ground trying to get over the bar.
Greatness is all around us!
It's easy to be great because great people will help you.
What is fantastic about all the conventions I go to is that
the great in the business will come
and share their ideas, their methods and their techniques with everyone else.
I have seen the greatest salesmen open up
and show young salesmen exactly how they did it.
They don't hold back.
I have also found it true in the world of sports.

I'll never forget the time I was trying to break Dutch Warmerdam's record.
I was about a foot below his record, so I called him on the phone. I said
"Dutch, can you help me? I've seemed to level off; I can't get any higher."
He said, *"Sure, Bob, come on up to visit me and I'll give you all I got."*

I spent three days with the master, *the greatest* pole vaulter in the world.
For three days, Dutch gave me everything that he had seen.
There were things that I was doing wrong and he corrected them.
To make a long story short, I went up eight inches.
I've found that *sports champions and heroes*
willingly do this just *to help you become great.*

John Wooden had a philosophy
that every day he was supposed to <u>help someone</u>
<u>who can never reciprocate;</u> that was his obligation.

Great people will share, and that is what makes others great in the world.
Great people will tell you their secrets.
Look for them, call them on the phone or buy their books.
Go where they are, get around them, talk to them.
It is easy to be great when you get around great people.

The Request

A man came home from work late again, tired and irritated, to find his
five-year-old son waiting for him at the door.
"Daddy, may I ask you a question?"
"Yeah, sure, what is it, son?" replied the father.
"Daddy, how much money do you make an hour?"
"That's none of your business! What makes you ask such a thing?" the father said.
"I just want to know. Please tell me, how much do you make an hour?"
pleaded the little boy.

"If you must know, son, I make $20.00 an hour."

"Oh," the little boy replied, head bowed. Looking up, he said,
"Daddy, may I borrow $10.00 please?"

The father was furious and said, *"If the only reason you wanted to know how
much money I make is just so you can borrow some to buy a silly toy or some
other nonsense, then you march yourself straight to your room and go to bed.
Think about why you're being so selfish. I work long, hard hours
everyday and don't have time for such childish games."*

The little boy quietly went to his room and shut the door.
The father sat down and started to get even madder about the little boy's questioning.
How dare he ask such questions only to get some money?
After an hour or so, the father had calmed down,
and started to think he may have been a little hard on his son.
Maybe there was something he really needed to buy with that $10.00,
and he really didn't ask for money very often.
The father went to the door of the little boy's room and opened the door.
"Are you asleep son?" he asked.

"No daddy, I'm awake," replied the boy.
"I've been thinking, maybe I was too hard on you earlier," said the father
*"It's been a long day and I took my aggravation out on you.
Here's that $10.00 you asked for."*

The little boy sat straight up, beaming. *"Oh, thank you daddy!"* he yelled.
Then, reaching under his pillow, he pulled out some more crumpled up
bills. The father, seeing that the boy already had money, started to get angry
again. The little boy slowly counted out his money, and then looked up at the father.
"Why did you want more money if you already had some?" the father grumbled.

"Because I didn't have enough, but now I do," the little boy replied.
"Daddy, I have $20.00 now. Can I buy an hour of your time?"

The Tators

("*Tators*" -Southern for Potatoes)

Some people are very bossy and like to tell others what to do,
but don't want to soil their own hands.

They are called *"Dick Tators."*

Some people never seem motivated to participate,
but are just content to watch while others do the work.

They are called *"Speck Tator*s.*"*

Some people never do anything to help,
but are gifted at finding fault with the way others do the work.

They are called *"Comment Tators."*

Some people are always looking to cause challenges by asking others to agree with
them. It is too hot or too cold, too sour or too sweet.

They are called *"Agie Tators."*

There are those who say they will help, but somehow just never
get around to actually doing the promised help.

They are called *"Hezzie Tators."*

Some people can put up a front and pretend to be someone they are not.

They are called *"Emma Tators."*

Then there are those who love and do what they say they will.
They are always prepared to stop whatever they are doing and lend a helping hand.
They bring real sunshine into the lives of others.

They are called *"Sweet Tators."*

The Ten Steps To Getting Rich

Craig Lock

1. Accept that you can achieve financial success and make a commitment to
   yourself to attain it. It is within your grasp if you really want it.
   Really **believe** it - that is the most important step. Only then will the incredible
   power of the human mind work out a means of achieving it.
   Reject the idea that work is simply something you have to do
   until the age of retirement.

2. Ask yourself this: Where do you want to be in 2, 5, 10 year's time?
   If you could do absolutely anything with your life, what would you do? If you had
   unlimited money or found out you only had a month to live, what would you do?

3. Establish your current financial position. What is the cash inflow
   and outflow? Which areas can be improved upon?

4. Develop your *new* plans. Decide what action you are going to take that
   will move you closer to the achievement of your goals?
   All goals should be specific and have a time deadline.

5. Closely monitor the performance of your investments and your rate of savings.

6. Try to put extra savings into investment (it could be your own business)

7. Review and reward yourself annually if your targets are met.

8. Pursue your personal goals and business ideas with all you've got.
   With real **passion** and **purpose**. If you really believe in them, they are
   far more likely to be achieved.

9. Still try to live a balanced life... or as balanced as you can make it.

10. The highest cost of all is the cost of waiting to **take action** to
    change your current circumstances in life. It is up to you to do
    things differently. **So take action now**- to change course.

True prosperity is created from within. All prosperity is created in
the mind. You are only as wealthy, happy or as prosperous as what you feel...
and what you make up your mind to be. And money is not everything.
Aim high, dream high.
If you aim for the treetops, you might not get off the ground...
so why not aim for the stars.

142

The Trouble Tree

The carpenter I hired to help me restore an old farmhouse had just
finished a rough first day on the job.

A flat tire made him lose an
hour of work, his electric saw quit, and now his
ancient pickup truck refused to start.

While I drove him home, he sat in stone silence.
On arriving, he invited me in to meet his family.
As we walked toward the front door he paused briefly at a small tree,
touching the tips of the branches with both hands.
After opening the door, he underwent an amazing transformation.

His tanned face was wreathed in smiles and he hugged
his two small children and gave his wife a kiss.
Afterward he walked me to the car.
We passed the tree and my curiosity got the better of me.
I asked him about what I had seen him do earlier.

"Oh, that's my trouble tree," he replied.

"I know I can't help having troubles on the job,
but one thing for sure,
troubles don't belong in the house with my wife and children.

So I just hang them up on the tree every night when I come
home. Then in the morning I pick them up again."
"Funny thing is," he smiled,

" when I come out in the morning to pick 'em up, there aren't
nearly as many as I remember hanging up the night before."

The Wise Man
Bruce Barton

God made the world;
but He does not make your world.

He provides the raw materials,
and out of them every man selects what he wants and
builds an individual world for himself.

The fool looks over the wealth of material provided,
and selects a few plates of ham and eggs, a few pairs of trousers,
a few dollar bills and is satisfied.

*The wise man builds his world out of wonderful sunsets,
and thrilling experiences and the song of the stars,
and the romance and miracles.*

Nothing wonderful ever happens in the life of a fool,
an electric light is simply an electric light; a telephone is only a telephone -
nothing unusual at all.

But *the wise man never ceases to wonder*
how a tiny speck of seed, apparently dead and buried,
can produce a beautiful yellow flower.
He never lifts a telephone receiver or switches on an electric light
without a certain feeling of awe.

Thoughts on Getting Rich
Pastor Russell Conwell

It's Your Duty To Get Rich:

"The opportunity to get rich, to attain unto great wealth, is here right here now, within the reach of almost every person who hears me speak. I have not come to this platform even under these circumstances to recite something to you. I have come to tell you what I believe to be the truth, and if the years of life have been of any value to me in the attainment of common sense, I know I am right; that the people sitting here, who found it difficult perhaps to buy a ticket to this presentation, have within their reach "acres of diamonds" opportunities to get largely wealthy. There never was a place on earth more adapted than our civilization today, and never in the history of the world did a poor man without capital have such an opportunity to get rich quickly and honestly as he has now. I have no time to waste in any such talk, but to say the things I believe, and unless some of you get richer for what I am saying, my time is wasted."

I say, *"You ought to get rich, and it is your duty to get rich."*

Many of my pious brethren say to me,

"Do you, a minister, spend your time going up and down the country advising young people to get rich, to get money?"

I say, *"Yes, of course I do."*

They say, *"Isn't that awful! Why don't you preach the gospel instead of preaching about man's making money?"*

I say, *"Because to make money honestly is to preach the gospel. The men who get rich may be the most honest men you find in the community."*

They say, *"Oh, I have been told all my life that if a person has money he is very dishonest and dishonorable and mean and contemptible."*

I say, *"My friend, that is the reason why you have none, because you have that idea of those people you are listening to. The foundation of your faith is altogether false. Let me say here clearly, ninety-eight out of one hundred of the rich people are honest. That is why they are rich. That is why they are trusted with money. That is why they carry on great enterprises and find plenty of people to work with them. It is because they are honest people."*

They say, *"I hear sometimes of people that get millions of dollars dishonestly."*

I say, *"Yes, of course you do, and so do I. But they are so rare a thing in fact that the newspapers talk about them all the time as a matter of news until you get the idea that all the other rich people got rich dishonestly. My friend, you take and drive me into the suburbs of our community, and introduce me to the people who own their homes around this great city and I will introduce you to the very best people in character as well as in enterprise in our city, and you know I will."*

"For a man to have money, even in large sums, is not an inconsistent thing. We preach against covetousness, and you know we do, in the pulpit, and oftentimes preach against it so long and use the terms about "filthy lucre" so extremely that Christians get the idea that when we stand in the pulpit we believe it is wicked for any man to have money—until the collection-basket goes around, and then we almost swear at the people because they don't give more money. Oh, the inconsistency of such doctrines as that!"

Money is Power:

"Money is power, and you ought to be reasonably ambitious to have it. You ought because you can do more good with it than you could without it. Money printed your Bible, money builds your churches, money sends your missionaries, and money pays your preachers, and you would not have many of them, either, if you did not pay them. I am always willing that my church should raise my salary, because the church that pays the largest salary always raises it the easiest. You never knew an exception to it in your life. The man who gets the largest salary can do the most good with the power that is furnished to him. Of course he can if his spirit is right to use it for what it is given to him. I say, then, you ought to have money. If you can honestly attain unto riches in your life, it is your Godly duty to do so. It is an awful mistake of these pious people to think you must be awfully poor in order to be pious."

What About The Poor People?:

They say, *"Don't you sympathize with the poor people?"*

I say, *"Of course I do, or else I would not have been lecturing these years. I sympathize with the poor, but the numbers of poor who are to be sympathized with is very small. To sympathize with a man whom God has punished for his sins, thus to help him when God would still continue a just punishment, is to do wrong, no doubt about it, and we do that more than we help those who deserve. While we should sympathize with the poor—that is, those who cannot help themselves—let us remember there is not a poor person in the United States who was not made poor by his own shortcomings, or by the shortcomings of some one else. It is all-wrong to be poor, anyhow."*

They say, *"Don't you think there are some things in this world that are better than money?"*

I say, *"Of course I do, but I am talking about money now. Of course there are some things higher than money. Oh yes, I know by the grave that has left me standing alone that there are some things in this world that are higher and sweeter and purer than money. Well do I know there are some things higher and grander than gold. Love is the grandest thing on God's earth, but fortunate the lover who has plenty of money. Money is power, money is force, money will do good as well as harm. In the hands of good men and women it could accomplish, and it has accomplished, good."*

146

I heard a man rise in a prayer meeting and thank the Lord he was *"one of God's poor."*

I said: *"Well, I wonder what his wife thinks about that? She earns all the money that comes into that house, and he smokes a part of that on the veranda. I don't want to see any more of the Lord's poor of that kind, and I don't believe the Lord does. And yet there are some people who think in order to be pious you must be awfully poor and awfully dirty. That does not follow at all. While we sympathize with the poor, let us not teach a doctrine like that."*

Is Money The Root of All Evil?:

Our age is so prejudiced against advising a Godly man from attaining unto wealth. The prejudice is so universal and the years are far enough back. Years ago there was a young man in our theological school who thought he was the only pious student in that department.

He said: *"I heard you say during a presentation, that you thought it was an honorable ambition for a young man to desire to have wealth, and that you thought it made him temperate, made him anxious to have a good name, and made him industrious. You spoke about man's ambition to have money helping to make him a good man. Sir, I have come to tell you the Holy Bible says that money is the root of all evil."*

I said,   *"I have never seen that doctrine in the Bible, please go get the Bible and show me the place you have found this truth."*

So out he went for the Bible, and soon he stalked into my office with the Bible open, with all the bigoted pride of the narrow sectarian, or of one who founds his belief on some misinterpretation of Scripture. He flung the Bible down on my desk, and

He said,   *"There it is; you can read it for yourself."*

I said: *"Well, young man, you will learn when you get a little older that you cannot trust another denomination to read the Bible for you. You belong to another denomination. You are taught in the theological school, however, that emphasis is exegesis. Now, will you take that Bible and read it yourself, and give the proper emphasis to it?'"*

He took the Bible, and proudly read, *"The love of money is the root of all evil."*

Then he had it right, and when one does quote aright from that same old Book he quotes the absolute truth. I have lived through fifty years of the mightiest battle that old Book has ever fought, and I have lived to see its banners flying free; for never in the history of this world did the great minds of earth so universally agree that the Bible is true—all true—as they do at this very hour. So I say that when he quoted right, of course he quoted the absolute truth. *"The love of money is the root of all evil."* He who tries to attain unto it too quickly, or dishonestly, will fall into many snares, no doubt about that.

147

The Love of Money:

The love of money. What is that? It is making an idol of money, and idolatry pure and simple everywhere is condemned by the Holy Scriptures and by man's common sense. The man that worships the dollar instead of thinking of the purposes for which it ought to be used, the man who idolizes simply money, the miser that hordes his money in the cellar, or hides it in his stocking, or refuses to invest it where it will do the world good, that man who hugs the dollar until the eagle squeals has in him the root of all evil.

They say, *"Is there opportunity to get rich today?"*

I say, *"Well, now, how simple a thing it is to see where it is, and the instant you see where it is it is yours."*

They say, *"You have you lived in this city for thirty-one years and don't know that the time has gone by when you can make anything in this city?"*

I say, *"No, I don't think it is."*

They say, *"Yes, it is; I have tried it."*

I say, *"What business are you in?'"*

They say, *"I kept a store here in this city for twenty years, and never made over a thousand dollars in the whole twenty years."*

I say, *"Well, then, you can measure the good you have been to this city by what this city has paid you, because a man can judge very well what he is worth by what he receives; that is, in what he is to the world at this time. If you have not made over a thousand dollars in twenty years in your store, it would have been better for your city if they had kicked you out of the city nineteen years and nine months ago. A man has no right to keep a store twenty years and not make at least five hundred thousand dollars even though it is a corner grocery.*

They say *"You cannot make five thousand dollars in a store now."*

I say, *"If you will just take only four blocks around you, and find out what the people want and what you ought to supply and set them down with your pencil and figure up the profits you would make if you did supply them, you would very soon see it. There is wealth right within the sound of your voice."*

They say, *"You don't know anything about business. A preacher never knows a thing about business."*

Change Your Attitude:

I say, *"I will have to prove that I am an expert. My father kept a country store, and if there is any place under the stars where a man gets all sorts of experience in every kind of transactions, it is in the country store. Sometimes when my father was away he would leave me in charge of the store. This is what did occur many times:*

A man would come in the store, and say to me,
> *"Do you keep jack-knives?"*

I say,   *"No, we don't keep jack-knives,"* and I went off whistling a tune.

Then another man would come in and say,
> *"Do you keep jack-knives?"*

I say,   *"No, we don't keep jack-knives,"* and I went off and whistled another tune.

Then a third man came in and said,
> *"Do you keep jack-knives?"*

I say,   *"No. Why is every one around here asking for jack-knives? Do you suppose we are keeping this store to supply the whole neighborhood with jack-knives?"*

Do you carry on your life and business like that? The difficulty was I had not then learned that the foundation of Godliness and the foundation principle of success in business are both the same precisely. The man who says, *"I cannot carry my religion into business,"* advertises himself either as being an imbecile in business, or on the road to bankruptcy, or a thief, one of the three, sure. He will fail within a very few years. He certainly will if he doesn't carry his religion into business. If I had been carrying on my father's store on a Godly plan, I would have had a jack-knife for the third man when he called for it. Then I would have actually done him a kindness, and I would have received a reward myself, which it would have been my duty to take.

There are some over-pious religious people who think if you take any profit on anything you sell that you are an unrighteous person. On the contrary, you would be a criminal to sell goods for less than they cost. You have no right to do that. You cannot trust a person with your money who cannot take care of his own. You cannot trust a man in your family that is not true to his own wife. You cannot trust a man in the world that does not begin with his own heart, his own character, and his own life. It would have been my duty to have furnished a jack-knife to the third man, or the second, and to have sold it to him and actually profited myself. I have no more right to sell goods without making a profit on them than I have to overcharge him dishonestly beyond what they are worth. But I should so sell each bill of goods that the person to whom I sell shall make as much as I make.

Change Your Thinking:
The man who said he could not make anything in his store has been carrying his store on the wrong principle. Suppose I go into your store tomorrow morning and

I ask,   *"Do you know neighbor A, who lives one square away, at house No. 1240?"*

You say,   *"Oh yes, I have met him. He deals here at the corner store."*

I say,   *"Where did he come from?"*

You say,   *"I don't know."*

I say,   *"How many does he have in his family?"*

You say,   *"I don't know."*

I say,   *"What ticket does he vote?"*

149

You say, *"I don't know."*

I say, *"What church does he go to?"*

You say, *"I don't know, and don't care. What are you asking all these questions for?"*

If you had a store would you answer me like that? If so, then you are conducting your business just as I carried on my father's business in. You don't know where your neighbor came from when he moved to your city, and you don't care. If you had cared you would be rich now. If you had cared enough about him to take an interest in his affairs, to find out what he needed, you would have been rich. But you go through the world saying, *"There is no opportunity to get rich,"* and there is the fault right at your own door.

Enjoy this Life:

"To live and let live is the principle of every day common sense. Oh, hear me; live as you go along. Do not wait until you have reached my years before you begin to enjoy anything of this life. If I had the millions back, or fifty cents of it, which I have tried to earn in these years, it would not do me anything like the good that it does me now in this almost sacred presentation tonight. Oh, yes, I am paid over and over a hundredfold tonight for dividing as I have tried to do in some measure as I went along through the years. I ought not speak that way, it sounds egotistic, but I am old enough now to be excused for that. I should have helped my fellow men, which I have tried to do, and every one should try to do, and get the happiness of it. The man who goes home with the sense that he has stolen a dollar that day, that he has robbed a man of what was his honest due, is not going to sweet rest. He arises tired in the morning, and goes with an unclean conscience to his work the next day. He is not a successful man at all, although he may have laid up millions. But the man who has gone through life dividing always with his fellow-men, making and demanding his own rights and his own profits, and giving to every other man his rights and profits, lives every day, and not only that, but it is the royal road to great wealth. The history of the thousands of millionaires shows that to be the case."

"*Tough times never last,
but tough people do!*"

Dr. Robert Schuller

150

What It Takes To Be Number One

Vince Lombardi, NFL Coach

You've got to pay the price. Winning is not a sometime thing; it's an all-the-time thing. You don't win once in a while, you don't do things right once in a while; you do them right all the time.

Winning is a habit. Unfortunately, so is losing.
There is no room for second place.
There is only one place in my game and that is first place.

I have finished second twice in my time at Green Bay and I don't ever want to finish second again. There is a second place bowl game, but it is a game for losers played by losers. It is and always has been an American zeal to be first in anything we do

and to win and to win and to win.

Every time a football player goes out to ply his trade, he's got to play from the ground up, from the soles of his feet right up to his head. Every inch of him has to play. Some guys play with their heads. That's O.K. you've got to be smart to be number one in any business. But more important, you've got to play with your heart, worth every fiber of your body. If you are lucky enough to find a guy with a lot of head and a lot of heart,

he's never going to come off the field second.

Running a football team is no different from running any other kind of organization, an army, a political party, or a business. The principles are the same. The object is to win, to beat the other guy. Maybe that sounds hard or cruel, I don't think it is. It's a reality of life that men are competitive and the most competitive games draw the most competitive men. That's why they are there, to compete. They know the rules and the objectives when they get into the game. The objective is to win, fairly, squarely, decently, by the rules, but to win. And in truth, I've never known a man worth his salt who in the long run, deep down in his heart, didn't appreciate the grind, the discipline. There is something in good men that really yearns for the discipline and the harsh reality of head to head combat. I don't say these things because I believe in the brute nature of man or that men must be brutalized to be combative. I believe in God, and I believe in human decency. But I firmly believe that any man's finest hour, his greatest fulfillment to all he holds dear, is that moment when he has worked his heart out in a good cause and lies exhausted on the field of battle, victorious.

There is no room for second place.
The objective is to win.
First Place is Our Objective.

Winners vs. Losers
Pat Williams, NBA General Manager

When a winner makes a mistake, he says, *"I was wrong."*
When a loser makes a mistake, he says, *"It wasn't my fault."*

A winner works harder than a loser and has more time.
A loser is always *"too busy"* to do what is necessary.

A winner goes through a challenge.
A loser goes around it, and never gets past it.

A winner makes commitments.
A loser makes promises.

A winner says, *"I'm good, but not as good as I ought to be."*
A loser says, *"I'm not as bad as a lot of other people."*

A winner listens.
A loser just waits until it's his turn to talk.

**A winner respects those who are superior to him and
tries to learn something from them.**
A loser resents those who are superior to him and tries to find chinks in their armor.

A winner feels responsible for more than his job.
A loser says, *"I only work here."*

A winner says, *"There ought to be a better way to do it."*
A loser says, *"That's the way it's always been done here."*

152

You'd Better Slow Down

Have you ever watched kids on a merry-go-round or listened to the rain
lapping on the ground? Ever followed a butterfly's erratic flight
or gazed at the sun into the fading night?

You better slow down.
Don't dance so fast.
Time is short.
The music won't last.

Do you run through each day on the fly?
When you ask *"How are you?"* Do you hear the reply?
When the day is done, do you lie in your bed
with the next hundred chores running through your head?

You'd better slow down.
Don't dance so fast.
Time is short.
The music won't last.

Ever told your child, *"We'll do it tomorrow."*
And in your haste, not see his sorrow?
Ever lost touch, let a good friendship die cause you never had time to call and say

"Hi?"

You'd better slow down.
Don't dance so fast.
Time is short.
The music won't last.

When you run so fast to get somewhere you miss half the fun of getting there.
When you worry and hurry through your day,
It is like an unopened gift....thrown away...
Life is not a race. Do take it slower.
Hear the music. Before the song is over.

Presentations Are Everywhere

Cathy Barber's Canadian team attended
Jan's Nuts $ Bolts Presentation in Aspen.
In less than one year, her business tripled!

Celebrate with enthusiastic people!
Jan Ruhe's leaders celebrating in Kentucky!

Chapter

Giving the Presentation

"Fortune Favors the Brave."
Virgil

The Warm Up:

Do the great athletes of the world warm up prior to their event? Do the great actors of the world warm up prior to going on stage? Do the great singers of the world warm up their voices prior to singing? Why not you? Before you go on stage do a few stretching exercises, use your voice, but most important get psyched up! Some presenters have been known to meditate prior to speaking. Something that works for Jan Ruhe is for the hour preceding her presentations she silently repeats to herself: *"I own this room!"* and *"I own this audience."*

Beginning the Presentation:

You have four minutes to set the climate! Don't rely on the introduction you have been given. Before you lose your audience, grab them with a powerful opening. See the list of openings in the Appendix.

Carol Waugh shares: *"What do you want in your life that's not there now? What do you need and what are you willing to do to get it?*

Dr. Joe Rubino shares: *"My commitment is to see if there might be something here that would significantly contribute to your life."*

 Tip → *Watch your audience's reaction to the way you act. Check yourself while actually giving a presentation or ask for feedback.*

155

Eva Zimmerman shares: *"Be and stay honest. The presentation has to be coming from the depth of your heart and you have to mean everything you say."*

Hilton Johnson shares: *"We had a discussion earlier Ms. Customer regarding my program. I came here to explain everything to you but before we get started, what is your perspective on what we have already discussed?"* Whatever they say gives me a basis to build my presentation around their needs.

Kathy Riley shares: *"Get in step with your customer by using little phrases that demonstrate you heard what they said, cared what they said, and don't think what they said was stupid." "I appreciate your comment!" "I understand your point!" "I see how you feel!" "I know what you mean!"*

Joshua Shafran shares: *"Get inside the hearts and minds of your audience in your presentation."*

Kathy Roland Smith shares: *"Hi my name is Kathy Roland Smith and for those of you who have already forgotten, my name is Kathy Roland Smith."*

Linzi Day shares: *"Give the audience the best you that you can and be the real you. Richard Bach, author of <u>Jonathan Livingston Seagull</u> and <u>Illusions</u> advises, if you let the real you shine out true and clear you will attract like-minded people to you."*

Pam Evans shares: *"Welcome to a fun evening! I am so excited to have all of you here tonight."*

Peter Raynard shares: *"Start your presentations off by telling the people how and why you are involved with your company and what you used to do prior to what you are doing today."*

Randy Gage shares: *"The most successful people are the ones with the best presentation."*

Simon Hamer shares:
- Tell what you're going to tell them.
- Tell Them .....and then,
- Tell Them what you've told them.

"It's a time old adage. Everyone has poor general retention, it is better you make sure you get the message heard and understood, rather than just have people listen. You are making the presentation to impart your message, make sure you do."

Tip ➜ *Be careful of telling your full story the first time you are in front of the customer. The customer wants to know about how the product and opportunity will benefit them. When you tell your story, begin with how you got happily involved. Keep your story interesting to the customer. It's actually better not to talk about yourself. Keep your story focused on the prospect.*

Suzanne Olejnik shares: *"Just like those first impressions when you first meet someone, the first few minutes of your presentation are the most critical. You must take this opportunity to recognize your Host and make them feel special. By complimenting and thanking them you will be asked back. The others in the audience will see the rapport that you have established with the host, and want to hear you again."*

Teresa Epps shares: *"I really cannot emphasize enough the importance of visuals in your presentation. Be the benefit of joining your business by presenting yourself in a put together, organized professional manner."*

Have People Talk to Each Other:

You say: *"Take the next five minutes to turn to someone right next to you and discuss the two best ideas you learned today and how you are going to put them into practice in your business or at home."*

Visuals in the Audience:

Use beach balls or soft Frisbees. Whoever catches it offers an idea and tosses the ball to the next person. This works great in a big audience!

Avoid Trying to Get Anyone Who is Reluctant to Speak:

Many people fear public speaking. Don't push someone who does not want to speak who really does not choose to do so. Honor and respect that person. Give them lots of opportunities in the future.

Audience Participation:

- •Ask questions; get them to nod with you.
- •Get your audience participating.
- •Have people take notes. For maximum results have handouts or workbooks.
- •Have someone volunteer to come on the stage to role-play.
- •Separate people into small groups.

Use Charts and Graphs:

•Charts and graphs can accomplish more in a few seconds than minutes or even hours of recited information.

•Place charts where the prospect can easily see them.

•Rehearse your use of your charts until you can smoothly handle them without awkwardness.

•Take your time showing charts, it will take a person longer to absorb one kind of chart information than another.

•When you present a chart or graph, explain briefly what it shows or make an explanatory comment.

Use Visuals:

•Along with each step in your presentation make note of the comments or *benefit* descriptions that will accompany it.

•A visual presentation tells your prospect more than you can explain in twice the time by words alone, and much more clearly. This is because seeing is the most important of the five senses for comprehension.

•If your product presentation or opportunity is lengthy or involved, fit it into the outline in steps.

•Provide for using visuals in the presentation when making your outline.

•Statistics show these startling facts:

•The best presentation is an in-use presentation. Show products as you talk about them.

•The best way to convey to a prospect the *benefits* gained by buying your product is by a visual demonstration.

  •The eyes are eight to nine times more effective than mental registration.

  •The eyes increase absorption possibilities 35% in the same length of time.

  •The eyes increase retention possibilities 55%.

•When you show a prospect how to use your product or the *benefits* the prospect will get from using your product you give the prospect confidence in you, it shows that you have faith in your product.

•While you are working on your outline for your presentation you can decide where the visual presentation belongs.

Show a Video:

•Act as though you are showing the video for the first time, no matter how often you have seen it.

•Do not show a video that is old and includes outdated information.

•If you show a video or slides, make sure the equipment is working before you start.

•Point out to your prospects beforehand what to look for.

•Summarize at the end and ask for questions.

•Videos are valuable in describing complicated subjects in the shortest time.

•Visuals amplify your words. As you speak, the customer sees.

Use Pictures:
- A picture of places or people that your prospect knows personally has the greatest convincing power of all.
- A picture says 1,000 words.
- Be your own camera person.
- Show before and after pictures.
- Take tons of photos.

Put a Surprise Under Various Chairs in the Room:
Scotch tape one-ten dollar bills under chairs and then say to the audience,
"You never know when you are sitting on a gold mine! Look under your chair and see what's there, if you are sitting on a gold mine and don't even know it wave what you find up in the air for all to see!"

The Voice Mail Presentation:
When you can't get past a person's voice mail, always leave a message. If you don't get a call back, call again and leave another message. Always leave an upbeat brief message and let the person know that you will keep calling until you get to talk to them. Leave a different message every time you call. On the first message you leave tell the person that you have something valuable, exciting or something that will interest them (time savings, save money, improve lifestyle, etc.) When you call the second time refer to the first call and keep going until they call you back.

Power Phoning:
Work every day from 8am to 2pm with no breaks, no lunch, no eating on the job, just hard driving and smart work. Only exceptions are appointments with buyers, or sellers or emergencies.

Power Talking:
Whatever your telephone presentation, it really boils down to creating relationships with someone you can't see. Your success depends on your skills in three areas:

1) **Starting relationships**...respond professionally and promptly...communicate superbly...use "C.P.R." (Consult, Personalize, Recommend).

2) **Nurturing them**...Stay in touch...maintain positive contact...consistently exceed customer expectations...under promise...upgrade, cross-sell and prompt referrals to strengthen relationships.

3) **Rekindling them**...find out what's wrong and take action to fix it...encourage and welcome complaints...use "S.O.A.R." (Solicit feedback, Open communication flow, Appreciate input, Reward behavior)

Telephone Presentation Skills:

- Ask: *"Is this a good time?"*
- Always assume that people want your products.
- Be genuinely enthusiastic.
- Be ready for objections.
- Compliment your prospect.
- Transfer your enthusiasm.

Power Telephone Skills:

While there are numerous techniques that you could employ to more effectively use the phone in your business, here are three that will significantly improve your business telephone relationships:

1) **End Phone Tag**...how time wasting is it when the person you are calling is not available? Try these techniques:
   a) Ask is there is another number to call or if someone else can handle your request now.
   b) Leave a thorough message detailing what you want. Set a specific time for them to call you back.
   c) Set an appointment for your call back.

2) **Save Phone Time**...you only have so much time to get the customer's attention regarding the purpose of your call, so...
   a) It's better to call than be called. You'll be better prepared and focused and you won't get caught off guard with your mind somewhere else.
   b) Prepare for your call before you dial. Focus on your objectives for the call. Make notes.
   c) Work out a system for handling calls with your spouse or other business partner. Make sure they know when you are available for calls and have them schedule them for you.

3) **Penetrate Screens**...ever feel that your calls are being screened and you can't get through to your prospect? Well...
   a) Call when you know that you'll get through.
   b) Consider the person answering as an ally. Briefly state your reason for calling, be happy to hold, develop rapport, get a name. Set an assumptive appointment: *"She's available Thursday? Good. I will make it a point to call at 10:30 a.m., if that looks good or I can call at 1:30 p.m. Which would be better?"*
   c) Use the person who answers and is attempting to screen as a resource. Ask questions about your prospect's schedule, the best time to call or when are they the least busy?

Tip → *Watch your tone of voice:*
- *If you are talking in a monotone, emphasize key words by moving up or down the scale.*
- *If you sound tired, speed up your delivery.*
- *If your tone of voice is too high, deepen it.*
- *Radio announcers read about 150 words a minute.*

Phone Phrases to Avoid:

There are certain words to use and certain words to avoid. Certainly use all the positive words you can in your telephone presentation. Here are some phrases that are a must to purge from your phone presentation:

But.................by using the word "*but*" you are devaluing the phrase before or after it. The listener will prepare to do battle with you. Instead say..."*and*"

Disagree..........by using this you create immediate conflict because the listener believes that you are telling them that they are wrong. Instead say... "*I understand, let's consider another viewpoint.*"

Failed..............don't look at failure as failure but a learning experience. Instead say... "*I've learned.*"

I'll have to......sounds like your being imposed upon and don't want to help. Instead say... "*I'll be glad to...*"

I'll try.............sounds like you're tentative and unsure about what you'll really do. Instead say... "*I will...*"

Lucky..............don't attribute your successes to flukes, rather give yourself credit for creating positive outcomes. Instead say... "*My hard work paid off.*"

Only................you lessen your credibility by using diminishers. Instead say... "*I am.*" or "*I believe.*"

Problem..........this stifles creativity. Instead say..."*This sounds like a challenge...*"

Should.............this sounds indefinite and unreliable. Instead say... "*I will...*"

Truthfully.......sounds to the listener that you're not always honest. Don't use this in your presentation. Get to the point and be honest always.

You make me..you're sounding like a victim, not in control of the situation. Instead say... "*I feel...*"

Tip → *You are "sized up" based on the words you use. Remember the listener can't see you so they will decide if they'll cooperate with you based on how you communicate and by the words you use.*

An Exercise for Presenting on the Telephone:

This telephone exercise is known as the *"Family Recipe Exercise"* and goes like this: You ask the members of the audience to choose a partner. You then ask them to think for a minute about an old favorite family recipe. Next, ask them to decide who will be Partner A and who will be Partner B. The A's will go first. Then say, *"Everyone sit on your hands, I don't want you using your hands, just your words. Now when I say three Partner A will start reciting his favorite family recipe, and oh yes did I tell you that since on the phone you can't see each other I'm going to turn off the lights. One, two, three...recite your recipe!"*

The audience will have fun with this, so at the appropriate time tell them to stop and have Partner B recite a recipe. After the exercise is complete, the obvious comes out. On the telephone you have to use words that describe your enthusiasm, enthusiasm that you would normally emote with body language or gesture. You've gotten your point across.

Your Phone is Your Friend:

Consider your telephone to be alive and helpful to you in getting your job done. Check yours now for cleanliness. Tell it that you love it. Maybe even give it a name (I like Mr. Holmes) Really start to use it to its best advantage. Let this be the beginning of a beautiful relationship between yourself, your customers and your goals. Be committed to care for and work with your telephone for the success of all concerned. Give up your negative attitude about your telephone and greet it with, *"Good morning, Mr. Holmes! How about some great appointments today? It's you and me all the way."*

Telephone Affirmations

- I appreciate my telephone.
- My telephone is indispensible. It is reliable, loyal, faithful and dependable; and, it is never late for work!
- My telephone is necessary in order to arrange appointments with a customer.
- My telephone is the most powerful tool in my office.
- My telephone is vitally important in terms of dollars and time.
- The key to my success is right on my desk.

Chapter

Ending the Presentation

"Thank your guests for attending."
Janet Wakeland

Jan Ruhe Closes Her Presentations:
"Now is the time!" or *"Begin today to live your life 'as if' you are the person 'you want to be!'"* or *"Go for greatness, prepare for prosperity and abundance, never give up, dream big, I believe in you, and as I say to you now and always, don't be average, be a Champion!"*

Ending The Presentation:
Many salespeople do a good job with every step of the selling process until they get to the close, and then that is where they falter. Work on your closing presentation skills. 95% of the presentation time should go into the close. Most average sales people spend 95% of their time into selling the product. Sales are lost every day because there is no close of the presentation. You have to be a strong closer to make top-level income at selling. Learning how to close is something that is simple to master, something that will repay you with high earnings for the rest of your life. Become a student of closing skills.

 Tip ➜ *"Make 'em laugh, make 'em cry and end on dancing feet."*

*"An ounce of energy
is worth a pound of technique."*

Roger Ailes

Closing the Presentation:

"All I have learned about closing the presentation I learned from my mentor Tom Hopkins. I have attended his seminars for years; I devoured his books, outlined them; memorized his closing statements and questions and made a fortune. Through the years, I have cherished a few stories on closing skills. And now they are in this guide. I have adapted them for inclusion in this guide." -Jan Ruhe

Close Through Their Eyes:

Several years ago I attended a huge banquet for sales agents as a speaker. Before I gave my presentation, the main speaker introduced someone in the audience and said, *"This woman earned twice the national average in sales in our industry last year..."* The speaker's manner suggested that is was quite an achievement. Everyone craned their necks and looked in puzzlement at the woman who was introduced. *"...and she's totally blind."* There was a burst of applause. When that quieted, the speaker said, *'I'm sure that many of us are wondering how you got into the top third in sales achievement with that handicap."* *"Wait a minute,"* the blind woman replied, *"I don't have a handicap, I have an advantage over every other salesperson in this area. I've never seen a product I've sold, so I have to close my buyers through their eyes. What I'm forced to do, all you sighted people could do, and you'd serve your clients better and make more money if you did."*

It was quiet in the auditorium for a moment while everyone pondered what she said, and then there was another spontaneous round of applause for this courageous woman who could hold her own, selling blind, and still offer sage advice to the rest of us.

The point is, you must see the benefits and features and limitations of your product or service or opportunity from your potential buyers' viewpoint; you must weight them on their scale of values, not your own; you must close on the benefits that are of value to them. And you must radiate the conviction that you can satisfy their needs. After you've qualified them and discovered their true motives, you must start radiating confidence that you know how to handle their requirements. If, instead of that you radiate a profound doubt about your ability to fill their wants, why do they need you? Buyers need to have a feeling of confidence before they can rationalize the decision they really want to make.

The last time you bought an automobile, did you spend more than you wanted to? If it was a new car, did you go into the showroom with the firm intention of not buying any extras—and drive out loaded with options? If so, you met a professional salesperson who helped you rationalize the decision you really wanted to make.

Aren't you glad when you tilt the seat back, adjust the right hand mirror from the inside, listen to the sound system and relax in cool air when it's sweltering outside? Of course you are, and the small additional cost on your monthly investment is forgotten.

164

Be Like A Matador:

When watching a bullfight on TV, about three minutes or less into it, you will begin to see parallels between the aspects of bullfighting and selling. So come with me to the arena, where thousands of people are watching—like all the people you know are watching the progress of your own career.

A roar goes up as a ton of live beef charges onto the sand. The bull, the customer, has entered the arena.

Next, the matador comes out and all of a sudden it gets quiet, like when you go in to make your presentation.
Who has the advantage now?

The bull outweighs a dozen matadors and is armed with animal fury and sharp horns. The matador at this point is armed only with a cloth cape and courageous skill.
Isn't that the usual sales situation?

The customer has the absolute power to buy or not buy from you, and you have only your technique and courage.

You can't overpower your customer for the same reason the matador can't overpower his—the strength is all on the other side. Like the matador, you must have *superior skill* to win against the odds you face every time you step out onto the hot sand of the presentation arena.

The first thing the matador uses is the cape—
to lead the bull and establish moral ascendancy over him.

Do the same in closing your customers. Lead them with questions. Develop a sense in them of your expertise on your presentation of your product.

When your customer snorts, stomps the ground and then charges at you, do you meet that charge head on? Not unless you want to be carried out on a stretcher. Of course, your wounds won't be visible. You'll walk out on your own two feet. But you'll be hurt in your pocketbook, confidence and pride.

No, you don't clash heads when your customer charges into you. Instead, you step aside like a matador and let the customer run. You listen to his grunts and stompings and watch which way he hooks with his horns like the matador does. *And then* you work with him, getting closer all the time, leading with questions and more questions.

"Tell me more," he says. *"Tell me more,"* you think. You ask and you answer. You use

your cape with exquisite technique and finesse and in a predetermined sequence gain control of your more powerful opponent.

To hold the crowd's admiration and end the match cleanly, the matador must go in over the bull's horns at exactly the right time and put the tip of his sword through a point the size of a quarter. That's a good description of a skillful closing of a large and difficult presentation. Both in bullfighting and in presenting, the time of greatest danger comes at the close of the performance and the matador's final thrust is much like your final close. For the unskilled, the unpracticed, the unprepared, the close in presenting is like the matador's estocada over the horns of a fighting bull. In both cases, it's all or nothing; the only things that count are knowledge, technique and courage.

Future Flash:

Many people fight trying techniques that are proven and tried. As you read this guide, make a conscious and highly emotional decision to throw away your fears and give your presentations *all you have*. Have the confidence in your heart and the determination in your mind that you should, apply everything you can and decide to decide to improve your presentation skills. Decide to go to the top in your company. Go over your notes from this guide. You will forget much of what you read, so for sixty days review what you have learned. Go over what you highlight, master the concepts, adapt every technique you can and practice every skill until you can own them. Your income will shoot up, it will double and double again and will keep on growing. Set goals of increasing your business and dream big and your income will become outrageous.

Master the techniques we are sharing in this guide, and you will discover something new and exciting that you can use in your presentations. Remember, among the greatest closers of presentations and sales, the best average at about five closing attempts. That is, the great ones usually close after their fifth attempt. You are not going to go too far in presentations if you only know one or two presentations. Once people have heard you, normally you won't be invited back over and over and over if you only know one presentation. People want what is new and fresh and they will ask you back once they realize you know many presentations and that you have confidence in presenting.

> *"Fortune Favors the Brave."*
>
> **Jan Ruhe**

Tip → *Remember, there is an alternative to learning and growing and paying the full price of switching to success—you can try to stay just as you are.*

Presenter's Closing Check-Off List:

Always having your closing materials with you. Be ready to close anytime and anywhere. Presentations are made on golf courses, tennis courts, spas, on boats, jogging trails, tracks, ski slopes, hiking trails, and anywhere in fact where people play, work, exercise or relax. Lots of business is done outside offices and showrooms. Many sales are lost because the presenter forgot the paperwork and has to get back with the prospect. By the time you get back with the prospect the prospect may have had a change of mind. Just keep your closing materials with you in your brief case, club locker, overnight bag, car trunk and your office desk.

☐ **Clean Forms:** Use crisp new forms, not the ones all waded up in your handbag or briefcase. If you pull out a form that has coffee spots all over it, your prospect will think you haven't closed a presentation in months and he won't want to break your streak!

☐ **Figure out Money Calculations using a calculator:** Today's champions presenters sell using a calculator, not a pencil. Don't make a human mistake; trust a calculator over your memory of math.

☐ **Use test or trial closes:** *"Which is better for you, the first or the fifteenth?"*
•Answer the objection.
•Don't argue.
•Don't attack when overcoming objections.
•Feed the objection back.
•Hear them out.
•Lead them to answer their own objections.
•Question the objection.

☐ **Go for the close:** say, *"So, how does that sound?"* And then shut up.

☐ **The first person who talks loses.**

When you go into your final close change your body language. To signal that the last step is over and you are going into your final close, just turn the page on your proposal, shift in your chair and say: *"By the way, are you ready to join me so that your life will be bigger better and more exciting than you ever dreamed of..."* Or *"By the way, how does this sound, are you ready to go ahead and get your credit card out?"*

Most presenters like to wing it. Average presenters like to wing their closings. Champions like to make money. So they don't wing it, they prepare intensely for the close.

☐ SPR - The Difference between have and have not:

Right now, you are as good as your R's and not a bit better. Your R's might not be great because you haven't taken a good P yet. It's almost impossible to take a good P unless someone gives you a good S.

Stimulus, pause and response theory:

If you walk into your den tonight and, failing to see your cat, step on its tail, you'll get a *stimulus*. Your cat will have an immediate *response*. It won't *pause* and think, "All right, I'm going to get even later, but first I'd better make a noise and get out from under this humans foot." The animal's instant reaction is S-R, stimulus-response.

We as humans have a great ability to respond to stimulus. We can receive a stimulus, pause to consider what our best response will be and then respond. Here is a formula for human reaction:

Stimulus-Pause-Response

You must close in a stimulating way, then pause and let the customer respond to your stimulus.

You have turned yourself into a presenting machine; now turn that machine on! The moment you go into high gear and start using your presentation material efficiently, you'll glimpse your bight new destiny. At that moment you'll be ready to break out above the average and join the ranks of the excellent. When you achieve the status of super professional presenter you will be tempted to throw out the very labors and methods that put you there. You don't want to dwell on past difficulties except to laugh about them. Guard the golden hours of your day jealously and use them effectively. Put a note in your calendar to review this book in a year. Don't limit the effectiveness of your learning. Don't put a ceiling on your income earning potential. Enhance your knowledge. Add to it. Collect closings.

The presenter's main closing tool, just like a golf club is to a golfer, is his mouth. You must use your mouth with confidence. Concentrate on learning to say the right words. Accept the fact that what you say will sometimes come out badly. Attend more seminars. Learn new material. Use it daily. When you create desire and the proper training, you will get the income you want.

 Tip ➔ *Curb your urge to tell all. Some presenters get so excited they can't stop talking and end their presentations. Close your presentations like you would slam a car door shut!*

Write your favorite closing here:

"*There's no business like show business.*"
Ethel Merman

Presentations Are Everywhere

Have Photos Taken With Your Mentors, Don't Miss This Opportunity!

Jan Ruhe with William Bates & Jim Rohn

Jan Ruhe with Tom Hopkins

Chapter

After The Presentation

*"Stick around after the Presentation, you
never know who you will meet"*
Priscilla Harrison

After a Presentation:

Walk up and stand by the speaker. Powerful professionals gather around a prominent speaker. Extend your hand, introduce yourself, network, get acquainted, gather business cards. Have your photo taken with the speaker.

Thank The Person for Bringing in the Speaker:

The day after the event, call the person in charge of bringing in the speaker. Thank the decision maker for sponsoring the seminar. Every time you have a chance, call the person in charge of bringing in the speaker. The more you do, the more your name will come up and you will be surprised after only a few times that you will be considered valuable to the person in charge of bringing in the speaker.

Use Your Last Presentation as a Blueprint for the Next Presentation:

- •After the presentation make notes in a spiral notebook of what produced good audience response.
- •Ask yourself, what can be improved upon?
- •Determine what contributed to your success?
- •Have your audience do an evaluation, written, verbal or both.
- •Then revise and refine the presentation.

Beware the Critics!:

Prepare yourself speakers! When you are a presenter there will be critics. The best advice is to either ignore the critics or *use criticism to motivate you.* A critic is someone who makes negative judgments and statements about others. Master presenters are focused on how others can improve themselves. Critics want to tear down hopes and dreams. They seem to enjoy watching people fail. Most critics are jealous of people with *real talent,* the people with the will to succeed. There are so many examples of critics who try to destroy the dreams of ambitious people. Critics are a necessary part of success. They screen out those who lack the courage and resolve to take criticism and succeed in spite of them. Those who would succeed in spite of the critics are the champions. Be careful to whom you listen. Be sensitive to the motives of so-called advisers. Be clear on this, the successful speakers are more heavily criticized than the unsuccessful.

Successful speakers are different; they don't follow the crowd, and those who don't follow the crowd are often criticized for being different. Speaking success comes at a price of not being one of the people in the audience. Remember in the stage play The Lion King when the predator animals sing *"It's time to Chow-Down!"*

 Tip ➔ *Let criticism motivate you!*

Here is What the Critics Will Mainly Say About Speakers:

- *No one is interested in what you have to say.*
- *Powerful women speakers threaten men.*
- *What makes you the expert?*
- *You are too ambitious, and you are a threat to some people.*
- *You can't succeed.*
- *You lack the intellect to be a great speaker.*

Suzanne Olejnik shares: *"The higher up in the company you move, the more critics you will have. Just remember, 'no matter how hard you dance, some people are just not going to clap.'"*

Handling Complaints:

Fact: Complainers are more likely than non-complainers to do business with a company again, even if the complaint is not resolved to their satisfaction.

Fact: The average business never hears from 96% of its unhappy customers.

Fact: For every complaint received a business will have twenty-six others that are unreported, six which are "*serious.*"

Fact: Non-complainers complain to nine or ten other people.

- Be firm. Keep your temper and stand on the fact.
- Don't argue. Explain you are eager to do what is fair and right.
- Here is how the champions handle complaints:
    - Be courteous. Courtesy has been called many things: pleasantness and politeness, thoughtfulness, tact, good cheer, charm and company manners. It means just being nice to people. It's not always easy.
    - Dump up. If you have a complaint about your company go to your Upline, your Boss or someone in the company who can handle the complaint. Do not go to everyone in your organization or company.
- It's tough to say "*no*" to a customer, but when the circumstances justify it you have no choice. Of this you can be sure: once you agree to an outrageous proposal there will be no end to it.
- Let your customers keep their dignity. State your position politely and reasonably.
- When a customer makes an unreasonable demand, the customer is usually keenly aware of it. The customer may not really expect you to agree to it at all.

Using Humor:

- The real wit tells jokes to make others feel superior, only the half-wit tells them to make others feel small.
- Make others the hero.
- Even is you have heard a joke or a story, never interrupt someone telling a joke or story.

 Tip ➔ *You are the only person in existence who can use your potential, use it now!*

You should listen to the critics but do not support them. There is really no such thing as constructive criticism. Most criticism is destructive because more often than not, the person doing the criticizing will be criticizing the performer and not the performance. Something is very wrong in that kind of criticism. Ignore this kind of criticism, it has no value. Look for someone you respect and ask them to give you positive feedback.

Challenges:

Expect to have trying and tough times. Expect upheavals, difficult people, naysayers, critics, and hypocrites. Don't be surprised, shaken or discouraged when you run into them. When they come, here is what to do:

•Clear your mind of all negative thoughts.

•Enjoy time with positive people.

•Reconnect with positive people and go looking for new and better relationships.

•Set new goals.

"Challenges are only illusions, in reality they are only decisions waiting to be made."

"Every challenge has a solution someplace that can match it."

"Every obstacle is an opportunity, to learn, to grow. This is great news!"

"When faced with a mountain, I will not quit! I will keep on striving until I climb over, find a pass through, tunnel underneath, or build a bridge."

•Take time for yourself.

The High Achievement of Triumph:

This is one of the most impressive and impacting philosophies ever written. It was a thought expressed about critics by one of the greatest competitors of our time, the twenty-sixth President of the United States, Theodore Roosevelt. It embodies the basic truths as to what is really success. The same philosophy applies to just about every phase in life. The common thread of thought for people who are going for greatness is to always try, try and try again, to know in your heart that although you might have slipped that you did your best. However, if victory does arrive, you will know that you made a very special contribution to your team, to your organization and/or to the world.

It is not the critic, who counts,
not the man who points out how the strong man stumbles or
where the doer of deeds could have done them better.
The credit belongs to the man, who is actually in the arena,
whose face is marred by dust and sweat and blood,
who strives valiantly, who errs and comes short again and again,
because there is no effort without error and shortcomings,
who knows the great devotion, who spends himself in a worthy cause,
who at the best knows in the end the high achievement of triumph and
who at worst, if he fails while daring greatly,
knows his place shall never be with those
timid and cold souls who know neither victory nor defeat.

Theodore Roosevelt

Tips on Handling Critics:

You shouldn't become angry with the people who try to block your path any more than you would with a tree, which the wind blew across the road. Acquire the habit of not hating gossips anymore than you do a person who is foolish enough to neglect his teeth. You don't have to like gossips, few people do and you don't have to like pettiness. Look upon the gossips, the hypocrites and the critics that they have foolish behavior rather than evil behavior.

Start a rumor by saying *"I sure like that person."* This gets back to them and many times they say, *"Well, I always liked her or him too."*

There is always a temptation to listen to gossip, just remember, while you are on the listening end with the gossiper, the next time you will be on the receiving end when the gossiper goes to the next person who will listen to them. Beware of the gossip and the critic. Avoid them. Don't give them a chance to even be with you, find something out about you, and then carry that gossip into another circle. If you must gossip, gossip about how nice people are. The 'gossip carriers" in every circle will soon carry that back to the other person, and you've made a friend. Let the gossip carriers carry good things, not bad things. Know this that the gossips will spin everything you say. If you want to stop a critic say these words to them: *"If you don't stop criticizing me, I will start telling the truth about you!"*

The purse robber is punished; but the reputation robber goes free. Don't worry; Karma will get them. If you hear a fire alarm you run out of the building, whether there is a fire or not. It might be a false alarm, but you take action just as if there were a fire. The critic spreads some gossip. Later you see that critic talking to someone else and you feel maybe you are now being talked about. And guess what, you probably are.

The open mouth catches the most flies. The champions conceal bad thoughts.

If you have a challenge with someone, go to that person and air out your differences, never try to get a group of people together to turn on someone who has built a business. Seek first to understand, then to be clearly understood. Shame on the person who tries to break up a church, an organization, a team, a business. You might have a short term of fame, but believe this, it will come back to haunt you.

> *"What you think, what you say and what you do are inextricably intertwined."*
> **George Walthen**

Don't Be Average, Be A Champion!

- Avoid gossip, jealousy and negative thinking.
- Be cautious of false relationships. When you feel that a friendship has turned cold, remind yourself that it most likely was not a friendship in the first place. Real friends do not criticize one another.
- Control your own ego and make other people feel important.
- Critics free you from unhealthy relationships you think were important but actually do nothing to further your business or yourself.
- Don't hang on to the past; the past is a bucket of ashes.
- Each day, well spent, brings a lifetime of happiness.
- Have a strong drive to meet your career goals.
- If you can't say anything nice, don't say anything at all.
- Keep on keepin' on.
- Make a conscious effort to hold loving and beautiful thoughts in your mind.
- Never allow negative input into you mind, choose to be happy.
- Never take rejection personally.
- The average are the best of the worst and the worst of the best. Don't be average!
- The past is forever gone; the future is an uncertainty, so be happy and thankful for each moment.
- There are no statutes erected to the critics.
- Want, but don't need everyone's approval.

 Tip ➔ *There are no statutes built to the critics!*

Presenter's Affirmations

- Activity leads to productivity.
- Be caring.
- Be courteous.
- Be disciplined.
- Do what it takes.
- Keep your word.
- Take urgent action.
- Tell the truth.

Presentations Are Everywhere!

What a fabulous name:
Cape of Good Hope!

Nairobi Train Station

Arrivals --
How do you present your
arrivals?

Have fun with your name!

What are you presenting?

Presentations Are Everywhere

The Masai - a nomadic tribe roaming
in the Mara of Kenya present themselves
in red as a badge of their courage.

Jan and Bill with Sue and Pëet duPreez
Bahati, South Africa 1999

Jan in the Bahati Land Rover with
Pëet, Sue and friends

Giraffes are curious -
are you curious?

Appendix

Presentation Manners

When you are a presenter, you have an image that many other people are envious of. You can go through this check off list and see how many manners your parents and grandparents, coaches, teachers, spouses and others have taught you in the past. This is just a place to start. Your manners are part of your image. It doesn't matter how handsome or beautiful you are, if you do not have good manners, people notice and you will hurt and tarnish your own image. Pay attention to these manners. They are very important. You never know who is watching you to make a decision to invite you to be a speaker. Having good manners is one very special way of drawing the right kind of attention to you and your message.

In a world of cellular phones and business luncheons, proper presentations are emerging. Presentation manners are not about dos and don'ts, but about common sense and good old fashion courtesy. Good manners means thinking of others, being there when you say you will be there. Included here are modern points of etiquette such as how to respond to voice mail and answering machine messages and how to deal with E-mail in a courteous manner. This information is indispensable for people who aspire to be speakers. You have to have good manners to be a pro. Having good manners requires a little logic, a bit of forethought and a great deal of consideration for others. Clayton, Jan's son, says *"It is not about complicated rules and convoluted instructions. It is about honestly and sincerely being a nice person."* Simply acting courteous is not enough. It is being courteous that is important and that means thinking of others. It is what you do and who you are, an accumulation of above and beyond behaviors over the course of a lifetime that make you a pro. People watch the manners of presenters. Mind your manners!

As a presenter, you must be so very careful of your manners:
- Always carry breath mints.
- Always turn your beeper off.
- Always turn your cellphone off in a restaurant. If you need to make a call, leave the restaurant, go outside, do not have people listen to your conversations. Very rude.
- Be considerate of other speakers. Do not go past your allotted time so that the next person has less time to make a presentation.
- Be considerate of special needs of senior citizens and physically challenged people.
- Cologne-only wear expensive cologne, nothing but the best. Men should wear very little cologne or after shave and it should be meant for someone who gets very close to him. Reminder, do not wear inexpensive cologne.

A2

- Establish a friendly relationship with the hotel concierge for some necessary service, one that is important enough to justify a substantial tip.
- Gentlemen:
  - do not have creases ironed into the legs of your jeans.
  - do not wear hats inside a public building or home.
  - never wear a tuxedo before six o'clock, no matter what anyone else does.
  - shine their shoes.
  - when you wear a cummerbund, make sure the pleats are turned up.
  - when you wear vests, always leave the bottom button undone.
- If a bellhop offers to assist you in hailing a cab or a limo, accept the offer, understanding that a tip is implied.
- If necessary, get your shoes resoled.
- If someone offers you an apology accept it with grace. Consider it past history and move on.
- Keep an apology simple.
- Keep your address book up to date. Don't always depend on someone else to find a number for you.
- Look nice when you exit your home.
- Make every effort to prevent dandruff.
- Make others feel comfortable.
- Make sure to have a manicure.
- Never share a revolving door section with another person. Respect their space.
- Never ask a woman if she is pregnant.
- Only argue over an issue that could save a life.
- Recognize that other people's beliefs are valid.
- Respect the fact that your friends have busy schedules.
- There is no such word as *"irregardless."*
- Think before you speak.
- Think before you offer your opinions. You are justified in having your own opinions.
- Trim your mustache or beard. Do not have a mustache that falls down the sides of your face.
- Use your personal stationary to write thank you notes. If you have to say, *"I am sorry,"* use the telephone.
- Wash your hair.
- Watch going through doors. Never slam a door in another person's face.
- When describing an unpleasant person, do not stretch the truth. Goodness, when accurately described will stand on its own.
- When you get out of a car, be careful. Do not bang your car door into the car next to you. If you scratch another car, leave a note.
- When you outgrow your clothes, give them away to charity.
- Your shoes and handbag must be up to date.

Dining Tips:

- A good opening at a party is *"This is a nice party, isn't it"*.
- Always have dental floss with you.
- Always place your napkin in your lap. Never tuck it into your belt or under your chin.
- If at a restaurant your food is slow to arrive from the kitchen and others at the table have been served, urge them *"Please go ahead without me."* And mean it.
- Leave at least 15 percent of your total bill for gratuity. Excellent service justifies 20 percent or more.
- Never crunch ice cubes.
- Never tell jokes that may embarrass others, even if those people are not in the room.
- Never use a straw.
- Observe the established dress code.
- Remember, *"please"* and *"thank you"* are still the magic words.
- Stay away from sore subjects.
- Turn your cell phone off.

If you are:

- a vegetarian, inform your host or hostess about it ahead of time so that the proper arrangements can be made.
- if lost, admit it and ask for directions.
- on a diet, do not talk about it at the table.
- pouring wine, the gentleman always pours the wine and finishes by turning the bottle slightly, which prevents unsightly dribbles and drips.
- subjected to a conscious insult, either in public or private, say nothing at all.

If you:

- arrive late, wait until there is a timely intermission for you to be presented.
- borrow something from someone, there should be a deadline set by which you will return it. Then, keep to that deadline and return the property in good condition.
- decide to go a different direction that you have been going, don't burn your bridges.
- discover something lodged in your teeth, excuse yourself and head for the restroom.
- have a cold, especially if you are running a fever, decline all speaking engagements.
- have a tendency to cough, always carry a cough drop.
- have an unpleasant time in a restaurant, do not badger the wait staff. Make your complaint with the management and only quietly and not in sight of others.
- have not made a dinner reservation, accept the fact and wait in the bar.
- leave the table leave your napkin in your chair.
- must park your own car at a restaurant or any other place of entertainment, offer to let your passengers out at the door.
- start coughing uncontrollably, leave the room.

If you are invited to stay in a private home as a guest:

- check your room upon departure and make sure you have packed all belongings.
- do not ever make phone calls during the dinner hour.
- do not make long distance phone calls from other people's homes unless you use your cell phone or use a credit card.
- eat what is served and do not complain.
- leave nothing but pleasant memories behind.
- make your bed in the morning.
- prior to agreeing with someone that you will stay in their home, make sure to ask if they have pets that you might be allergic to.
- rise and retire according to the household schedule.
- stick to your arrival and departure plans.

Presenting Food:

- If you are at someone's home and you break something, you just apologize and replace the broken item as soon as possible without fanfare.
- Never, never rush your friends to leave the table after a satisfying meal.
- Serve dessert and coffee or tea.
- Serve the dinner plates in the kitchen or bring out the main course and its side dishes to the table where the guests serve themselves.
- Take the empty plates away.
- When entertaining, use your good china. If a piece is broken accidentally, do not make a scene and do not accept a guest's offer to pay for its replacement.
- When guests have finished the main course, take away the dinner plates along with the dinner forks and knives.
- When pouring wine make sure that you pour it with the label facing the person who will be drinking the wine.
- When you are faced with a plate of pasta, such as spaghetti, linguine or fettuccine, resist every temptation to chop it up with your knife and fork. Instead, twirl a small mouthful around the tines of your fork and with the help of your spoon; transfer it to your mouth.

Airline Travel Manners:

- Be careful when you stow luggage into the overhead to prevent injury to your fellow passengers and to yourself.
- Do not feel obligated to give up your rightful seat to another person.
- Do not feel the need to get acquainted with everyone on the airplane.
- Do not have a loud obnoxious laugh; many people try to rest on the airplane.
- Do not intrude on the space that is allotted for another passenger's use.
- Give all young children a small amount of Tylenol to help their little eardrums, so that you are not trying to calm a child down the entire flight while ruining the flight for the rest of the passengers, be considerate.

•If you sit in the wrong seat and are asked to move, do not argue about it. Move.
•If your bag is small enough, stow it under the seat in front of you.
•Keep your voice low. No loud talk or laughter, be considerate.
•Leave your seat once an hour to stretch and get your blood circulating.
•Sit in the seat assigned to you.
•Take on board only the amount of luggage that is permitted.
•Tell all young children traveling with you not to bang the drop down table nor kick the seat in front of you.
•When putting your bags overhead, be careful not to smash another's belongings.

Do not:
•answer the phone during dinner.
•applaud until you are directed to do so by the senior person in the room.
•bite your nails.
•brag about leaving a generous gratuity.
•carry unnecessary paraphernalia in your pockets.
•complain or whine during dinner.
•correct another person's grammar unless you are very close friends.
•extend last-minute invitations.
•file or cut your nails around others. Do this in private.
•fret over broken glassware or scratches on the furniture. This is part of entertaining if you have someone making a presentation in your home.
•hesitate to screen your calls.
•hold a grudge.
•interrupt.
•make phone calls prior to 8:00am or after 9:00pm to a private residence.
•make threats.
•offer an insincere apology.
•salt food before tasting it. It's insulting to the chef.
•shift about in your chair unnecessarily.
•smoke.
•stare.
•talk during a presentation, even during the very loudest music or sound effects.
•talk with your mouth full.
•touch other people's children unless you are invited to do so.
•walk into a room talking. Someone else may be talking, wait until you enter the room.

Presentation Tips

Here are some presentation tips; ideas that you can use to help you in your presentations. Review these ideas often to find out any weaknesses and ways to improve your presentation. These ideas will help you to find areas in which you need to improve so as to be more successful in your presentations. Whenever you feel like you are not working your business properly or you are in a rut, review these ideas and find out what you might not be doing right.

Headlines For a Presentation:
- aren't catchy or cute.
- avoid headlines that don't excite curiosity.
- if it can be misunderstood, it will be.
- motivate action by stirring an emotion.
- never use all uppercase, rather use upper and lowercase in Times Roman.
- put quotations around the headline.
- the more you tell, the more you sell.
- use short words that create images or pictures.
- use verbs which are vital and strong.

Using Stories:
- A well-told story is interesting and entertaining as well as instructive.
- If your story tells about someone the audience knows, its convincing effect is greatly increased.
- Imagination is the magic power that lets the customer visualize instead of just comprehending.
- Most sales are not made until visualizing is accomplished and the audience turns words into pictures.
- People enjoy hearing stories.
  - Stories can be used in any stage of the interview.
  - Stories can get the attention of and motivate the person to join you or buy from you.
  - Stories enable the audience to visualize the *benefits* to them.
  - Stories enable the audience to picture themselves in the same circumstances.
  - Stories put the imagination to work.
  - The best stories are ones illustrating the *benefits* that others received from your product or service.
- The story should make a point.

Presentation Image:

The objective of dressing right for a presentation is to project an image of calm control, authority, quiet affluence, assurance and power. You don't want your audience to comment on the way you look unless it is with praise. Your clothes must assist you in delivering your presentation.

Here are some dos and don'ts on dress:

Never appear to be more casually dressed than your audience. It is professional to always begin your presentation fully dressed. Don't be putting on your jacket or taking it off after you begin your presentation.

Colors: Send a powerful message. Select those that reinforce you as an authority.

  Blue: A safe power color. Blue for hundreds of years represented prestige, power and authority. It is equally suitable for men and women and for all types of presentations.

  White: To set off blue, white is a great choice. Blue and white do not distract your listeners from your message but do reinforce you as an individual of power and distinction.

  Red: A dash of red, either as a tie (for men) or as an accessory for women is a good idea. Red indicates energy and is a powerful attractant.

Colors to avoid: Orange, magenta, bright green, hot pink.

Fibers: Always dress in natural fibers. Polyesters are out. Do not go trendy or ultra chic. People will be concentrating on the way you look rather than on what you have to say.

Hair: Have an up-to-date haircut.

Jewelry: Make it expensive. Costume jewelry is fine, but no dangley earrings. Diamonds and fine jewels say you are powerful and know what you are talking about.

Nails: Always have a manicure, this goes for both men and women.

Shoes: Shoes usually tell an individual's personality type quicker than anything else. Do you need to have new heels put on your shoes? Never make a presentation with run down shoes on. Keep them polished. If you wear tennis shoes, make them bright white and clean!

Hints: Men…black shoes, dull shine.
Women…stiletto heels are not acceptable. Scuffed shoes are ridiculous. You don't want to wear shoes that are too tight or too high.

Choosing a Topic:

You will want to choose your own topic or ask the people hiring you to speak for the topics they wish to speak about. Here is a shopping list of topics to choose from:

Advertising	Merchandising
Arts/culture/music	Motivation
Athletics/sports	Negotiation
Attitude	Network Marketing
Business	Nuts $ Bolts
Careers	Organization
Change	Patriotism
Communication	Performance
Computers	Politics
Consulting	Presentations
Continuing Education	Productivity
Creativity	Psychology
Customer service	Public relations
Design	Quality Management
Diversity	Real estate
Education	Recruiting
Empowerment	Relationships
Engineering	Religion
Enthusiasm	Retirement
Estate planning	Sales
Family	Science
Finances	Self-esteem
Future	Self management
Gender issues	Service provider
Government	Spouse programs
Growing Older	Strategic planning
Health and nutrition	Stress
Human resources	Success
Humor	Tax planning
Image	Teaching
Inspiration	Team building
International affairs	Teamwork
Labor relations	Technology
Law	Time management
Leadership	Training
Magic	Travel
Marketing	Writing

Presentation Ideas

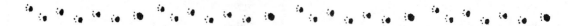

1. A presentation is likened to a symphony and you the presenter are the conductor.
2. Adult learners crave structure. Break down the presentation by topic. Use words, *"moving along," "next"…, "as I promised you."*
3. Advanced planning pays off in time saved in the end.
4. After you have done a couple of presentations, you will find them getting easier and easier.
5. Agree with or show respect for what the customer says.
6. Always carry your notes on the plane with you if you are traveling by air. Never pack your notes.
7. Always make sure that you have a glass of water on a table close to where you are speaking. Drink your water slowly.
8. Always make sure you have mastered the name of the person who introduces you. Thank this person from the platform.
9. Answer these questions of the customer: *"How do I know that it will do what you say?"* and *"Can I count on it to work for me?"*
10. Appeal to their senses.
11. Appreciate the opportunity, always.
12. Arouse interest by describing ***benefits*** to the customer, remember the two words the customer wants to hear more than any other words: ***"You Get."***
13. Arrange to show your products in use.
14. Ask:
    - advice. Somewhere in your presentation you can arrange to ask the customer what the customer thinks of a point you have made. The answer may give you important clues to the customer's buying motives.
    - everyone to join your opportunity, you never know where the next leader will come from.
    - everyone to turn off cell phones before you start. Including yourself, don't interrupt your own presentation.
    - for the order.
    - questions as you go along.
    - questions at intervals to make sure that the customer understands the points you are making.
15. Associate with positive speaking people. Birds of a feather, flock together, beware.
16. At first, when building your speaking business, be prepared to drop everything and go speak for free if a time and place is offered to you. People get sick at the last minute. Be prepared to fill in.

17. Attend seminars of those living the lifestyle you want.
18. Avoid tentative or non-committal statements.
19. Be:
    - alert and eager to serve.
    - alert for the opportunity to take advantage of something the customer says to further your presentation.
    - aware of your own stinking thinking.
    - dependable.
    - flexible.
    - on the lookout for reactions that will reveal what the customer likes about your presentation.
    - patient. Be willing to put forth effort so that you can earn the big money.
    - prepared to insert trial closings during your *"live performance."*
    - sincere. Stick to the facts, be sincere in presenting them and in promoting the customer's benefit and your presentation will acquire strength. A new customer doesn't know you and perhaps doesn't know about your product or your company. Your sincerity will help build a bridge of assurance and will win the buyers' confidence.
    - very careful whom you choose as friends. Friendships take a lot of time.
    - well prepared.
20. Believe in and use your products.
21. Believe that *"if it is to be, it's up to me."*
22. Believe that *"if not now, then when, if not me, then who?"*
23. Bless and release as quickly as possible all those who don't lead or follow you. Wash your hands of them completely; throw out photos, mementos, everything about them as soon as possible. They were in your life for a reason, a season but not a lifetime.
24. Caution= Don't confuse confidence with boastfulness or arrogance. The goal is to be strong in your expression of assurance.
25. Cherish books, tapes and relationships with your teachers and those who have mentored you through the years. Protect their image and their name and never be the one who says unkind things about them.
26. Choose glamour words: *glide with silky smooth power, the rich colors, the easy-chair comfort, etc.*
27. Clearly and adequately explain, in a convincing manner, what is being sold and the **benefits** the customer will get from using your product or getting happily involved with your company.
28. Close the sale at the earliest opportunity. Don't wait until the end of your presentation.
29. Compliment the customer's responsible position, reputation, even family photos in their home or office.
30. Conflict should be resolved, not avoided.
31. Consider other peoples needs.
32. Create an atmosphere that makes the audience feel comfortable.

33. Create interest, start the customer thinking.
34. Customers judge from your first call or first conversation that your attitude will be after the order is placed or if they join you. Buyers like to deal with salespeople who will follow up, offer helpful advice and be there when they are needed.
35. Date and identify any printed material you prepare.
36. Delete "*I*" and "*me*" and "*mine.*"
37. Depend on yourself to increase the business.
38. Do not:
    - badmouth other companies.
    - be a know it all; continue to learn from the Masters.
    - *be average, Be a Champion.*
    - be easily influenced by negative comments from family members, relatives, distributors, employees and friends. Listen to the positive side.
    - believe in rumors. Check out all the facts. Do not be gullible to listen to a person who is unfit and who only presents one side of a situation. Check out the facts yourself. There are always two sides to the story.
    - be lazy.
    - be only interested in personal profits. Care about the needs of others. Run contests; put money earned back into luncheons, rooms at convention, parties in your suite, gifts and surprises.
    - be overbearing.
    - distribute unprofessional, sloppy, poor copies of information.
    - dwell on the past; you can't change what happened five minutes ago.
    - get discouraged by small people, their cheap shots, and their criticism and don't let them inconvenience you for one second of your life. Do not take any negatives from their criticism inside of you, let it go. Bless and release easily.
    - get involved in Chain Letters, illegal pyramids, emails that use scriptures to support those who are hypocrites who use their faith to justify their lack of success or any other scheme.
    - get paid for number of years "*in,*" you get paid for results.
    - have unrealistic expectations for time spent on business. Stick with it.
    - knock your competition. You gain stature with most buyers by welcoming comparison and by tending to emphasize your strong benefit points rather than your competitor's weak ones.
    - look at the ceiling or at your hands, but the people in the audience.
    - panic on the platform.
    - meander, wander or go in different directions.
    - put your hands in your pockets.
    - speak in a monotone. Vary the tone and the pace.
    - speak over 30 minutes. Most people can't pay attention without a break for more than 30 minutes.
    - spend one moment in regret.

- •spend too much time getting organized at the presentation.
- •stand behind a podium.
- •wait around and expect someone to make you successful.
- •wait too long for late-comers. Don't penalize those who get there on time.

39. Drive a clean car.
40. Emphasize the points to which your customer responds the best. If the customer seems to light up when you mention appearance, act as though appearance is a major benefit to owning your product or getting involved with your opportunity.
41. Envision a better future.
42. Establish that the product or service being presented will definitely satisfy one or more of the customer's buying motives.
43. Expect greatness.
44. Explain ease of joining.
45. Explain ease of operation.
46. Find people who are strong in areas you are weak and become their student.
47. Find the customer's needs and provide service.
48. Finish early.
49. First you must sell the audience on you and then they will be more likely to listen to what you have to say.
50. Follow up on customers. Care.
51. Four things are musts in buying a product or joining an opportunity. Dependability, Performance, Quality and Value.
52. From the platform, whether you are giving a one-day speech or a multi-day seminar, take on the better characteristics of a cheerleader. Radiate intensity.
53. Get:
    - •affirmative response.
    - •and stay committed.
    - •customer to take action and place the order or get happily involved with your opportunity.
    - •customer to use the word "*yes*".
    - •the customer interested in desiring the ***benefits***.
    - •the customer's attention (immediately after introducing yourself.)
54. Give no excuses.
55. Go for getting the order as soon as possible and as often after that as necessary.
56. Go into your audience and move about.
57. Handle distributor complaints.
58. Have:
    - •a Plan B.
    - •a professional appearance.
    - •emergency meetings when you get new information to present.
    - •energy.
    - •lots of practical tips.

•your answering machine on at all times. Be reached easily.
•no need to stand up and speak and train to whoever will listen to you if you have little to no results yourself. Be careful to whom you listen to. Be very careful. Do not waste your time going to insignificant seminars taught by people whose ego needs to be witty up in front of the room. Do not waste your time.
•people move around the room every twenty minutes.

59. Hold the person's interest throughout the presentation.
60. If:
•a person interrupts you simply say *"I am interested in what you have to say. Let's take a couple of minutes at the break and I'll see what I can do about answering your points."*
•two people are talking or whispering together, walk to their vicinity. Stand right beside them if you can and while taking no official notice of what they are doing, stand there for a minute. They will stop what they are doing, but you won't have to stop what you are doing!
•you can, get massages in between speaking days.
•you get flustered on the platform, know that people are not interested in your challenges, they are paying attention about the way you master any challenges on the platform and the less said about it the better.
•you have been standing all day, sit on a stool.
•you have no one to introduce you, give the audience a few friendly but firm statements of introduction focusing specifically on why you are where you are.
•you plan, prepare and rehearse your presentation, you will conquer the butterflies. If the butterflies are all flying in the same direction in formation, you're doing fine!
•you speak in the evening, don't pack in too much information, make it humorous and motivational.
•you use words that are *"jargon"* to your business, don't think everyone will understand you, define your *"jargon"* words.

61. Introduce yourself.
62. Involve your guests in the presentation. Don't be the only one speaking.
63. It is your responsibility to stimulate enthusiasm in your presentations.
64. Keep:
•agreements and appointments, don't be late, be on time. It's rude to be late, no excuses.
•an organized office.
•at least one copy or the original of any material you mail.
•high expectations for the high effort you put out.
•in mind selling is fun, selling is easy, selling is important!
•your family your priority.
•your self-esteem.
•records.

A14

•your enthusiasm high. People buy from enthusiastic salespeople. You can never afford to merely *"go through the motions"* when you are giving your presentation.

65. KISD= Keep it simple and duplicatable, it's not what you know, it's what you show.
66. Know that setbacks are stepping stones to comebacks.
67. Laugh all the way to the bank, keep your sense of humor.
68. Learn the final version of your presentation by heart.
69. Learn the customer's name.
70. Let the customer feel the product.
71. Let only the people who have mastered the business who are at the top teach you.
72. Listen to positive tapes.
73. Make:
    •a point of being open minded.
    •every one want all the products you present.
    •first impressions work for you.
    •proposals to decision makers. Even if they don't respect the proposals, care enough to make proposals.
    •the ending hit the high spots. In summarizing your points, stress those statements or benefits that seemed to impress the customer most when they were first heard.
    •the customer decide that he/she wants to own your products.
    •your presentation like a winner!
74. Most customers will give little indication of their feeling, most will give signs of agreement or disagreement that will be your cue.
75. Most recruiting and sales come from leading the customer through each step of the presentation.
76. Move fast away from disappointments and toward opportunities.
77. Move with power strides to the podium, make them quick movements.
78. Never apologize to your audience.
79. Never call a meeting just to call a meeting.
80. Never say anything unkind about others. Not once, not ever.
81. Nobody makes any money until someone sells something, so focus on really making your products and opportunity come alive!
82. No clutter is welcome into your life.
83. No guts, no glory. Have guts.
84. Nothing helps your confidence like knowing what you are going to say and do during the presentation.
85. One of the difficulties of the seminar and lecture circuit is maintaining the appearance of excitement after you have given the seminar again and again. Each audience you face is entitled to the best of you, you must do whatever it takes to bring yourself to the highest level of performance.
86. Overcome or answer to the satisfaction of the customer all questions and objections.

87. Paint the picture of how the customer will feel using your products and being part of your opportunity.
88. Pass timely information to your organization immediately. Don't block powerful information from those who are living the lifestyle you want.
89. Pay attention to these details:
    - be courteous.
    - be in a positive and friendly frame of mind.
    - do everything you can to avoid having your appearance act as a detriment to the presentation.
    - get the customer's name right and refer to the name during the introduction and through your presentation. If you mispronounce a name, you might lose the sale.
    - have a natural and confident manner.
    - smile to build rapport.
90. People never read introductions the way they should be read. Encourage the individual introducing you to read over the introduction you have prepared to avoid errors.
91. People want to buy from a strong, competent, reliable person.
92. PDR = **P**lan, **D**rill and **R**ehearse your presentation.
93. Plan to succeed.
94. Praise, recognize, and appreciate loyal top people.
95. Precede criticism with at least two words of praise.
96. Promote events where there are people who have not stabbed you in the back on stage or in front of your people.
97. Promote events where there are successful people building businesses, improving their sales skills and who are not gossips.
98. Put key points on index cards.
99. Read and keep up with the latest happenings in the industry.
100. Read books that teach you something positive (join the Jan Ruhe Book Club at www.janruhe.com).
101. Read, readers are leaders and leaders are readers.
102. Recognize and praise successline achievers.
103. Refrain from smoking and chewing gum.
104. Rehearse your presentation until you can handle it all, the words and any visual aids without stumbling.
105. Remember always that your audience wants you to succeed.
106. Remember that when you have a lot of products it is impossible to present every item in detail. Choose one to five products as your main focus point, mention a few aspects and benefits of the other products and leave something for the next presentation with the same crowd of guests. If they get to hear and see everything at the first presentation, why would they want to come back for more?
107. Repeat a point to give it greater force.
108. Repeat the customer's own words.

A16

109. Respect those who are able to professionally partner with you. Just because they have a title and a check from your efforts and just because they think they are in a powerful position in the company, does not mean they are the one to partner with. For people to be a partner, there must be respect.

110. Return all calls promptly whether you want to or not, be professional about returning phone calls.

111. Review this list often.

112. Say your presentation with integrity and only make outstanding **benefit** claims.

113. Seek out the leaders in your field, learn from the right people.

114. Sell with a flair: if your product has parts then present the product and show how to put it together easily.

115. Sell the benefits, sell the benefits...

116. Shine your light on the people who want it, go to the bank on the people who don't.

117. Should guests already be looking at the products before the presentation starts (That's a good sign that they will buy....), just ask them politely if they don't mind all sitting down for a while so that you can do a short presentation.

118. Show loyalty to your product. If you show lack of respect for, or confidence in, the product or it's benefits, so will your customer.

119. Slow down your speech, it's hard to keep up with a fast speaker.

120. Smile, laugh, blink, maintain eye contact, enjoy the moment, be passionate.

121. Some sales people include facts, make the best use of the facts, **benefits**, and figures, testimonials and similar convincers during the presentation, making conviction a constant process.

122. Speak as though you firmly believe and want the customer to believe what you say.

123. Speak forcefully. Project your voice. Convey confidence by speaking with authority and with emphasis.

124. Spellbinding…

125. Spend a lot of time with people. You are in the people business.

126. Sponsor people and help them learn *how to* become a top producer. It's better to be sponsored by a top producer than to sponsor one. That way they can learn how a top producer achieves. Mentioning that your sponsor is a *top producer* is a great recruiting tool!

127. Stand on principle. Don't care if people think you are unreasonable. What they think of you is none of your business. Stay clear on principle.

128. Start your formal presentation no longer than 15 minutes after you have promised the guests that you will start. Do your best to start on time.

129. Stay:
    •fired up through tough times. Tough times never last, but tough people do.
    •in communication via email with your leaders on a regular basis.
    •informed on how to succeed in building a business. Keep your interest in learning.
    •serious about building leaders and making them successful.
    •up-to-date on technology.

130. Stimulate desire for *benefits*.
131. Stop yourself when you hear yourself saying something negative.
132. Stress that the *benefits* described are true.
133. Strive to do your best.
134. Surround and identify yourself with successful people.
135. Take a couple of good deep breathes before advancing to the platform.
136. Take action. Activity breeds productivity.
137. Take risks.
138. Talk about:
    - the fact that business is booming.
    - the Initial Investment- when you begin.
    - the Net Investment- quality shows in the end.
    - the Real Investment- the cost of not having it!
    - the Running Investment- here is where you consider things like daily costs of operation, business cards, getting involved in leadership, buying and moving products and catalogs, attending seminars, buying books and tapes.
    - time saving benefits.
139. The audience must be convinced, must believe with all their heart that they are getting information they need in a form that they cannot get anywhere else.
140. The audience must be touched by intense enthusiasm which must not wane.
141. The best kind of humor is spontaneous.
142. The best place to start speaking is to have a small group over to your home. Do a book report on a favorite book. Ask for feedback.
143. Think for yourself.
144. Thought provoking…
145. Train yourself to view challenges as opportunities.
146. Trial closings should be placed at intervals in your presentation to see what the customer is thinking. For example, use these scripts:
    "Do you feel that this is a fit for you?"
    "Does this meet your bottom line requirements?"
    "Is what we have to offer something that you can see yourself benefiting from."
    "So, how does that sound?"
147. Trial closes fit naturally into your planned presentation after your strong points and when your presentation ends.
148. Use:
    - a microphone for over fifty people. Do not put excess stress on your vocal chords.
    - a stool on the platform.
    - body language. Lean into your audience when you want to stress a point.
    - dramatic comparisons and illustrations. Example: the *biggest* football player could stand on it and not harm it.
    - examples.
    - parallel situations.

A18

- pauses and changes of tempo. If you see that a point has hit home, don't be in a hurry to move on. A pause gives a good point time to sink in.
- personal effort.
- simplicity in your words. No need to use words people don't understand.
- the word *"new"*, this one word will make you money. Listen to what TV announcers use and note how many times you will hear the word *"new"* mentioned. It's repeated over and over again. It's repeated and repeated. Why? The pros know that the audience will listen when something is described as *"new."* And when you get your customers listening you are well on the way to a sale or sponsoring new people. Talk about the *new* **benefits** of your opportunity.
- vivid picture words to sell quality in looks, sound and performance.
- *"you"* and *"your"* and *"our"* and *"let's"* emphasis frequently.
- your body language. Point, lean forward
- your products, be proud of your products, give them as gifts.
- your voice to add emphasis. Change the pitch, volume or excitement in your voice.
- your voice with expression.

149. When bogged down…move on…it'll be there when you come back.
150. When the customer talks, listen.
151. Whether we acknowledge it or not, we are all born sellers. We sell and negotiate all day long with spouses, children, parents.
152. Work your business daily.
153. Work on your presentation skills.
154. Work with those who want leadership and let go totally and completely those who don't.
155. Write down goals. Know what you want out of life. Get a direction or some dreams. Don't be confused and lost.
156. Write your own introduction; don't leave this to an inexperienced speaker.
157. You are expected to know your business.
158. You must use humor in your presentations. However, do not make any comments about sex, political, religious ideas or humor. Not acceptable.
159. You never have a second chance to make a first impression.
160. Your presentation is your ship and you are the captain.
161. Zoom in on your target, your goal, you products, your opportunity, and your **benefits.**

"You are the Captain of your future!"

Jayne Leach

Presentation Openings

•*A man spends the first half of his life learning habits that shorten the latter half of his life...*

•*A monumental feat was just accomplished by...*

•*And while we are on that subject...*

•*A new organization is being born today...*

•*A question mark hangs over us today...*

•*A remarkable step upward happened this month...*

•*Aren't we?*

•*A savings of several hundred to thousands of dollars a year would be nice to have, wouldn't it?*

•*A sound idea is only the tip of the iceberg in any course of action. It's the action we take that shows our ability to achieve success...*

•*A story like a fire is very hard to stop once it gets started...*

•*A truly happy person is one who can enjoy the scenery on a detour...*

•*A wise person tests....*

•*Actions speak louder than words and the best actions are prefaced by words. I am here to call you to action.*

•*Actions speak louder than words...*

•*Adversity is a school of hard knocks; but its alumni often shine. This year you will face some adversity but I want you to stand like a stone wall and navigate through the tough times. What will history say of you if you do not quit?*

•*All the world is a stage, Shakespeare wrote. But some of the events are staged in our lives...*

•*Anything goes...*

•*April showers may bring May flowers, but June brings the end of the school year and the beginning of summer holidays. Many weddings traditionally take place this month. Today I would like to talk to you about the importance of working your business throughout the summer.*

•*April showers may bring May flowers, but today I am going to spring ahead to the business at hand. I am going to plant some new ideas in your head and see which ones sprout.*

•*Are you a dream?*

•*Are you a pioneer? Pioneers are people who make a new path for others to follow, they go where others have feared to go, reached higher peaks, solve mysteries and go for greatness...*

A20

- *Are you a white knight?*
- *Are you counting the moments until…*
- *Are you ready to get fired up?*
- *Are you ready to go for greatness?*
- *Are you sick and tired of being sick and tired?*
- *Aren't we?*
- *As a wise person said: Might does not always make right. Today I would like to discuss with you how we could do what is right without using might.*
- *As I look around the room…*
- *As I stand before you…*
- *As I stand before you, I want you to know that you and I do indeed speak the same language…*
- *As I stand here surveying this room…*
- *As this day in history demonstrates…*
- *As we know from the history books…*
- *As we look back on what we accomplished last year…*
- *As we ponder our future, let us remember our not-so-distant past…*
- *As what I have shown and told you suggests…*
- *As you grow in understanding it is like building blocks in your solid foundation of your future…*
- *As you may or may not recall…*
- *Ask for help. I am here today to help you…*
- *At every step of the process of joining my team, if you have any questions, stop me so I can explain the benefits…*
- *Back in the 1990's…*
- *Be a fountainhead of great advice…*
- *Be wiser than other people if you can, but do not tell them so…*
- *Before I begin today, can you keep a secret?*
- *Being on a 125 ft. yacht was astonishing…*
- *Benefits for you…*
- *Birthdays are good for you - the more you have the longer you live…*
- *Bon voyage!*
- *Build your life into a masterpiece…*
- *By aiming for our goals, we push others and ourselves to great achievements…*
- *Bya Danke (Afrikaans for thank you)*
- *Caed Melia Falcha! (Irish for 100,000 welcomes)*
- *Can you have your cake and eat it too? Today it's going to be hard to convince me you can't…*
- *Can you imagine the world without safety pins, washing machines, hairdryers, computers, golf clubs?*
- *Changes can sometimes be so subtle as to go unnoticed for a long time…*
- *Changing your future takes working every moment toward your goal…*

•*Charity starts at home...*
•*Come on over and check out our one-hour opportunity presentation.*
•*Come stroll down a future memory lane with me...*
•*Destiny is what we ourselves make it. Today I am announcing that we have a new motto: Anything can be done. Anything can be done!*
•*Did you ever dream of being a princess?*
•*Did you ever stop to think about...*
•*Did you ever stop to think that...*
•*Did you know that experts recommend forming a corporation for a home based business once it starts generating $1000 per month or more in income? It allows you to maximize your tax savings and protect your personal assets.*
•*Don't you agree?*
•*Do something good that needs doing...*
•*Do you:*
 •*desire to be profitably decisive?*
 •*ever stop to think how our children will talk about the good old days that we are living in...*
 •*have a pioneering spirit?*
 •*have star potential?*
 •*have the hope of attaining a better way of life?*
 •*know how persistence and concentration help you win...*
 •*know how to make sure your business is classified as a business instead of a hobby?*
 •*know how to present your opportunity on a napkin?*
 •*know it's important to drive an SUV? Doing so could mean an immediate, reduction in your taxes using a small business tax loophole that most accountants don't know about.*
 •*know that positive thinking begins your success process?*
 •*know that September 19 is Mickey Mouse's birthday?*
 •*know to deduct every meal you go out to eat, professional sports game you attend and entertainment event you pay for?*
 •*like to cook?*
 •*love Indian Summers?*
 •*own a camera?*
 •*pride yourself on being a team player?*
 •*remember last year at this time?*
 •*think all the planets have been discovered?*
 •*treat others, as you would have them do unto you?*
 •*want the best future you can possibly have?*
 •*wonder about...*
 •*work for a playcheck or a paycheck?*
•*Don't 'take care;' 'take charge'...*
•*Don't cry because its over, smile because it happened...*

A22

•*Don't hide a good idea...*
•*Dream of things that haven't been accomplished yet and then say to yourself, "why not?"*
•*Dreams sometimes do come true...*
•*Each of us must ask, what do we make of it when we have a great opportunity right in our hands?*
•*Earn while you learn, learn to live and live to learn...*
•*Effective leaders inspire their followers through sound judgment and good example. I plan to inspire you for a few minutes today and promise that if you take action that you will not believe the results that you will have...*
•*Even if you are not a leader, building trust and confidence is only the tip of the iceberg; maintaining that trust takes a lifetime of hard and honest work.*
•*Events have consequences that cannot be foreseen. Today, I think we have a winning combination of ideas and I want everyone to share them...*
•*Every act of heroism is memorable. Today I want to talk to you about the hero within you.*
•*Every civilization, every tribe, every culture, every nation has contributed to the treasury of wisdom in our world. It takes great wisdom to know how to use and preserve the riches of this planet.*
•*Every one of you in this room today is capable of doing better...*
•*Every time...*
•*Everybody has his or her own personal definition of Utopia...*
•*Everyone has the right to freedom of thought...*
•*Everyone in the world deserves independence and freedom...*
•*Everything should be made as simple as possible, but no simpler...*
•*February is a month close to our hearts. It's a month for romance; it's a reminder to tell those we love how important they are to us.*
•*Five years from now...*
•*Following in the footsteps of our leader, I will make my points brief...*
•*For the golfers here today, I plan to tee off properly, aim true and finish with as few strokes that are necessary...for them.*
•*For those of you who might be unfamiliar with...*
•*Fortunately I can let you all know that we have a beautiful year ahead and that we have come a long way...*
•*Freedom must never be taken for granted. Many people have paid a high price for freedom...How valuable is your freedom to you?*
•*Friendship is a powerful asset. When you have friends, you have support...Building friendships takes time and effort, but when the chips are down, you can always rely on friends to be there for you...*
•*Get going as fast as you can...*
•*Get up, get going, and let's make something happen early in the year...*
•*Great and long-lasting unions deserve all the honor, respect and praise we can give them...*

•Great meetings don't have to become great firefights; they can be a powerful
 introduction to mutual admiration...
•Happiness comes through doors you didn't even know you left open...
•Happy New Year!
•Has the greatest company President been hired?
•Hasn't it?
•Have:
 •the greatest company VP's been hired?
 •the greatest paintings been painted?
 •the greatest songs been composed?
 •the greatest successlines been built?
 •you come here eager and ready to take action?
 •you ever been out sailing in Vancouver?
 •you ever felt like a movie star?
 •you ever gotten lost while driving on a road trip? What do you do? Have you
 ever pulled into a filling station or asked for directions or picked up a map to help
 you find your way? Well, today I hope that you will just consider me a friendly
 person who has the directions to help you find your way...
•Have you ever seen a baby sable in the wild?
•Have you experienced a Spa?
•Having lived through...
•Here are some bright ideas about some areas where I believe we need to shed new
 light...
•Here is a photo of our headquarters. Our home office is a progressive company with a
 25 year reputation...
•Here is how to make decisions for personal profit...
•Here is how to make money every time your neighbor uses the telephone...
•Here is why it's so important for you to get involved...
•Hear me roar...
•Herman Melville wrote in Moby Dick: "I love to sail forbidden seas, and land
 on barbarous costs." If you are disenchanted with your lifestyle you are going to love
 what I have to offer you...
•Hmmmm, let's see!
•Hope springs eternal...
•How:
 •can we embrace change?
 •do you want to be treated in your golden years?
 •However slowly progress moves, we do make progress...
 •goals generate the vision to keep you going...
 •interesting it is to...
 •long a minute is depends on what side of the bathroom door you're on...
 •many more springs do you have in your life...
 •persistence and concentration help you win...
 •positive thinking begins your success process...

A24

•*professional skills contribute to success...*
•*to be profitably decisive...*
•*to feel like you are 16 years old again...but with better judgment...*
•*to give yourself a bonus...*
•*to make decisions for personal profit...*
•*to make money every time your neighbor uses the telephone...*
•*to think constructively to create your success...*
•*Humans are creatures of hope. We must keep on trying over and over and that's what I am here to speak to you on today...trying just a little more...*
•*I always love to come to this group...*
•*I am:*
  always looking for better ways to bring people closer together, and that is why I am speaking to you today...
•*clear as I stand before you today that ...*
•*encouraged to start my speech today by noting that one of the wisest people in our company is in the room...*
•*going to keep this short before the MEGO factor kicks in. That stands for My Eyes Glaze Over.*
•*going to teach you the power of words and their delivery today...*
•*happy to announce that for the first time...*
•*happy to point out that, since we are all together today, we can celebrate right now this incredible achievement...*
•*happy to report to you all that we have reached our goal...*
•*happy to tell you that my speech today is presented to a distinctly selective audience.*
•*here to keep the lines of communication open. I want consistent interaction and communication with all of you. Communication and keeping in touch cements all kinds of relationships. Even when links are broken, it doesn't mean they can't be mended. Those of us together today may not have truly communicated with each other for a long time. Wouldn't you agree that now is a great time to renew our relationships by opening up communication with each other?*
•*here today not to simply utter a few words or to hear myself speak, but rather to raise a few questions and to give you some information, which, I hope, will raise your curiosity...*
•*here today to talk with you about how to view your own personal success with some consideration of what it can do to help others...*
•*here today with a call to believe as well as a call to act...*
•*really impressed with your choice of a speaker today. As a matter of fact, I can hardly wait to hear what I have to say...*
•*reminded of...*
•*so thrilled to be back in...*
•*I ask you to donate a small portion of your time to listen to what I have to share with you today...*
•*I believe that most products stand or fall on the basis of their own performance...*

A25

•*I can't hide my enthusiasm for…While I was preparing to give you this presentation I found…*
•*I cannot help but think how much we really take for granted…*
•*I care about you, everyone one of you every day…*
•*I certainly hope that today will inspire you to get fired up and go for your dreams…*
•*I certainly won't let this opportunity pass me by…*
•*I do not believe you are lost or need me to show you the way, however, I would like to put up a signpost or two in the hope that they will help you at some point…*
•*I do not come here today with all the answers…*
•*I do not have the patent on having the total truth…*
•*I don't think what I am about to tell you will shock you…*
•*I don't want half of anything, I want it all, do you…*
•*If you make the investment to join right now, you'll save…*
•*I greet you on Valentine's Day…*
•*I guess everybody knows the story of…*
•*I have:*
  •*a bit of interesting financial news…*
  •*a dream and I want to share it with you…*
  •*a few ideas to help you concentrate your efforts…*
  •*borrowed part of this presentation today from…and let me tell you why…*
  •*covered this point sufficiently so I am going to move right in to my prepared remarks…*
  •*major mixed emotions, I am so grateful, so excited and love being here with you all…*
  •*missed you all so much and love it when we get together…*
  •*noticed that the people who are late are often so much jollier than the people who have to wait…*
  •*some burning ideas of my own that I would like to share with you…Have you heard the illustration that when two people are sting in a boat, it doesn't make much sense for one of them to point an accusing finger at the other and say. "Your end of the boat is sinking." Let's take a look at both ends of the boat…*
  •*some ideas worth pursuing with you here today, an all-star hope for tomorrow…*
  •*some jolly thoughts to share with you…*
  •*stood by my convictions no matter what. How many of you would be willing to publicly make a commitment out loud today to increase your business? This is what I want to consider with you today.*
  •*taken pains to plan a presentation that was short…*
  •*to paint my pictures with words; word pictures tell a story…I have some stories to share with you today…*
•*I hope:*
  •*all of you will be inspired by this story…*
  •*that our coming together today is a great omen of good things to come…*
  •*that what you here today will help you make some important choices…*
  •*today you will listen intently…*

A26

- *I know that in this room there are...*
- *I know that some people have been the first into a company or in on the ground floor, but what I am going to address to you today is that many people have succeeded who were not the first or not in on the ground floor...*
- *I know that today some of you are going through some tough times...*
- *I know there are some of you who...*
- *I promise to make all of my points perfectly clear...*
- *I remember before Walmarts, before the Bic pen, cell phones, computers, CD players, big screen TV's DVD's, answering machines, scanners, coca-cola in a can, pure spring water, pampers, credit cards...*
- *I rise today with a Diamond salute to the past and to the future of our great organization.*
- *I see your lights shining at the end of my tunnel...*
- *I should like tonight to call your attention to a fantastic opportunity...*
- *I thank you for being excited...*
- *I thank you for being here today...*
- *I thank you for giving me the opportunity this afternoon to...*
- *I thank you for listening...*
- *I thank you for the opportunity to speak with you about...*
- *I thank you for your attention today as I find it a pleasure and a privilege...*
- *I thank you for your enthusiasm...*
- *I thank you for your interest...*
- *I think we should talk today on the importance of never quitting and staying in for the long haul, don't you agree?*
- *I want you all to be examples of shining, burning brighter with each new day...*
- *I want you to get fired up with me today...*
- *I want you to know that it took a lot of work to get me here today. Once you get into the habit of working, it's hard to take off. I expect to go on working even if I only work at taking things easier. When I started my business, we didn't have all these modern technologies. I was well in my career before so many wonderful new ideas came into being.*
- *I welcome this opportunity to make a presentation to you...*
- *I welcome this opportunity to speak to you today...*
- *I will take a deep breath and begin speaking on the importance of breathing...*
- *I wish I had millions to give away, but my words will have to suffice...*
- *I wish the buck stopped here. I could use a few...*
- *I wonder:*
  - *how many of you know about...*
  - *how many of you know...*
  - *how many of you remember...*
  - *if it was mere coincidence that...*
  - *what would happen today if we toast the guest of honor right now...*
  - *what you are already thinking about...*
- *I would:*
  - *like to discuss with you how your business has changed for the better...*

A27

•*like to open my presentation today by saluting...*
•*like to present to you today...*
•*like to quote Victor Hugo to say: "There is one thing stronger than all the armies in the world, and that is an idea whose time has come."*
•*like to take you on a comfortable ride to success, not a bumpy ride...*
•*like you to take a look at our opportunity....*
•*like to play the game of "How come" with you right now...*
•*like to play the game of "What if" with you right now...*
•*like to start the year off asking each of you a question, "Are we really that different deep down inside where it counts?"*
•*I'll have you know...*
•*If:*
 •*fate comes knocking on your door, are you ready to rise to the occasion without expectations of fame and glory?*
 •*I could make a video of your future, you would quit worrying...*
 •*ignorance is bliss, why aren't more people happy?*
 •*one individual has the courage to cut a path, others can surely follow...*
 •*Wal-Mart is lowering prices every day, how come nothing in the store is free yet?*
 •*we look back at some of the steps we did early in our business...*
 •*we'd stop trying to be happy we could have a pretty good time...*
 •*you aim high, you will stand a little bit taller...*
 •*you believe in something passionately, you should be prepared to do something for that belief...*
 •*you care enough you can do enough...*
 •*you make the investment to join right now, you'll save.....*
 •*you think thirteen is an unlucky number, then think again...I am here today to let you know that thirteen is anything but unlucky...*
 •*you think times have changed...*
 •*you want to go down in history as the first to achieve something, keep a detailed record of how you did it...*
•*Imagine all the people, living life in peace...*
•*Imagine what it would be like to spend 10 days at a Spa in Evian...*
•*Imagine what you could do if you could see the future in one place...*
•*In a period of 4 weeks...*
•*In any conflict, is there a winner?*
•*In some parts of this country...*
•*Inspiration comes from many sources and blooms in many forms. It is up to each of us to derive what we can from those moments and share them with others...*
•*Inspired by what we are accomplishing, I hope to begin a new forum for discussion and plan on a bountiful outcome...*
•*Isn't it:*
 •*amazing what a little encouragement can do?*
 •*ironic that...*
 •*refreshing to know that...*

A28

•right that...
•true that...
•It has been said that every deed is just another stepping-stone on an eternal road...
•It is a privilege to be free to speak your mind, to share your opinions, today you will be safe with me, no one will make you feel ignorant or stupid...
•It is:
  •a reminder that...
  •a twist of fate that...
  •in the spirit of...
  •interesting to note...
  •It is said that the pen is mightier than the sword. I have put in writing some of my beliefs for you today...
  •sometimes both comforting and shocking to recall what some wise people have said and done in the past...
  •the ideal time to step forward...
  •true, it is more blessed to give than to receive. Today you must be richly blessed for you have given so much to me. I appreciate you all so very very much...
  •worth noting...
•It isn't always what is done, but who does it that counts...
•It isn't often that a new product is exciting enough to deserve this much attention. But our products are exciting and here are the articles!"
•It may not seem very fast by our standards, however...
•It might come as a surprise to you...
•It might interest you to know...
•It takes commitment and persistence to gain the title of champion in any field of endeavor. And it takes real focus to keep one's title from being grabbed by strong competitors. Champions don't get to be champions easily, it's no accident that we have a true champion today in this room...
•It was amazing to view Victoria Falls in Zimbabwe...
•It was considered to be...
•It was more than one year after...
•It would be flattering today as your presenter if you were to agree with everything I said. But it would be far more rewarding if what I said started you thinking about why you agree or disagree with me...
•It's a good time to raise the question on how much we can contribute to someone's success and what we can expect in return...
•It's:
  •a relief to know that...
  •amazing to think that I have been in 11 countries in one year...
  •amazing what you can do when you set your sights on achieving your goals...
  •been a long time since...
  •been said that if March comes in like a lion, it will go out like a lamb. With that in mind I would like to roar about some great news that will definitely get you excited while we are waiting for spring to arrive!

•extremely important to take the initiative in a situation, rather than passively waiting to react to whatever comes along...

•hard to stop the winds of change. I have been through a lot of changes and here today to give you some refreshing words...

•not uncommon...

•the set of the sail that will get and keep you going, not the wind...

•time to exceed your expectations of yourself...

•time to set your goals high. Who knows what new heights together we could reach...

•true that pictures say a thousand words...

•up to each of us to provide our children and grandchildren with supportive standards to become fine young citizens...

•up to you to take copious notes today and listen carefully to what I have to share with you...

•Jambo! (Swahili for hello)

•Jetting to Bahati, which is a private game camp, in a private plane was amazing...

•Just because you have done something once doesn't mean you have to do it again. Some things only need to be experienced once for lessons to be learned, allowing us to move on to greater things...

•Just one idea can change your life forever...

•Just think back to this same time last year...

•Laughter is the shortest distance between two people...

•Lead me, follow me or get out of my way, I am going to the top...

•Less than a year ago...

•Let me:
  •give you a couple of examples...
  •go back to the present and tell you about our future...
  •say in all languages I am happy to be here...
  •tell you about the piñata party we had in Cancun...
  •tell you about...
  •tell you what we all stand to achieve...

•Let's:
  •look at this opportunity and see if there is a match for you to get happily involved...
  •contemplate...
  •discuss today how we can succeed despite the alleged odds...
  •give a great champion well-deserved recognition...
  •look today at how each of us can rise to greater personal heights...
  •pause for a moment to remember...
  •remember that today's superhighway is tomorrow's Route 66...
  •consider how we can make this our best year ever...
  •discuss how we can explode our business...
  •do it...
  •face it...

A30

•start a sensible trend...
•talk about giving our spouses unconditional love...
•talk about how goals generate the vision to keep you going...
•talk about how we can bring out the good in anyone...
•talk about the fact that it is proper to return phone calls...
•talk about the fact that no individual or group should control the thoughts of
 another...
•talk today not only about what seems to be happening, but why...
•welcome the new season...
•work together to find the best fit for all of us...
•Life:
 •is a series of struggles and today I want you to know that we have some great
  news to help you through this first month...
 •is an inspirational experience that can become art in itself if we only stop for a
  moment to appreciate it...
 •is discovery and exploration...
 •is not always what we make it; sometimes life is what other people make
  or us. With that in mind, let's take a look at what is going on in our lives...
 •is what you make of it...kind of like Play-Doh...
•Light is not simply a source of illumination. It can burn. If you shine a light that's
 very bright, it can have a blinding effect...
•Living on Earth is expensive, but it does include a free trip around the sun...
•Look what I've discovered...
•Looking back on what we have accomplished, I have come to the conclusion that it's a
 good day to be here talking with you...
•Make a career of selling your opinions...
•Make every day January 1...
•Make your own Disneyland...
•Making connections isn't always a simple task...
•Many consider...
•Many of you might be faced with some major decisions this month. Few people ever
 have the kind of choices that we have...
•Many of you might not know this...
•Many people are convinced that...
•Many people think that their journey has come to a successful end, but ours is just
 beginning. I'd like to take you on a journey across some uncharted territory...
•Many times an ambitious idea grows larger than you can ever imagine...
•Many years ago...
•Memories of former glory don't pay today's bills or solve today's challenges...
•Mind can win over matter despite the odds...
•Moral support can be found in many places reaching out to us and bringing us together...
•More than 20 years ago I started my career...today I am here to share with you a
 tested road map to success...

•Most:
  •changes happen one small step after another...
  •conflict is not between good and evil, right and wrong, but between two opposing sides who are convinced that they are in the right. The big challenge arises from those who don't believe there is a right or wrong, who don't take a stand. I think it's time we talk about ethics...
  •of us go to our grave with our music still inside us...
  •of us have an old photo of ancestors...
  •traditional beliefs at one time were regarded to be radical concepts. I am here to remind you of this simple truth and hope you find that what I have to say is somewhat radical...
•My commitment is to see if there might be something here that would significantly contribute to your life...
•My intention is to explore the possibilities with you to see if there might be some mutual interest in our working together or benefit that could come from...
•My special reason for calling you today is that we are offering a special this month that enables you to...
•My subject today is simply this, "In times like ours what is there that we can call our own and nobody else's? And is this what we truly desire?
•Nature cannot be replaced, but thankfully it can sometimes be restored...
•Necessity is the mother of further invention...
•Never ever ever ever quit...it's always too soon to quit...
•New limitless boundaries are all around us. I would like to discuss some of them with you here today...
•New Years Day gives us an opportunity to resolve to do things differently and to have an incredible new year. It's in the spirit of abundance and prosperity that I would like to speak to you today...
•No man is an Island...
•No matter how large or strong a barricade is, you cannot stop people from choosing their own destinies...
•No matter how much time it takes, all great achievers share two things in common; self- confidence and persistence, let's talk about those today...
•No matter what someone does against another, it's always a great idea to turn the other cheek...
•No need to push the panic button...
•No one can predetermine every situation. Despite all of our preparations, or lack of them, fate often plays a critical role in the final outcome of any situation...
•No person can be denied the right to reach the heights if you are determined to be the best...
•None of us knows what lies ahead. We must take action as soon as we can. Tomorrow, after all, depends on what we do today...
•Not too long ago...
•Not too many of you know what's possible to achieve, today I am here to share this with you...

A32

•*Now I know some of you in this audience who sincerely hope you have a great year...here are some ideas of how to get started...*

•*Now is the time when...*

•*Now today happens to be...*

•*Of all the days of the year, none has a more glorious starting point for a speaker than today, Independence Day...*

•*On the average, about 20 million people have their birthdays on any given day of the year. If they all decided to celebrate together, they'd have to have a birthday country...*

•*One might think...*

•*One misplaced word can have fatal results...*

•*One of our organizations best...*

•*One of the great pleasures of our life is ...*

•*One of the most wonderful parts of being here today is for me to look around the room and see the wonderful friends we have and the way our work has grown and prospered so many people. You have made me proud...*

•*One way people attempt to resolve a common cause is by gathering regularly to discuss their opinions...today I am so happy that we have once again gathered...*

•*On the other hand, do you think?*

•*Opinions are triggered by events...*

•*Opportunities are abundant for those who focus on being there when opportunity comes knocking. Today, I am knocking on your door...please be willing to listen to what I want to share with you...*

•*Opportunity does knock more than once for some people...*

•*Our business brings out competitiveness, tension and incredible rewards for those going for greatness...today I believe this is a worth while theme to explore at this time and in this place...*

•*Our lives are closely intertwined in both destiny and friendship...*

•*Our organization's greatest achievements...*

•*Our products are made for people like yourself who want better than ordinary results...*

•*Our products enable you to...*

•*Over the course of the last several months...*

•*Ownership is a serious responsibility...*

•*Paris is an incredible city to visit...*

•*People are remembered for the strangest reason. Once set loose, a misconception can be more powerful and widespread than the truth. Today I am here to set a few facts straight...*

•*People believe what they want to believe...*

•*People who live in glass houses shouldn't throw stones...*

•*Perhaps in the future some speakers will be talking to groups sitting in front of their individual home computers...I wouldn't trade anything for all the great speeches that I have attended. I invested in my mind and needed to see the person speaking up close and personal...today I am so glad you are here...*

•*Perhaps it will comfort you to know...*
•*Perhaps you saw the amazing results of how your skin reacted so great to this product?*
•*Picture wagon trains streaming across endless prairies...*
•*Picture yourself jetting off for Monte Carlo...*
•*Ponder what I have to say to you...*
•*Precedents are made to be challenged...*
•*Probably the reason why people become champions in our industry is...*
•*Progress is the development of options...*
•*Public service normally runs in the family; if we want our children to carry this legacy, we must first be fine examples...*
•*Riding up the gondola in Aspen...*
•*Send your mother flowers on your birthday...*
•*Shakespeare's writings are excellent training grounds for the realities of life, including the realities of life today...*
•*Should we trust tradition or science? Maybe both and here is why...*
•*Small beginnings can grow into more productive endings, which is what I will be presenting to you today...*
•*Some:*
  •*champions rest on their laurels while others take action...*
  •*mistakes are too much fun to only make once...*
  •*of you are today only to listen to me because...*
  •*of you undoubtedly are getting ready to...*
  •*people are not affected by criticism. To make a mark in this world, you must forge ahead despite bad reviews from shortsighted critics...*
  •*people get hungry when they smell dinner cooking...*
  •*Some people leave their mark on the world...*
  •*people's heart beats faster when the flag goes marching by...*
  •*products have a particular smell that triggers a craving or an appreciation...*
  •*things are just mysteries...*
  •*traditions never lose their charm...*
•*Somebody once said...*
•*Sometimes:*
  •*I wonder...*
  •*it is hard to imagine how one single action can inspire the world to follow suit...*
  •*our heroes and sheros have feet of clay and sometimes we fail to give them their well deserved recognition, today we are going to take the time to do just that...*
  •*success is achieved because the person is in just the right position at the right time...*
  •*the best source of inspiration for younger people is found right at home...*
  •*when you search hard for something you don't even realize that you have reached your goal when you are there...*
  •*a person's place in history is secured by accident, not only by design...*

A34

•being the only one to accomplish a particular goal means being the last of your kind for a long time, and not everyone has the desire or inclination to be unique. Hard work and commitment are the deciding factors that single out certain people for a particular status in our company's standard bearers. Today I would like to call your attention to someone in our company who is unique, who will remain unequaled for years to come...

•Somewhere in my presentation I will share with you my trials...

•Speak for yourself is the topic today...

•Speeches, like books cover the entire spectrum from great to bad. Today, I hope my remarks will fall into the great section...

•Spending time at Entebanie at the Wildside and Ravineside in South Africa was one of the best memories of my life...

•Springing forward has to be the theme of the first month of the year. Let's take advantage of this first month of a new year by making a fresh start. Here is what we can do...

•Stack your successes upon your successes...

•Stand on the winners platform today...

•Take the time to listen to what I have to say, ponder it, if it works for you fine, use it, if it does not work for you, throw it away...

•Taking the first step in creating your business sometimes is worrisome. But taking the next step and the next step without knowing the outcome requires the fortitude to go forward. I am here today to help you take your first steps...

•Tell me a little bit about yourself...

•Tell me more...

•Thank you for coming today, I know you invested your money and time to be here to spend a day with me and I am trading a day of my life to spend it with you as well...I take that seriously...

•The battle for a better life is what I will be speaking about today...

•The best ingredient for a happy life today is the hope of tomorrow...

•The culture of the Masai people...

•The day was...

•The easiest way to...

•The first product I would like to show you is the modern ...

•The first product I would like to show you is the up to date, state of the art...

•The first time I drove my new Porsche...

•The future is bright...expect abundance and prosperity, they are coming your way...

•The future of the world...

•The gift of words is a great gift indeed. Today, let's use our words to sort out how we can increase our bottom line...

•The greatest medicine in the world, for old and young alike, is the knowledge that someone cares...

•The greatest speeches are those coming from the heart...

•*The information is so important you won't want to miss it...*
•*The leaders in our organization are generally remembered for their triumphs. Today I am here to recognize a special individual...*
•*The lesson to be learned today is...*
•*The message you have asked me to speak on is so important. The most cherished thing in the world is the esteem of one's friends and loved ones. Today you have made me very wealthy in spirit and I thank you from the bottom of my heart...*
•*The month of May comes from the word Maia, the goddess of spring and fertility...*
•*The more you give the more you get...*
•*The one unchanging rule of life is change...*
•*The only thing we can do in sight of the unforeseen and unforeseeable is to have patience and never give up hope...*
•*The past is a reflective reference for the future...*
•*The past is not a stained mirror of what could have been...*
•*The past may have been the good or bad old days. One thing we know, we can't go back in time. We cannot live in the past, but we can learn from it...*
•*The person who reaches for the heights doesn't always get there..*
•*The point I'd like to make...*
•*The show must go on...*
•*The sky is not falling...I can assure you of that...in fact...*
•*The spirit of adventure is in our company...*
•*The struggle to be heard ...*
•*The way to be a bore is to say everything...so today I am only going to share some of my experiences with you...*
•*The wisest leaders know not only when to stand firm, but also when to move with the times. Take our own times as an example...*
•*The year was...*
•*There are any number of amazing events which we file away in our memories...*
•*There are present day heroes like....*
•*There is:*
  •*a four-letter word that has inspired more hope in making and opened more new lands than any other...Gold...*
  •*a lesson ...*
  •*a lesson that goes far beyond what we are doing today...*
  •*a story about...*
  •*an old saying that if a dog bites a man, it's not news. But if a man bites a dog, that's news.*
  •*excitement in the air...*
  •*hope for all of us. I am such an optimistic person that I have to share this with you...*
  •*living proof in our audience today that individual achievement can break barriers...*

A36

•more to life than just living in the here and now. Visions of the future inspire us to live more fully and to go for greatness. Today's visions are often tomorrow's realities, so what do we envision for this year?
•no patent on miracles...
•no place like being at the top...
•nothing like the feeling of jetting off for Hawaii or the Bahamas...
•no way for me not to be melodramatic about this...
•There was a famous...
•There was a very festive day when...
•There's no way for you to tell from the way I come out how long my speech is going to be. I assure you I will only be speaking for 20 minutes...
•Things are popping in our business...
•Think what it would be like if you would be willing to...
•Think with me...
•This fall:
  •we are opening up in this part of the country or world. Of course, you are wondering what this means to you...
  •our generation has a rendezvous with destiny...
  •is a perfect day to talk about...
  •is a time for our hearts to be light, and today I will be speaking of pleasant, happy and fun things...
  •is a very big day...
  •is going to change your life...
  •is not the time to give up trying...
  •is the beginning...
  •is the first time I have had an interpreter to help me spread my wisdom to your language...
  •means two things for you...
  •opportunity is filled with the following benefits for you....
•Thorough analysis of a challenge can lead to surprising solutions and today after much consideration I am happy to announce that we have a solution for our present situation...
•Those who are unwilling to accept the status quo often change it more than they intended.
•Those who expect to reap the blessings of having a great lifestyle, must undergo the fatigue of getting there...
•Today:
  •commemorates...
  •I am going to explain the good and the bad on forming a corporation for your business. Doing it right could double your tax savings; doing it the wrong way could cost you a small fortune...
  •I am here to ask you how we can create an organized team of our own?
  •I am here to ask you what do you want out of this new year?
  •I am here to introduce you to a sparkling example of...
  •I am here to remind you of what you can achieve by taking massive action...

•*I am here to voice a few concepts with you…*
•*I am saluting the men and women whose virtues and talents epitomize what we have been striving to accomplish…*
•*I am speaking in confidence and have a word to the wise…*
•*I have a question for you…should we practice what we preach, or preach what we practice…*
•*I here to speak to you on education. We have known for years that there is always more to be learned, more to see, and more to be explored. I want you to feed your mind and here is what I suggest…*
•*I hope to talk my way into your hearts…*
•*I just want to focus on love-love your team, love your family, love your nation, love our industry, love your products, love your neighbors, love your spouse, love your parents, love your children, love each other…*
•*I plan to make a few big points and take a position from which I will not shift…*
•*I propose…*
•*I urge you to look at the marvelous opportunity…*
•*I want to share our success with you…*
•*I want you to direct your goals to greater heights than you ever thought possible, then work like you are a bird dog until you reach those goals…*
•*I want you to know that maybe we need to look at the bigger picture…*
•*I wish to salute…*
•*I would like to focus on courage, dedication and determination…*
•*I would like to honor the courageous people who turned a deaf ear to those who said it couldn't be done…*
•*I would like to share with you the abundance of information I've found on this rich resource…*
•*I would like to speak to you about relationships…*
•*is a day of inspiration and renewal for all of us; a day that reminds us that our organization is as great as it's people…*
•*is a day to feast and celebrate…*
•*is a day to reach great heights…*
•*is a very significant anniversary for…*
•*is quite a day to…*
•*it is timely to talk about the importance of your name…*
•*let's clear the air before situations begin to smolder…*
•*let's give thanks for the abundance that surrounds us…*
•*let's mutually pledge to each other that we are going to honor each other and listen to each other…*
•*marks a few meetings of great minds…*
•*my purpose is to inspire all of you to wish and to dream…*
•*we are entering a drastic transitional phase…*
•*we are going to compare…*

A38

•we are meeting on an historic anniversary...
•we celebrate the unalienable right to the pursuit of happiness...
•we salute a landmark milestone...
•we should be mindful...
•you can decide to agree or disagree with my opinions...
•I suggest that we consider...
•I'd like to open up new frontiers...
•let us dedicate ourselves to this goal both individually and as a team...
•let's celebrate a noble attempt and a great start...
•let's look at the results of...
•you will discover some nice surprises I have arranged for you...
• topic is on building the fire of desire...
•Tomorrow is the heir of yesterday and today is the legacy we leave for tomorrow...
•Tomorrow we will look toward the future...
•Traditions can be replaced by new traditions...
•Tune in, turn on ...
•Utter the "you" twenty times where you once utter the "I"...
•Wait until you hear what I have to tell you...
•Wake up and dream...
•Watching my son break three Colorado State football records made me think of...
•We:
  •always aspire to be the best...
  •are a very independent group of people. With a common passion, we can forget
   our differences and unite to create a powerful future...
  •are bound to do good to all and evil to none...
  •are gathered here today...
  •are generally familiar with...
  •are in the midst of a technology explosion...
  •are more alike than we are different...
  •are not here today as spectators but to look to see if we can discover more
   ideas to help us help ourselves...
  •are on the cutting edge...
  •are part of a royal community...
  •can influence a lot of people. Here is what I have in mind...
  •can recall the past but we cannot relive it. What we can do today is to plan for a
   better future. I have some thoughts and ideas on some ways that we can do that...
  •cannot anticipate the unexpected events that lie ahead of us. The future is a
   mystery...
  •cannot deny the power of well-written ideas, nor the empowerment great books
   inspire for those going for greatness...
  •could learn a lot from crayons: some are sharp, some are pretty, some are dull,
   some have weird colors...

•*face mysteries today, why certain people behave as they do, why certain leaders choose to make a mountain of some particular molehill. Asking why reveals the extent of this never-ending puzzle...*
•*first learned about...*
•*got ourselves through another year...*
•*have a monumental opportunity. What is it? I am here to report some exciting facts that I think you might like to know...*
•*have been in business...*
•*have learned how to...*
•*have plenty of opportunities to dig right in...*
•*have the right to choose our destiny and I propose that we do that starting today...*
•*live in a world that is quite different from what it was ten years ago...*
•*must always try to look beyond today...*
•*must apply our thoughts and our efforts today so that we can have a broader frame work...*
•*must look forward and place the past where it belongs...*
•*need more people with courage now...*
•*need to pause and remember to thank the Native Americans for the blessings these people left the Americans...*
•*need to take the time and appreciate our heritage and the bond of mankind...*
•*often find ourselves wondering...*
•*pride ourselves on providing great leadership...*
•*progress; we invest; we change. We need to find alternative ways to do our business and find options that will make our outcomes better for everyone in our organization...*
•*should all reflect right now on an important event that just has happened in our organization...*
•*should never take education for granted. We should never deny any individual the right to learn...*
•*should pay attention to crayons. They all have different names, and all are different colors ... but they all have to learn to live in the same box...*
•*sometimes forget...*
•*What:*
•*does today's presentation mean to you? Well, it means that if you get happily involved now that you will...*
•*do you mean?*
•*has just happened has inspired me to reach out to all of you today...*
•*I am about to say will make some of your dreams and wishes come true...*
•*I am about to tell you comes from the heart...*
•*I stopped in to tell you about is...*
•*if we were all gifted with the ability to...*
•*kind of Spring can we look forward to...*
•*professional skills do you need to learn to contribute to success?*

A40

•sort of a lifestyle do you wish to create for yourself?
•When:
•I think of...
•I was jetting to Nairobi with my daughter to meet her sister...
•I was preparing my remarks for this occasion, I found something both interesting
  to share with you This is one of those days...
•King Henry VIII spoke, people listened...
•my grandfather, Harry Penniman, Jr. first saw me he said my song would be,
  "Don't fence me in"...
•our business first started...
•the announcer of the University of Alabama football games announces 'Ladies
  and Gentlemen, this is AlaBAMA football, I feel...
•the jet takes off...
•the Rovos Rail takes off from Johannesburg to go across the lower Karoo...
•the University of Texas band plays "The Eyes of Texas"...
•we consider our achievements...
•we get discouraged and need to be inspired, we should watch a spider. A spider
  spins and spins and spins until it finally finishes it's web...
•we were in St. Tropez...
•you autograph the paperwork, you get 10% for joining before the 15th...
•you first go into a business that you have little or no knowledge of without
  assistance or means of understanding it takes more than fortitude. It takes becoming
  a student and listening and seeking out those who have succeeded before you...
•you join our team, you will not be orphaned by your circumstances anymore...
•you look up into the stars at night, its probably hard to pick out the planets
  among the stars. Let's consider how we can reach farther than our eyes can see...
•While I am not expecting to set any records today, I want to join the others who have
  gone before me and "go boldly where no woman has gone before."
•While most of us think...
•While my remarks today might raise a few eyebrows, I hope that rather than looking
  for what you don't agree with, that you will look past me to the message I bring...
•Who ever said it can't be done?
•Who would succeed in the world should be wise in the use of pronouns...
•Why adversity is essential for rising beyond your limitations...
•Why disappointment becomes the cradle of ambition...
•Why integrity is the only foundation that can support success...
•Why you don't have a chance to win without motivation...
•Will you join me in wishing a happy birthday and happy anniversary to...
•With so many events far behind us, we should be well prepared for the events ahead...
•With the excitement in this room today, we can double or triple our business...
•With your permission, I would like to begin by quoting...

- *Working together is not always easy. It's always better to communicate than to remain silent. As an audience, however, you listen to a speaker and make your own conclusions. You do, of course, retain the option of applauding today if you would like...*
- *Would increasing your child's test scores be something that would interest you?*
- *Would you like to feel like you are 16 years old again...but with better judgment...*
- *Would you like to give yourself a bonus?*
- *Wouldn't it be boring if we all thought the same way...*
- *Wouldn't it be fun to travel through the future thinking together?*
- *Wouldn't it be wonderful if all of us could maintain the spirit of a child like wonder every moment of life?*
- *Yesterday's heroism may have made things easier today, but keep your eyes on the future...*
- *You:*
- *all know how difficult it is...*
- *are going to reap the benefits when we expand later this year...*
- *are in for a treat, today I am going to give you complete, simple, step-by-step information on how to file your tax forms yourself and save an immediate $1000 by not paying an accountant to "shuffle papers" around on his desk.*
- *are liable for the future of that which you own...*
- *can take a situation and create your own borderlines. This is easy when you have a complicated subject or new subject. Today I am going to address myself to what I believe is the real issue, the core of the matter...*
- *can't believe everything you see, but I assure you, you can believe everything you hear from me today...*
- *can't keep a good idea down...*
- *cannot stop ideas, even bad ones. You can only stop bad or hurtful ideas by spreading better concepts...*
- *don't have to chase your destiny, it will find you...*
- *don't have to put your name on your work to be proud of your creations. Just knowing you've done your best is sometimes its own reward...*
- *have the freedom to voice your opinions...*
- *may be only one person in the world, but you may also be the world to one person...*
- *may not know it but...*
- *might think that...*
- *must think constructively to create your success...*
- *never know when opportunity will come knocking on your door and today's meeting is a prime example. Opportunity knocks on everyone's door at one time or another. The only preparation any of us needs to make is to keep our eyes and hearts open...*
- *You're the top...*

A42

Words to Use

Words are like sunbeams, once they are spoken, they are on their merry way. Words on the loose-how they can damage, chew up, tear apart, rip a reputation, inspire, lift up, elevate! You cannot erase words once they are spoken. They leap at people, penetrate their hearts, pierce their brain, leave a wonderful thought or buy a bad one. Use three little words that make people feel important: *"I need you!"*

Resolve right now to use words to build up people, to make them feel better, to make them feel important, successful and happy. Tell them how well they look and they will actually feel better. Speak about cheerful things and you will see them cheer up. Don't be a prophet of doom and gloom, always talking about depression, hard times, sickness and trouble. Don't tell them how bad you feel. Talk greatness and watch people flock around you!

"It is with a word as with an arrow - once let it loose, and it does not return."

Here are the five best words in the world to make people like you:
"I am proud of you."

Here are the four best words to gain willing information from others:
"What is your opinion?"

The twelve words to keep them talking:
"...and then what did you do?"
"...and then what did you say?"

As has been stated in this guide saying the right thing is most important. So in this section we provide you with the correct words and phrases to use as well as the words and phrases to avoid.

Powerful Words

Abbreviated
Absolute
Abundance
Abundant
Accommodating
Accomplished
Accountable
Accurate
Action
Adaptable
Adjustable
Admirable
Admired
Adventurous
Affectionate
Affirmative
Affluent
After
Aggressive
Agile
Agree
Agreeable
Agreement
Alike
Ambitious
Amiable
Ample
Analyze
Apathetic
Apparent
Appealing
Appreciated
Approachable
Aromatic
Artistic

Assorted
Attend
Attentive
Attractive
Autograph
Automatic
Awesome
Banquet
Bargain
Basic
Beautiful
Becoming
Belief
Believable
Belong
Belonging
Beloved
Benefits
Big
Billionaire
Blessed
Bold
Bountiful
Brave
Brief
Bright
Brilliant
Build
Building
Busy
Calm
Care
Careful
Caring
Cartier

Casual
Catching
Ceaseless
Celebrate
Celebrated
Celebration
Ceremony
Certain
Certainty
Challenge
Champion
Change
Changeable
Charitable
Charming
Cheerful
Cherished
Children
Choice
Choose
Chosen
Citizen
Classic
Clean
Clear
Clever
Colorful
Colossal
Comfortable
Commanding
Commendable
Commission
Commitment
Committed
Common Sense

Compelling
Compensation
Compete
Competitive
Complimentary
Concerned
Concise
Condensed
Confident
Congenial
Congratulations
Conscientious
Consider
Considerate
Consistent
Constant
Contact
Contagious
Continuous
Contribution
Convenient
Convincing
Cool
Correct
Courage
Courageous
Courteous
Coveted
Credit
Crucial
Cultured
Curious

A44

Daring	Emulate	Financial	Happy
Dashing	Enchanting	Finished	Harmless
Dear	Encouraging	Fire Up!	Harmonious
Debate	Endless	Firm	Healing
Decadent	Endorse	First	Healthy
Decisive	Enduring	Fit	Heavenly
Dedicated	Energetic	Flag	Help
Definite	Engaging	Flattering	Helpful
Deliberate	Enhance	Flawless	Hero
Delicate	Enlighten	Flexible	High
Dependable	Enthusiasm	Flow	High priority
Deserving	Environment	Follow	Honest
Desirable	Essential	Fond	Honor
Destination	Established	Forgivable	Hope
Destiny	Eternal	Formal	Hopeful
Develop	Euphoric	Formula	Hopes
Devine	Exalted	Fortunate	Hospitable
Devoted	Excellence	Fragrant	Hot
Diamond	Excite	Free	Huge
Direct	Excited	Freedom	Humane
Distinguished	Excitement	Frequent	Hungry
Dream	Exciting	Fresh	Idealistic
Dreams	Exclusive	Friend	Ideas
Duplicatable	Exemplary	Friendly	Immaculate
Duty	Experienced	Fruitful	Immediate
Dynamo	Explosive	Full	Impartial
Eager	Expressive	Fun	Important
Eagle	Extravagant	Future	Impressive
Earn	Extreme	Generous	Improved
Earning	Fabulous	Genius	Incentive
Easy	Fair	Genuine	Independent
Economical	Faithful	Gift	Inevitable
Educated	Familiar	Gifted	Infinite
Education	Family	Glad	Influence
Effective	Famous	Glitz	Influential
Efficient	Fanatical	Glorious	Informal
Elated	Fancy	Glory	Initiaitve
Electrifying	Fantastic	Gold	Initial Investment
Elegant	Fantasy	Gracious	Innovative
Elementary	Fascinating	Gradual	Inquisitive
Elevate	Fashionable	Grand	Insistent
Elevated	Fast	Grateful	Inspiration
Eligible	Favorable	Greatest	Inspired
Eloquent	Ferrari	Greatness	Instantaneous
Email	Fertile	Gripping	Instructive
Emerald	Fierce	Growth	Intellectual
Emphatic	Final	Handsome	
Empower	Finally	Happily Involve	

Industrious	Mastery	Patient	Provide
Intricate	Mature	Peace	Pure
Intuitive	Mega	Peaceful	Pursue
Inventive	Memorable	Perfect	Qualified
Invest	Mercedes	Perfection	Quick
Investment	Meticulous	Performance	Radiate
Inviting	Mighty	Permanent	Radical
Involved	Milestone	Perpetual	Rare
Join	Millionaire	Persistent	Read
Keen	Minimal	Picture	Ready
Keep	Miraculous	Pioneer	Real
Kind	Moblize	Placid	Realize
Knowledgeable	Modern	Plain	Reasonable
Lambergini	Monte Blanc	Planned	Recognize
Landmark	Moral	Playful	Recruit
Large	Motivation	Pleasant	Refined
Lasting	Mountains	Polished	Regular
Latest	Movement	Polite	Relationships
Lavish	Mover and shaker	Popular	Relaxed
Lead	Moving	Porsche	Relevant
Leader	Moving on	Positive	Reliable
Leadership	Moving up	Power	Remember
Learn	Natural	Powerful	Repeat
Legacy	Neat	Precious	Repitition
Legend	Necessary	Precise	Replaceable
Leisurely	Neighborly	Predetermined	Representative
Lets	New	Predictable	Require
Liberty	Nice	Premise	Resolute
Light	Noble	Prepared	Respond
Listen	Noticeable	Preserve	Responsible
Live a little	Numerous	Pretty	Rest
Local	Obvious	Pride	Review
Logical	Offer	Principle	Rich
Lovable	Official	Principled	Right
Lovely	Olympics	Pristine	Rights
Loyal	Open	Privileged	Rise
Lucky	Opportunity	Productive	Romance
Magnificent	Optimistic	Profitable	Run
Magnified	Organized	Promise	Safe
Majestic	Original	Promote	Secure
Mansion	Paperwork	Promotion	Selective
Marathon	Paradigm	Prosperity	Sell
Masarti	Passion	Prosperous	Sensitive
Master	Passionate	Protect	Sentimental
Masterpiece	Patience	Proud	Serious

A46

Serve	Sponsor	Tolerant	Versatile
Service	Spontaneous	Top	VIP
Sexy	Sports	Top of the list	Virtuous
Share	Spotless	Total Investment	Vision
Sharp	Standing room only	Touch	Visionary
Shero	Steadfast	Training	Vital
Shine	Sterling	Tranquility	Vivid
Shining	Straight	Travel	Warm
Shopping	Strength	Triumph	Waterford
Significant	Strong	True	We
Simple	Success	True Leader	Wealthy
Skiing	Successful	Truly	Welcome
Slim	Sure	Trust	Well Done
Smile	Sweet	Trustworthy	Wide
Smoldering	Sweetness	Truth	Winning
Smooth	System	Ultimate	Wisdom
Soft	Talent	Uncompromising	Wise
Solemn	Talented	Understandable	Witty
Solid	Tasteful	Unique	Yacht
	Tenacity	Universal	You
Soothing	Thankful	Urgent	Young
Sought after	Thick	Us	Youthful
Sound	Think	Useful	Zealous
Special	Thinking	Varied	
Spectacular	Timely	Vast	
Speed	Together	Vastness	

"May the road rise to meet you.
May the wind be always at your back,
the sun shine warm upon your face,
the rain fall soft upon your fields
and until we meet again may God
hold you in the hollow of his hand."

An Irish Blessing

Watch Your Words!
Actual Newspaper Headlines

- Air Head Fired.
- Arson Suspect is Held in Massachusetts Fire.
- British Left Waffles on Falkland Islands.
- Cold Wave Linked to Temperatures.
- Deer Kill 17,000.
- Drunk Gets Nine Months in Violin Case.
- Drunken Drivers paid $1,000 in '84.
- Enfields Couple Slain. Police Suspect Homicide.
- Enraged Cow Injures Farmer With Ax.
- Eye Drops Off Shelf.
- Farmer Bill Dies in House.
- Hospitals are sued by Seven Foot Doctors.
- If Strike Isn't Settled Quickly, It May Last a While.
- Iraqi Head Seeks Arms.
- Juvenile Court to Try Shooting Defendant.
- Kids Make Nutritious Snacks.
- Killer Sentenced to Die for Second Time in Ten Years.
- Man Struck by Lightening Faces Battery Charge.
- Miners Refuse to Work After Death.
- NJ Judge to Rule on Nude Beach.
- Old School Pillars are Replaced by Alumni.
- Panda Mating Fails; Veterinarian Takes Over.
- Plane Too Close to Ground, Crash Probe Told.
- Police Begin Campaign to Run Down Jaywalkers.
- Prostitutes Appeal to Pope.
- Reagan Wins on Budget, But More Lies Ahead.
- Red Tape Holds Up New Bridge.
- Safety Experts Say School Bus Passengers Should Be Belted.
- Shot Off Woman's Leg Helps Nicklaus to 66.
- Something Went Wrong in Jet Crash, Expert Says.
- Squad Helps Dog Bite Victim.
- Stolen Painting Found By Tree.
- Stud Tires Out.
- Survivor of Siamese Twins Joins Parents.
- Two Sister Reunited after 18 Years in Checkout Stand.
- Two Soviet Ships Collide, One Dies.

Phrases to Use

All roads lead to you...
Always allowing...
Always bear in mind that...
Always stood for...
America's Sweetheart...
And in the end...
Anything is possible...
At the age of...
Attitude of gratitude...
Awaken the passion...
Be brave...
Because of you...
Because you were...
Believe in hopes, dreams...
Bold enough...
Centuries before...
Class Act...
Come with me...
Dedicated to...
Divided we fall...
Do not give up or give in...
Don't be afraid...
Enriched our lives...
Everybody buys tickets...
Everybody is famous...
Extraordinary...
Faces we love...
Fairy Tale...
For the next few minutes, let us turn...
For those of us here tonight...
Fountain of ideas...
Fresh ideas...
Future of tomorrow...
Global Experience...
Good will...
Gratitude Attitude...
Great directions...
Great moments...
Great to be alive...

Learned his craft...
Measure goodness by...
Most influential...
New talent...
Not since...
Once in a lifetime honor...
One of the greatest...
One of the greatest geniuses...
Please welcome...
Privilege to know you...
Put the human into the hero...
Recognizing outstanding achievement...
Remarkable career...
Sense of purpose...
Serious activity...
Share this hour...
Shock waves through the industry...
Simply the best...
Soldier through tough times...
Sometimes the best way...
Special privilege to present to you...
Special recognition...
Stunned the world...
Sweet smell of success...
Talk about beginners luck...
Thank my Mother in heaven...
Thank you...
Thank you for sharing your passion...
The legend lives...
There are no better relationships...
This generation...
This glorious night...
This has to be a dream...it's not real...
This is the first award given to...
This is the first time...
Thrill to work with...
Thrilled to be honored...
To all the wizards...
To dream without boundaries...

Several Common Word Errors in Presenting Information

•*Demolish* and *destroy* mean to do away with completely. You cannot *partially* demolish or destroy. It is redundant to say *totally destroyed.*

•Do not say, *"Where is it at?"* Never end a sentence with a preposition.

•Ecology and *environment* are not the same. Ecology is the study of the relationship between organisms and their environment.

•*First annual.* If it is a first, it is not yet annual.

•*Funeral service* is redundant. A funeral is a service.

•People don't *head* up committees; they *head* them.

•*Presidents-elect*-not *president elects.*

•Speakers *imply*; listeners *infer*.

•Temperatures go *higher* or *lower*, not warmer or cooler.

•The whole is *comprised* of its parts, not *composed* of its parts.

•There is no such word as *ir-regardless.*

•*Unique-* means one of a kind. Nothing can be *rather unique, almost unique, nearly unique*, or *most unique.*

Oxymorons

Act naturally.
Advanced basic.
Airline food.
Almost exactly.
Alone together.
Business ethics.
Butt head.
Childproof.
Clearly misunderstood.
Computer jock.
Computer security.
Definite maybe.
Diet Ice Cream.
Exact estimate.
Extinct life.
Found missing.

Genuine imitation.
Good grief.
Government organization
Legally drunk.
Living dead.
Microsoft works.
Military intelligence.
New classic.
Passive aggression.
Peace force.
Plastic glasses.
Political science.
Pretty ugly.
Rap music.
Religious tolerance.
Resident alien.

Same difference.
Sanitary landfill.
Silent scream.
Small crowd.
Soft rock.
Software demonstration.
Sweet sorrow.
Synthetic natural gas.
Taped live.
Temporary tax increase.
Terribly pleased.
Tight slacks.
Twelve-ounce pound cake.
Working vacation.

Here Are Words to Avoid

It's easy to fall into the habit of using sayings like these, but if you want more sales, more influence over your prospects and customers do **everything** you can to avoid these words.

- *Be realistic!*
- *Contract.*
- *Get your head out of the clouds!*
- *Good things sell themselves.*
- *I have no time to read manuals.*
- *I'll contact my home office about that, not today though.*
- *I take things as they come.*
- *Just happened to be in the neighborhood.*
- *Old ways are the best.*
- *Only a few can earn big bucks.*
- *Problem.*
- *Quit dreaming!*
- *Sign here.*
- *Sign up.*
- *That's not my specialty.*
- *There is no power in words like "good," "fine," "nice" and other weak adjectives.*
- *You are wrong about that.*
- *You wouldn't be interested in that.*

> *"To laugh often and love much,*
> *to win the respect of intelligent*
> *persons and the affection of children;*
> *to earn the approbation of honest critics;*
> *to appreciate beauty; to give of one's self;*
> *to know even one life has breathed easier*
> *because you have lived,- that is to have succeeded."*
>
> **Harry Emerson Fosdick**

Most Often Misspelled Words

How do I spell that? Here is a list of words that have been found to be the most often misspelled in the English Language. These are the correct spellings of the words.

Abandoned
Abbreviate
Abbreviation
Abrupt
Absenteeism
Accelerated
Acceptable
Accessible
Accidentally
Accommodation
Accompanied
Accomplished
Accumulate
Accustomed
Acquaintance
Acquittal
Actuary
Adherent
Adhesive
Aeronautics
Affidavit
Affirmative
Affluent
Aluminum
Ambiguity
Analyze
Annoyance
Annuity
Anonymous
Antagonistic
Anxiety
Applicable
Approximately
Arguing

Argument
Artificial
Attorneys
Auxiliary
Awkward
Bankruptcy
Basically
Believable
Beneficiary
Bequeath
Binocular
Bookkeeping
Boundaries
Brochure
Bureaucracy
Business
Calculator
Camouflage
Career
Census
Chargeable
Clientele
Conscientious
Conscious
Conspicuous
Contagious
Contemptible
Contingent
Continuous
Controlling
Convenience
Conversion
Conveyance
Corporation

Courageous
Criticism
Decision
Deficiency
Definitely
Dehydrate
Dependent
Depression
Disappointment
Disbursement
Discrepancy
Disguise
Duplicator
Duress
Electrician
Eligible
Eliminate
Embarrass
Eminent
Encyclopedia
Endorsement
Enthusiastic
Envelope
Environment
Equitable
Eradicate
Etiquette
Exaggerate
Excellent
Excessive
Excusable
Executor
Existence
Extemporaneous

External
Extraordinary
Familiar
Fascination
Feasible
Feasibility
Flammable
Flexible
Fluorescent
Forcible
Foreclosure
Foreign
Forfeiture
Formally
Forwarded
Grammar
Gratuitous
Grievance
Haphazard
Hectic
Heir
Homogenize
Humanitarian
Hygiene
Hypocrisy
Illegality
Illegible
Illiterate
Immediately
Imminent
Impulse
Incidentally
Indemnity
Independence

A52

Inevitable	Miscellaneous	Reciprocate	Undoubtedly
Infinite	Misspell	Recommendation	Unique
Innovation	Morale	Reconcile	Usury
Intercede	Mortage	Referendum	Vacancies
Interference	Municipal	Referred	Vaccinate
Interpret	Nineteenth	Requisition	Vacuum
Interrupt	Ninety	Retrieve	Vandalism
Interstate	Ninth	Ridiculous	Variable
Intrastate	Noticeable	Satellite	Various
Irreparable	Oblige	Scarcity	Vein
Itinerary	Obvious	Scissors	Vengeance
Jeopardize	Occasionally	Separate	Verbatim
Judicious	Occruuing	Souvenir	Versatile
Justifiable	Omitted	Stationary	Versus
Knowledge	Optimism	Stationery	Vetoes
Knowledgeable	Pamphlet	Strategy	Vicinity
Legitimate	Parallel	Succeed	Visibility
Liaison	Parentheses	Sufficient	Voidable
Libel	Pasteurize	Supervisor	Volume
Librarian	Perseverance	Symbolic	Voluntary
Lieutenant	Personnel	Symmetrical	Waive
Limousine	Pharmacist	Sympathize	Warranty
Litigation	Phenomenon	Synonymous	Wealthiest
Luxury	Plaintiff	Synthetic	Weather
Magnificent	Prejudge	Systematic	Wherever
Maintenance	Prerequisite	Technique	Whether
Manageable	Privilege	Temperament	Withheld
Manipulate	Proceed	Theorize	Witnessed
Manuscript	Promissory	Tragedy	Wreak
Mathematics	Proprietor	Transaction	Wrought
Matriculate	Psychiatry	Treasurer	Yield
Mediocre	Psychological	Trivial	
Memorandum	Pursing	Twelfth	
Meticulous	Quantity	Unanimous	

Sample Presentation Music

Aida soundtrack
All I Have to Do is Dream
Anticipation
Back In Time
Be
Beautiful Noise
Body to Body
Born In The USA
Burning Down The House
Can You Feel the Love Tonight
Caribbean Queens
Chariots of Fire
Cherish
Conga
Country Road
Dare Me
Dirty Dancing
Don't Worry-Be Happy
Elvira
Emergency
Eye Of The Tiger
Faith
Feeling Alright
Fiddler on the Roof
Footloose
Four Strong Winds
Friends
Get Outta My Car
Gloria
Good Golly Miss Molly
Good Vibrations
Greatest Love Of All
Hakuna Matata
Heat Is On
Hero In You
Holding Out For A Hero
I Feel For You
I Found Somebody
I Heard it Through the Grapevine

I hope you'll dance
I Want To Live
I Will Survive
I'm So Excited
In The Air Tonight
Islands In the Sun
It Is Every One Of Us
It's All Right
I've had the time of my life
Jump
La Bomba
Lady Madonna
Land of 1000 Dances
Let It Be
Like A Virgin
Locomotion
Love America Style
Love Can Build a Bridge
Love Is All You Need
Mighty Wings
Miracle
Money Money
Mustang Sally
Nadia's Theme
Neutron Dance
Never Give Up
New Attitude
Old Time Rock and Roll
One Moment In Time
One Tin Solider
Paperback Writer
Peace Train
Power of Love
Pretty Young Thing
Put a Little Love in Your Heart
R.O.C.K. in the USA
Rhythm Is Gonna Get You

Rock Steady

Rocky

Shake Down. Break Down

She Loves You

Shower The People You Love with Love

Sitting On The Dock Of The Bay

Some Other Time

Stars Wars

Success Is Up To You

Take A Look At Me Now

Take My Breath Away

The Impossible Dream

The Letter

The Longest Time

The Power of Love

The Rose

Uptown Girl

Up Where We Belong

Walk Like An Egyptian

Walk Thru The Fire

Walking On Sunshine

Waltz

We Are the Champions

We are the World

What A Feeling

What A Wonderful World

Whip Cream

Wild Wild West

With a Little Help From My Friend

World Games

Yesterday Help

YMCA

You Are So Beautiful

You Belong To The City

You Can Do Magic

You Decorated My Life

You're the One that I Want

You've Got a Friend

"Music makes the meetings."

Ray Aziz

Almanac

Spice up your presentations by using interesting facts from history. Remember, you want to get your audience's attention. When you know you are giving a presentation, go to this Almanac and find out what happened in that month.

Here are some examples:

"Just like the Texas oil boom started in 1901, this month we are going to have a sales boom."

"Today our business is as fired up as the day the patent was granted for the match in 1836!"

"Almost twenty years ago today, Walt Disney World's 200-millionth guest, 1985 was registered coming through the gates. Think where we will be in two years from now if we build our business."

Century Events:

The 15th Century= Discovery that the world is round.

The 16th Century= Continents were discovered.

The 17th Century= Establishment of European colonies around the world.

The 18th Century= Patents almost happened daily from discoveries.

The 19th Century= Imperialism, colonialism, industrialization

The 20th Century= 1900-1999- The roaring 20's, The 60's, 2 World Wars, The Viet Nam War, the Holocaust, The Cold War, Communism, AIDS, Telephones, Electricity, Radio, TV's, DVD's, Videos, men walked on the moon, contact lenses, cures, the computer and technology explosion.

The 21st Century=This is when our grandchildren will live.

Monthly Events:

In January:
New Years Day.

King Henry VIII took the title of King of Ireland, 1542.

The first traveler's checks were issued in London.

The British settled Australia, 1778.

Tin canning process for food was patented, 1825.

President Lincoln issued the Emancipation Proclamation, 1863.

The electric light bulb was patented, 1880.

First drinking straw was patented by M.C. Stone, Washington, D.C., 1888.

The first basketball game was played, 1892.

Wilhem Roentgen discovered the x-ray, 1895.

The Texas oil boom started, 1901.

The Trans-Siberian Railway started its maiden voyage, 1905.

The March of Dimes was organized, 1938.

Pan Am Airlines complete the first around the world commercial flight, 1942.

Alaska became a state in the USA, 1959.

Surveyor VII landed on the moon, 1968.

The first successful human heart transplant operation was performed, 1968.

The Beatles have their last recording session at EMI studios, 1970.

Brooklyn merged with Manhattan, 1989.

The Dow Jones Industrial Average rose above the 2800 mark, 1990.

In February:
King James I of Scotland was murdered, 1437.

Galileo was born, 1546.

Popcorn was introduced, 1630.

France ceded Canada to England, 1763.

The US Postal Service was created, 1792.

Freedom of worship was established in France, 1795.

The Republican Party was founded, 1854.

First electric burglar alarm is installed in MA, 1858.

Four wheeled roller skates were patented by James Plimpton, NY, 1863.

First telephone book is issued, CT, 1878.

First Teddy Bear introduced in America, 1903.

Pluto was discovered, 1930.

The first singing telegram was sung, 1933.

Carol King was born, 1941.

George Harrison was born, 1943.

The first all-electric computer was introduced, 1946.
First electric typewriter placed on sale in NY, 1957.
Garth Brooks was born, 1962.
Great Britain and Ireland switched to decimal-based currency, 1971.
Fighting in Vietnam War came to a halt, 1973.

In March:

According to Shakespeare, this is the month Romeo and Juliet married.
St. Patrick's Day.
The Crowns of England and Scotland were joined, 1603.
George Washington's second inauguration speech (133 words), 1793.
The first washing machine was patented, 1797.
Artificial teeth were patented, 1822.
William Henry Harrison's longest inauguration speech (8,442 words), 1841.
Niagara Falls stopped flowing for one day because of an ice jam. 1848.
The USA government issued its first paper money, 1862.
The telephone was patented, 1876.
The first telephone call made by Alexander Graham Bell, 1876.
Ear mufflers were patented, 1877.
Dr. Seuss was born, 1904.
Time Magazine first published. 1923.
First U.S. permanent automobile license plates issued, CT 1937.
Academy Awards ceremony telecast for the first time, 1953.
Dr. Jonas Salk announced a new vaccine against polio. 1953.
Elvis Presley buys Graceland, 1957.
Hyman Lipman of Philadelphia patented the pencil with an attached eraser, 1858.
The Beatles make their first appearance at Liverpool's Cavern Club, 1961
John Lennon marries Yoko Ono in Gibraltar, 1969
Vietnam peace treaty was signed in Paris, 1973.

In April:

City of Rome founded, 753B.C.
Leonardo da Vinci born, 1452.
Wales became a part of England, 1536.
Yale University founded by Elihu Yale, 1649.
First Jewish congregation in USA consecrates synagogue, 1730.
First edition of Webster's Dictionary published, 1828.
First safety pin patented by Walter hunt of NY. He immediately sold the patent rights for
    $100, 1849.
US Congress authorized "In God We Trust" on coinage, 1864.
First dishwasher marketed in Chicago, Ill., 1889.
Man first reached the North Pole, 1909.

A58

The S.S.*Titanic* sank, 1912 at 2:20am.

The zipper was patented by Gideon Sundback of Hoboken, NJ., 1913.

William Shakespeare was born and died in this month.

First professional golf tournament held, 1916.

NY Yankees become first team to use numbers on uniforms, 1929.

Sir Watson-Watt is granted a patent for radar., 1935.

NASA announces first seven astronauts, 1959.

Dr. Martin Luther King. Jr. shot to death in Memphis, Tn., 1968.

Branch Davidian compound, Waco, Tx. Burned, killing dozens, 1993.

The Murrah Federal Building in Oklahoma City, OK, bombed, killing hundreds, 1995.

In May:

First merry-go-round seen at a fair in Turkey, 1620.

Indians "sell" Manhattan Island for $24 cloth and buttons, 1626.

Patrick Henry was born, 1736.

Napoleon became Emperor of France, 1804.

Lewis and Clark begin expedition of Louisiana Purchase with Sacajawea, 1804.

The Waltz is first introduced into English ballrooms. Most observes consider it immoral and disgusting, 1812.

Beethoven's Ninth Symphony presented for first time, 1824.

Dr. John Farrie, patented the refrigerator, 1851.

Sigmund Freud, psychologist born, 1856.

First Kentucky Derby run at Churchill Downs. Winner was Aristides, 1875.

John Wayne was born, 1907.

Indianapolis 500 car race run for first time. Winning driver Ray Harroun wins with 75 miles per hour, 1911.

Edwin Land founded instant photography (Polaroid), 1909.

Nylon stockings went on sale, 1940.

Patent filed in the US for the H-Bomb, 1946.

B.F. Goodrich manufactures the first tubeless tire, OH, 1947.

The Diner's Club issues it's first credit card, 1950.

The first jet airplane passenger service was launched, 1952.

Roger Bannister breaks the 4-minute mile in 3:59:4, 1954.

Nelson Mandela was sworn in as South Africa's first native-African president, 1994.

In June:

Mohammed. Prophet of Islam born, 0570.

The Black Prince- Edward, Prince of Wales-was born, 1329.

Henry VIII of England was born, 1491.

King George III of England was born, 1738.

The doughnut is invented, 1847.

Slavery is abolished in the USA, 1862.

The suction vacuum cleaner was patented, 1869.
The first settlers moved to Idaho, 1860.
Christopher Latham Sholes patents the typewriter, 1868.
The Statue of Liberty arrived in the United States, 1885.
The cork-centered baseball was patented, 1909.
The royal British family adopted the name Windsor, 1917.
Nelson Mandela born, 1918.
Sir Barton becomes the first horse to win the Triple Crown, 1919.
Gone with the Wind was published, 1936.
Queen Elizabeth II was crowned at Westminster Abbey, 1953.
Cable New Network made its debut, 1980.
Michael Jordan was signed to the Chicago Bulls, 1984.
Chinese government puts down student democracy protest in Beijing; thousand die in Tiananmen Square, 1989.
Jan Ruhe became one of the first American women millionaires in Network Marketing, 1995.

In July:
City of Quebec founded, 1698.
American colonies declare their independence from England, 1776.
The first US Customs Service is stared, 1789.
First American passport issued by the US State Department, 1796.
First postage stamps go on sale, 1847.
Margarine is patented in Paris, for the use of the French Navy, 1869.
Statue of Liberty was presented to the US in Paris, 1884.
First concrete-paved street built in Bellefountaine, OH, 1892.
Louis Lassing of Connecticut creates the hamburger, 1900.
The first ice cream cone was invented, 1904.
Ringo Starr was born, 1940.
First withholding tax from paychecks, 1943.
Construction began on Disneyland, 1954.
Disneyland opens it doors in rural Orange County, 1955.
Michael Jackson signs a $60 million contract with Sony Records (the largest-ever), 1991.
A telephone was first installed in the White House, 1880.

In August:
The first one way streets are established, London, 1617.
Alaska was discovered, 1741.
The Republic of Switzerland was founded, 1291.
Dom Perignon, invents Champagne, 1693.
John Hampson patents the Venetian blind, 1841.
Isaac Singer granted patent on the sewing machine, 1851.

A60

The yacht *America* wins the first Royal Yacht Squadron Cup, now known as the
 American's Cup, at a regatta in England, 1851.
The potato chips are prepared by Chef George Crum, Saratoga Springs, NY, 1853.
The waffle iron is invented, 1869.
Sir Alexander Fleming, discovered penicillin, 1881.
The world's first roller rink opens its doors, Newport, RI, 1866.
Theophilus VanKannel of Philadelphia receives a patent for revolving door, 1888.
The first beauty contest is held, Spa, Belgium, 1888.
United Parcel Service begins service, Seattle, Wa., 1907.
Mother Teresa was born, 1910.
First automobile exceeded 30mph, Sir Malcolm Campbell, 1935.
"The Wizard of Oz" premieres at the Grauman's Chinese Theater, Hollywood, Ca., 1939.
Atom Bomb dropped on Hiroshima by the "Enola Gay", 1945.
The Hawaiian Islands achieved American statehood, 1959.
Martin Luther King, Jr., gives *"I have a dream"* speech at Lincoln Memorial; 200,000
    demonstrate for equal rights, 1963.

In September:

The Mayflower sets sail from Plymouth with 102 Pilgrims, 1620.
Great London Fire begins in Pudding Lane. 80% of London is destroyed, 1666.
Queen Liliuokalani, last queen of Hawaii (1891-93), born, 1838
10,000 workers marched in the fist Labor Day parade in New York City, 1882.
First Cafeteria opens for business, New York City, 1885.
The typewriter ribbon patent, 1886.
George Eastman patents first roll-film camera and registers "Kodak", 1888.
Peter Sellers, England, actor (Pink Panther, Being There, Goon Show), born, 1925.
Japan surrenders ending WW II (US date, 9/2 in Japan), 1945.
Elvis Presley appears on national TV for 1st time (Ed Sullivan), 1956.
Bonanza premieres — in Color, 1959.
U.N. announces Earth population has hit 3 billion, 1962.
Supremes release "Baby Love," 1964.
Star Trek premiers on NBC TV, 1966.
Mission Impossible premieres on TV in the USA, 1967.
American swimmer Mark Spitz becomes the first athlete to win seven Olympic gold
    medals, 1972.
M*A*S*H premiers on TV, 1972.
Miami Vice premieres, 1984.
Walt Disney World's 200-millionth guest, 1985.
USSR recognizes independence of the 3 Baltic republics (Estonia, Lithuania and
    Latvia), 1996.

In October:

Martin Luther posts his 95 Theses, begins Protestant Reformation, 1517.

The back of a bar in New York is decorated with birds' tail feathers. Customer jokingly asks for glass of "cock tails," and a tradition is born, 1776.

Charles Macintosh of Scotland begins selling his raincoats, 1823.

The match is patented, 1836.

U.S. Naval Academy opens, Annapolis, Maryland, 1845.

First transcontinental telegram sent, 1861.

Model T revolutionized the automotive industry by providing an affordable, reliable car, When it was first introduced, the "Tin Lizzy" cost only $850 and seated two people, and by the time it was discontinued in 1927, nearly fifteen million Model Ts had been sold, 1908.

Nylon stockings first go on sale in the USA, 1939.

First Peanuts comic strip featuring Charlie Brown and Snoopy appears in nine newspapers, 1950.

Burglar Alarm patented, 1953.

I Love Lucy premiers, 1954.

Wake Up Little Susie - The Everly Brothers tops the charts, 1957

Chances Are/The Twelfth of Never - Johnny Mathis, tops the charts, 1957

Jailhouse Rock - Elvis Presley, tops the charts, 1957.

My Shoes Keep Walking Back to You - Ray Price, tops the charts, 1957.

Jacqueline Kennedy marries Aristotle Onassis, 1968.

"Saturday Night Live" premiers, 1975.

Julian Nott sets world hot-air balloon altitude record (16,806 m), 1980.

Elizabeth Taylor weds for the 8th time (Larry Fortensky), 1991.

In November:

First National Celebration of Thanksgiving in the USA, 1789.

Lewis and Clark first see the Pacific Ocean, 1805.

Moby Dick, by Herman Melville, is published, 1851.

President Lincoln delivers The Gettysburg Address, 1863.

The Suez Canal opens, 1869.

First intercollegiate football game played (Rutgers 6, Princeton 4), 1869.

First college football contest with uniforms, Harvard vs. Yale, 1875.

US Weather Bureau begins operations, 1870.

Susan B. Anthony arrested for attempting to vote, 1875.

First Cash registered patented by James Ritty, Ohio saloon, 1879.

First air-conditioned automobile, Packard, 1939.

The State Department starts requiring photographs for passports, 1940

Green Bay Packers become first NFL team to travel by plane, 1940.

To Sir with Love – Lulu, top of the charts, 1967.

A Natural Woman - Aretha Franklin, top of the charts, 1967.
I Don't Wanna Play House - Tammy Wynette, top of the charts, 1967.
Tom Dempsey of New Orleans Saints kicks NFL-record 63-yard field goal, 1970.
Cyclone kills 300,000 in Bangladesh, 1970.
Reverend Jim Jones led 911 people in suicide in Jonestown, Guyana.

In December:
Abel Tasman discovered New Zealand, 1642.
William Semple patented chewing gum, 1669.
Father Marquette builds first dwelling in what is now Chicago, 1674.
First edition of Encyclopedia Brittanica is published in Scotland, 1768.
New Orleans first flew the American flag, 1803.
A Christmas Carol, published in London by Charles Dickens, 1843.
The coffee percolator was patented, 1865.
Electric lights were installed on Broadway, 1880.
A telephone was first installed in the White House, 1880.
George Grant patents golf tee, 1899.
Walt Disney born, 1901.
The word Motel was first used in San Luis Obispo, Ca., 1925.
Bingo invented by Edwin Lowe, 1929
King Edward VIII of England abdicates for the woman he loves, 1936.
Snow White and the Seven Dwarfs premiered, 1937.
Japan attacks Pearl Harbor in the Hawaiian Islands, 1941.
John Denver born, 1943.
Rosa Parks refused to give up her seat on a city bus, 1955.
The Ford Foundation contributed $500 million to US colleges and universities, 1955.
Christmas Day.

Presentation Worksheet

Questions for an Audience Presentation:
- Do you know your audience?
- Do you need to define any unfamiliar terms for your audience?
- Have you focused on your topic rather than trying to cover too much?
- How is the room set up?
- How is your company perceived in the marketplace?
- How long and what's before me and after me?
- Identify 3-4 key points you want to make during your presentation and list them.
- Identify what information you want to use to back up your points.
- Is there anything special you need to acknowledge about people in the audience?
- Is there anything you can say to give them a compliment?
- What are: •the audience's feelings on the subject you will be discussing?
  - the biases or preconceived ideas that the audience may have?
  - personal stories or experiences you can share with the audience on your topic?
- What are the expectations of the person or organization who has invited you to speak?
- What are your ideas for your opening?
- What are your qualifications for giving the presentation?
- What are the three biggest challenges facing your industry today?
- What are the three biggest challenges that this audience faces?
- What is the appropriate subject?
- What is the overall mood in your company today?
- What is the theme of the meeting and why and how was it chosen?
- What is the total agenda?
- What kind of room do you have reserved?
- What makes you a credible authority?
- What is your topic?
- What three things do you want the audience to leave the meeting with?
- When will I be speaking?
- Where will the meeting be?
- Who will be the senior person in the room?
- Why is this meeting important?
- Why is your company a good company to work for?
- Will most of the audience be looking forward to attending this meeting?
- Write your topic in one or two sentences.

Questions for a one-on-one Presentation:

- Do you have a great Motto?
- Do you remember the first moment?
- Explain a typical day in your life…
- How did you come up with this great idea?
- How did you get interested in this?
- How did you get started?
- How did you meet your business partner?
- If you could take a dream vacation, where would it be?
- What are your dreams?
- What are your favorite leisure activities?
- What are your goals?
- What are your major challenges?
- What are your strategies to overcome them?
- What are your strategies to reach them?
- What did people in high school think you were like?
- When did you first know you wanted to advance in your company?
- What do you like to read?
- What happened first?
- What has been your most important personal experience?
- What have you learned about life?
- What is advice you would give to young people?
- What is one thing you would like to change about the world?
- What is one thing you would like to change about yourself?
- What is something you can't stand in people?
- What is something you hope you never have to do?
- What is something you wish you could stop doing?
- What issues matter to you?
- What is the biggest obstacle you have had to overcome in your life?
- What is the most boring thing you can imagine?
- What is the word that describes you the best?
- What is your favorite thing to do on a Sunday afternoon?
- What is your personal philosophy on…
- What is your pet peeve?
- What material things do you care about?
- What was it like to be in law school during that time?
- What was the last good movie you saw?
- What was your most important work experience?
- What was your worst job?
- What would you be doing if you weren't doing what you are doing?
- Who is someone you hope to meet?
- Who is your personal hero/shero?

Preparing Your Presentation:

•Now, outline your presentation.
    I am here to talk about:
    I will cover these 3-4 main points:
    You should care about these points because:

•My first point is:
    I will back this point up with:
    Personal story:
    I will use these quotes to reinforce my point:

•My second point is:
    I will back up this point with:
    Personal story:
    I will use these quotes to reinforce my point:

•My third point is:
    I will back up this point with:
    Personal story:
    I will use these quotes to reinforce my point:

•My ending:
    I will tell the audience to remember these main points:

•Finally I would like my audience to take these actions:

Sample Evaluation Form

*Please take a moment and share your
thoughts so that we may serve you better in the future.*

What did you like about this presentation?

How would you rate the content of this presentation?

Are there any specific areas you would like to see deleted? What?

Are there any parts that you would like me to go into further?

How do you see yourself taking action on this information?

Your overall comments about this presentation?

May we quote you?

Your Name:

Email Address:

Fire Up!
Thanks for sharing!
Jan Ruhe
www.janruhe.com

Ending

Congratulations! You have just taken a mega step forward in improving your presentation skills! If you skipped through this book you might have missed a million dollar idea. Go back through this book several times. Decide now to go for greatness in your presentations. You have the necessary tools. Now, it's up to you.

Make a promise to yourself that you will work on perfecting your presentation skills so that you will be highly successful. You and only you can decide to take action. Work hard on your presentation skills. In this guide are proven tested ideas and techniques and scripts for you to use to create a masterpiece of a life! Are you ready to be the best presenter you know so that you can have the life you deserve? Affirm that you will never shrink your dreams to match your income and that you will increase your income to match your dreams.

Dream big, work on your skills, and develop your presentation skills so that you are a pro when you give your presentations. As we have traveled the world, we ask people *"Do you want to be a motivational speaker? Do you want to write books?"* So many hands go up saying *"yes!"* There is huge desire to do one or the other or both. These ideas worked for me and they will work for you too. Become the student of the person living the lifestyle you want. Come to the table of plenty, the success platters are heaped with treasures for you. There is no crowd. There's lots of room at the top. Don't take the busy road where the average people travel, take the high road where the champions are. We are waiting for you with open arms. Prepare for prosperity and abundance.

Why not you and why not now?

See you at the top - just feed your mind, work on your skills and as we say to you now and always, don't be average, be a champion.

Jan & Bill Ruhe

The Curtain Closes
John David Mann

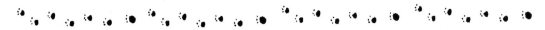

You've now read through what is probably the most thorough, most complete book on presentations ever assembled. What could I possibly add to send you off? Just this: A good presentation will do four things. A *great* presentation will do those four things, plus a fifth. A good presentation will sing and dance; it will laugh and cry. A *great* presentation will sing and dance, and laugh and cry—and tell the truth powerfully.

How does a presentation sing?
Through variation. A dull speaker speaks with the same pitch (high vs. low), same volume (loud vs. soft) and same pace (fast vs. slow) throughout. An engaging speaker plays with all three of these knobs. Your audience is drawn into your stories, vignettes and messages by the ebb and flow, the *movement* of your speaking. A good movie will do the same: some scenes are long and leisurely; then, as we move nearer to a key point of the story, the emotional intensity picks up—and so does the pace. The greatest story-tellers make their greatest impressions not in what they say, but in the silence—that magnificent pause before a punchline. Think of Johnny Carson, of Jack Benny. Think of George Burns: the funniest thing he ever *"said"* was the look that greeted Gracie's latest whackyism. The sharpest wordsmith is an even sharper pausesmith.

How does a presentation dance?
I'm not speaking here of the rhythm of your words, but the rhythm of your *images*. Imagine if John F. Kennedy had said simply, *"You should ask, what can you do for your country?"* Or if Neil Armstrong had pronounced, *"Well, that's one giant step for mankind."* Would we remember either phrase? I doubt it. Because neither image is paired with its contrast, its counterpointing partner. Neither image dances. Now, listen: *"Ask not what your country can do for you—ask what you can do for your country?"* *"That's one small step for man—one giant step for mankind."* The song Amazing Grace is one of my favorites, among other reasons, because it both sings and dances. *"I once was lost, but now I'm found; was blind, but now I see."* The good old *"feel, felt, found"* cliché doesn't get any more poetically expressed than that. Which brings up a good point: one reason that feel-felt-found (*"I know how you feel, Bob—I felt the same way, first time heard about this. But you know, here's what I found..."*) is so tried and true, is because that it has *rhythm*. It dances.

How does a presentation laugh and cry?

You know that people are motivated by two things: the desire to <u>secure</u> pleasure, and the desire to <u>avoid</u> pain. It's like the classic icon for the dramatic arts: the laughing mask (representing comedy) and the crying mask (representing tragedy). Amazing Grace sorts of stories *("I once was broke, but now I'm solvent; was enslaved, but now I'm a self-employed entrepreneur...").* A good presentation will not only contain a before-and-after story, but will also weave a little poignant imagery to more vividly evoke in the audience the feelings of pain and of joy. *"My little girl looked up at me and said, 'Mommy, how come you're always at work and I never see you except weekends?'"* The key is to find a gesture, a moment, that captures the pathos of a situation and gives it a human face. To say, *"I decided I didn't have enough time for my family,"* is abstract and dull. It conveys your point—but there is no laugh or cry in it. To say, *"... In that moment, it hit me: 'Bob, you're watching your own son grow up on video tape!'"*—it makes the same point, but makes it vivid and *real.*

How does a great presentation tell the truth powerfully?

Now, I do not mean that merely *good* presentations are not truthful. But in a *great* presentation, the speaker discovers and shares with the audience a powerful truth—a truth that is discovered in the moment, uniquely and for the first time ever. A *great* presentation is new. It has never been presented before—and never will again.

My father attended a very traditional, conservative university as a young man in pre-war Germany. He recalls one of his instructors looking up from his podium and announcing, *"At this point, I am accustomed to telling the following joke..."* That is precisely what does *not* make a great presentation. Can a great presentation include certain elements—specific stories, vignettes or images—that you have told before? Of course. It's not as if these elements of storytelling are used up after only one telling. But if you approach a presentation with a sense that it is routine, you eliminate any possibility of greatness—and cheat your audience as well as yourself.

Growing up as a performing musician, I am comfortable on stage. Still, I always prepare for every talk, no matter how brief or how elementary the topic. I have a goal of never giving exactly the same presentation twice—because I want to keep alive the possibility of conveying some powerful and newly grasped truth, each and every time I take an audience's time and attention. No matter how well you know your material, no matter how many times you have presented on this particular topic, no matter how easily you could go onto automatic pilot, here's what I urge you to do before each talk: Stop for a moment, adopt an attitude of taking absolutely nothing for granted, and ask yourself,

"What is the single most valuable thing I could possibly convey to these people?"

About the Author

This is yet *another* Presentation:
Include your bio and <u>sell</u> <u>yourself</u>

Network Marketing Lifestyles **Magazine (Feb/Mar 2001) calls Jan**
"one of the industry's most beloved and well-known author,
speaker and trainer."

Jan's passion to learn and feed her mind sent her to hundreds of expensive presentations as a student. With persistence and determination she put herself through an extensive personal growth and development program reading over 500 books and listening to hundreds of hours of tapes. While building her own business she has not only trained her own sales field but over 70,000 people worldwide! Bring Jan Ruhe in and your company will love you. Your company sales will increase and you will look like a hero.

Jan doesn't have to sell you on her qualifications, she can help you as well as your company find solutions to improve the bottom line.

Jan Ruhe:
- began doing a two day event worldwide for companies and successlines called Nuts $ Bolts seminars in 1998.
- formed her own workbook that covers over 1,000 Nuts $ Bolts for serious students to learn and duplicate and get massive results. People pay over $500 per ticket and the room is packed worldwide with people who feel their investment is the biggest bargain of their lives.
- entered public speaking in Reno, Nevada, USA in 1991 being asked by John Milton Fogg to be an Upline Master.
- focuses on being the best you can be, being a Master Presenter, a Master Prospector, a Master Trainer, people skills and a Master of yourself.
- provides instructions on how to build your business so that you will keep the fire of desire forever.
- rose from being a single mother of three children to a multi-millionaire to being a sought after worldwide speaker and trainer.

•was featured on the front cover in February 2001 on both *Network Marketing Lifestyles* in the USA and *Network Marketing News* in the UK.
•Weaves in humor, stories and spellbinds her audiences, they love her! No rah-rah or hype with Jan Ruhe, her presentations are packed with passion, fun and practical information you can use and duplicate and make your own.
•Will help you learn how to present yourself before, during and after a presentation so that your audience will be begging for more.

Jan Ruhe presents:

•from over two decades of true experience that gets results.
•her programs enlighten, entertain and empower your audience.
•like no one else.
•programs where she helps you overcome your fear of change and create positive change fast.

Jan Ruhe is:

•an internationally recognized speaker/trainer.
•a renowned public speaker, sales and marketing trainer and author.
•In her third decade as a Sales/Marketing/Leadership/Presentation Master consultant and professional speaker.
•One of the world's leading authorities in understanding, teaching and training presentation and leadership skills, utilizing powerful delivery and her special insights to teach, inspire and move people to new levels of achievement.
•The author of the highly acclaimed, successful and popular books Fire Up! and MLM Nuts $ Bolts. Fire Up! is now published in English and German and MLM Nuts $ Bolts is published in Korean and German. She co-authored True Leadership published in English and German. All available at www.janruhe.com.

Jan teaches how you can:

•get leaders and make them successful.
•how to set up and structure presentations so you get results you can only dream of!
•to contribute more than is expected of you, then you create a void, which the world is compelled to fill with goodness.
•you how to continue to do a little more than you think you can.
•you how to Master your presentations. If you continually learn more about how to present yourself and your products and opportunity, you will always be a leader. You will be purpose driven rather than process driven.
•you how to present so that people will listen to you, believe you and follow you.
•you that the way to advance is to advance others.

Jan has:

- an extremely active worldwide web at www.janruhe.com.
- contributed to many online chat rooms and on-line forums.
- has been an entrepreneur, meeting planner and a Diamond Distributor for her company for over twenty-one years that has sold in excess of $150 million in products with over 60,000 people in her organization cumulatively.
- has been published in hundreds of publications both nationally and internationally.
- has been sought by groups as far away as South Africa to Ireland, Germany, Scandanavia, Canada and all over the UK and in all of the United States.
- risen to be the number one female trainer in Network Marketing in the world.
- traveled the globe making presentations worldwide.

Jan delivers:

- a passionate message, which lets people know that they must shake off mediocrity and become the champion they are meant to be. It is a message Jan Ruhe has learned from her own life and one now she helps others apply to their lives.

Jan created:

- the Champion Network at her website to connect everyone together for a generic, free worldwide email loop.
- the Jan Ruhe Book of the Month Club in 1998 and now has membership worldwide.
- the Really Big Show and hosts this call with expert speakers monthly. Speakers have included Jim Rohn, Tom Hopkins, and many fantastic speakers.

J R Productions:

- In 1992, Bill Ruhe, Jan's husband, formed their international company; JR Productions.
- JR Productions provides motivational tapes and materials, seminars and personal/professional development and mentoring programs for groups, teams, companies and organizations.

Jan Ruhe's Website:

www.janruhe.com

Present Yourself:

When you want a speaker/consultant who:

- Combines knowledge, wit and sincerity to create a sensational presentation.
- Gives practical information you can really use.
- Has walked the walk.
- Is passionate and real and fun.
- Learned from actually building an incredible business herself.
- Will deliver a presentation that people will remember forever.
- Will help you learn sales marketing strategies and certain business building formulas, turn to the woman who has used them to make millions for herself and others.
- Worldwide "how-to" sales trainer…

Then *you* want Jan Ruhe
Seminar Presenter/Worldwide Consultant

To the Top:

That's where Jan Ruhe has been taking her clients for years. Besides Jan's best selling books, she has been quoted and written about in hundreds of books, articles, newspapers, publications, and international magazines. Her roster of clients is too long to list here but they have flown Jan and Bill all over the planet. Jan has emerged as one of the world's premier experts on Presentation Skills, Leadership, Sales and Marketing. Jan specializes in helping organizations like yours implement total excitement and explode the bottom line. When you want your business to grow, you need Jan Ruhe.

Jan Ruhe

A world class expert on

"Presentation Skills, Leadership Development, Sales and Marketing"

International Consultant

Author: <u>Fire Up!</u>, <u>MLM Nuts $ Bolts</u>, <u>The Master Presentation Guide</u>

Co-Author of <u>True Leadership</u>

xxii